LISTEN TO YOUR HEART

A DAILY DEVOTIONAL OF CALLING, PURPOSE AND NEW LIFE

Cover and interior art by Klocke Design.
Interior production by Katie McGuire Communications.

Author photo by Lifetouch Church Directories and Portraits, Inc. Lifetouch has granted permission to use the photo for this book.

Printed in the United States of America

ISBN: 979-8621926311

A Message to the Reader

You and I are meant to *be* who we *are*. Sounds simple enough, but I think we all get side-tracked by what *others expect of us*, what our *culture tells us* and what our *egos tell us* – or maybe a little of each. I believe that God – the *Love* that created *all that is* – has made each of us to be a *creative reflection* of this Love. Each of our lives is a creative adventure in discovering our *true selves!*

This book is my second devotional and is my gift in thanksgiving to all who have helped me to uncover who I am. My utmost gratitude goes to my greatest teacher, Jesus of Nazareth, as well as the living Christ. There are many others, especially authors like Thomas Merton, Richard Rohr and Ilia Delio.

If you are reading these words now, know that I wrote this book especially for *you* in the hopes that you would find a daily inspiration in discovering your *true self.*

Here is how to use the book effectively. As you start each day (or if you prefer, as you end each day), sit comfortably in the silence of God's loving Presence for a minute or two while acknowledging the One who is always with you. Then read the day's entry. Each begins with a title and then a scripture verse or two. Read them slowly and let them *soak in.* This will lead you into the practice of *Lectio Divina* whereby you silently reflect on the words and find rest there. Following a minute or two of rest, slowly read my reflection and again allow the words to speak to your heart. At the end of each reflection there is a suggested original song of mine to listen to. That is completely optional, but if you are a musical person, it will add another layer to your spiritual experience. Finally, thank God for the gift of life and for the inspiration you are receiving.

In my former life as a radio news journalist, I delivered an excess of *bad news.* When I followed the voice in my heart asking me to leave radio for ministry, I had a strong desire to continue the routine of writing daily to deliver news. This time, however, it would be the *Good News* of God's *unconditional love.* It began in 2008 as a daily scripture reflection that I emailed to the kids in my youth ministry and then expanded to an email to many of their parents and friends. Eventually, it turned into a daily blog at billtonnismusic.wordpress.com/todays-contemplation. Those posts are what led to my first book, *Mercy Reigns: A Daily Devotional of Compassion, Comfort & Healing* – and now, the book you are holding!

Reading and reflecting silently on the words of scripture helped change my life for the better. It will do the same for *you*, but you must find a *quiet* place to do it. As Jesus instructed, "When you pray, go to your inner room, close the door, and pray to your Father in secret." (Matthew 6:6).

The voice of God is *never* harsh. It is *always* merciful and compassionate. It will be a voice that tenderly says, *"You are my beloved."* May you hear that voice with each day's reflection and then *be* the *love* that *you are!*

Bill Tonnis

Cincinnati, Ohio

"Amen, amen, I say to you, unless a grain of wheat falls to the ground and dies, it remains just a grain of wheat; but if it dies, it produces much fruit."

John 12:24

TURN TOWARD LOVE

JANUARY
I

Matthew 4:17

From that time on, Jesus began to preach and say, "Repent, for the kingdom of heaven is at hand."

What *better* way to start the year than with the words of Jesus at the very beginning of his public ministry?

When John the Baptist was arrested Jesus' ministry began.

It was *time.*

Jesus started with the word *Repent*. This means: *Turn around!*

Turn *away* from the ways you are looking for fulfillment and happiness and turn *toward* the only source of fulfillment that can truly satisfy and bring you *peace* and *wholeness* (or *salvation*).

Jesus is "the way and the truth and the life." (John 14:6)

Follow Jesus and his ways and you will experience God's *unconditional love, mercy, grace, forgiveness and compassion.*

The "kingdom of heaven" will truly be at *hand*. Right here. Right *now*.

Listen to the song for the day "I Want to Follow You" on the *Listen to Your Heart* album.

JANUARY

2

LIVE IN LOVE

1 John 3:2

Beloved, we are God's children now; what we shall be has not yet been revealed. We do know that when it is revealed we shall be like Christ, for we shall see him as he is.

There is a beautiful plan unfolding.

Each of us is part of it.

God – or *Unconditional Love itself* – is still creating.
It is all evolving toward a *grand climax.*

Each of us is invited into the *creative dance.*

We have a choice of whether to take part in the *Divine Dance*, or the *human delusion* created by arrogance and greed.

If we *let go* of our ego-driven *false selves*, we will realize more and more who we truly are: *children of God.*

It is only then that we will be able to open our hearts to receive this Love and freely share it.

Be *co-creators* in this grand love story *in progress.*

Share your gifts!

Listen to the song for the day "Shall We Sing" on the *Listen to Your Heart* album.

THE WAY

John 1:38-39

Jesus turned and saw them following him and said to them, "What are you looking for?"
They said to him, "Rabbi, (which translated means Teacher) "where are you staying?"
He said to them, "Come, and you will see."

Put yourself in this scenario.

You meet Jesus and he asks you, *"What are you looking for?"*

Interesting question, isn't it?
What are ***you*** looking for?
Jesus is our great teacher in life.

He simply tells us:
"Come, and you will see."

That requires letting go of what our egos urge us to do. *Listen* to God's silent voice in your heart then *take a step* in the direction you think God is calling you.

Read in the gospels what Jesus *said* and *did* and then *follow his example.*

Life is not about attaining some *future heavenly reward.*
It *is* about being *compassionately present* to *each moment* of becoming more and more like Christ.

Listen to the song for the day "You'll Lead Me" on the *Listen to Your Heart* album.

JANUARY

4 JUST BE YOU

Psalm 98:1

Sing a new song to the LORD.

Is there a song inside of you waiting to be sung?
There is only one *you*.

Only *you* can sing *your* song.

You are unique and precious in God's eyes.
What you have to offer is also *unique* and *precious*.

**It doesn't have to be spectacular in the world's eyes.
It can be very *simple*.**

It is something *you alone* can offer.

**Love has breathed life into you.
How will you respond?**

For the kingdom of God to come alive in the present you must agree to cooperate.
Let all the masks you have worn to satisfy other voices fall to the ground.

It's time for your true *self* to *emerge*.

Be open and allow Love to express itself with your life.

God wants to sing and dance through *you*.

It's a *new year*.

How about offering a *new* song and dance?

Listen to the song for the day "Sing a New Song" on the *Live to Love* album.

STEP OUT

Luke 4:22

And all spoke highly of him and were amazed at the gracious words that came from his mouth. They also asked, "Isn't this the son of Joseph?"

The people who knew Jesus when he was growing up were amazed at his words as an adult, but they quickly turned on him.

When you follow your *calling*, you will be asked to step out of your *comfort zone*.

Sometimes the people *closest* to you may be the very ones who *block* your path.
They may respond like they did about Jesus,
"Isn't this Joseph's kid? The one who is a carpenter?
Who does he think he is?"

We cannot be concerned with what others say when we are trying to follow our callings.

Jesus is the perfect model to follow on the path to your *true self*.

He warned us that we would be persecuted on this journey to life.

Each of us is called to be a unique reflection of Love (God) to the world.
It will require courage to do it.

Others will feel threatened by the changes you make in your life.
They may ridicule and make fun of you.

Don't let that stop you!
You will be living the life you were meant to live.

Listen to the song for the day "Make Your Way" and the Mercy Reigns album.

JANUARY

6

FOLLOW THE LEADER

1 John 4:9

In this way the love of God was revealed to us: God sent his only Son into the world so that we might have life through him.

The bible tells us that God is Love – an incomprehensible, unconditional Love.

Jesus said, "If you know me, then you will also know my Father" (John 14:7).

Jesus showed us *Who God is* and *how God operates.*

What better example to follow in living our lives?

When we follow his example of living out the Beatitudes and the greatest two commandments of loving God and our neighbor as ourselves we will truly come to life.

When we *pour out* the love we've been given, we in turn discover who we *truly* are.

This is the *self-emptying path* that leads us to an *abundant life.*

Listen to the song for the day "Pour Me Out" on the *Give Praise and Thanks* album.

TOP PRIORITY

JANUARY

7

1 John 4:8

Whoever is without love does not know God, for God is love.

God is everywhere.

As St. Paul said, "In him we live and move and have our being." (Acts 17:28)

But some people are *unaware* of God.

They are estranged from Love because of human circumstances.
Sometimes they are *abused* by others.
That doesn't mean that God doesn't love them, for God is Love.

But sometimes God needs humans to be *channels of that Love to others.*

God loves *everyone* and *everything* unconditionally.

We are called to do the same.

How will Love be known if it is not shared?

Be that channel of Love *now* and *always.*

Listen to the song for the day "Make Me a Channel" on the *Listen to Your Heart* album.

JANUARY

8

ARE YOU LISTENING?

Luke 5:15-16

The report about him spread all the more, and great crowds assembled to listen to him and to be cured of their ailments, but he would withdraw to deserted places to pray.

Jesus modeled how to live our lives.

He took loving action with compassion for those in need, but then he took time to "withdraw to deserted places to pray."

He needed this *balance* between *action* and *contemplation.*

He needed to cultivate an interior *stillness* before he could be effective in the chaos of the world.

To do God's work he needed to take time to be in *intimate contact* with God.

So he went to "deserted places" to spend time in silence.

How can you hear God's *silent voice in your heart* if you never make the effort?

We are meant for an ongoing cycle of contemplation and action. Reflection followed by action, again and again.

How often do you set aside time to *let go* of your thoughts and simply be in the Presence of God?

How about *now*?

Listen to the song for the day "Turn Off the Noise" on the *Listen to Your Heart* album.

Mark 1:16-18

As he passed by the Sea of Galilee, he saw Simon and his brother Andrew casting their nets into the sea; they were fishermen. Jesus said to them, "Come after me, and I will make you fishers of men." Then they left their nets and followed him.

After John the Baptist was arrested, Jesus began his public ministry.

His message was: "The kingdom of God is *here*. *Change your direction* and believe the *Good News* that *God loves you unconditionally*."

Jesus wants each of us to hear that message now.
He also invites us to follow him.

When we follow Jesus we are on the path to becoming *aware* and *awakened* to *who we are* as *beloved daughters* and *sons* of God.

Following Jesus requires "repenting" or literally *"changing our direction."* For me, it meant leaving a radio news profession that was the only career I had ever known. Changes are never easy, but I can assure you that following Jesus will lead you to more joy, contentment and fulfillment than any other pursuit in this life.

The decision to follow is not a *one-time* deal. It is a *moment-to-moment lifelong* project.

A Great Love is calling *you*.

When you listen to the gentle, loving whisper in your heart, a great adventure will begin.

Listen to the song for the day "Changed" on the *Give Praise and Thanks* album.

JANUARY

10 WAKE UP

Mark 1:14-15

Jesus came to Galilee proclaiming the gospel of God:
"This is the time of fulfillment.
The kingdom of God is at hand."

This is such a simple statement; and yet, *it is profound.*
As we read in the Gospel of Matthew's account of this event, Jesus makes this enlightened message the *first* of his preaching ministry.

***Now* is the time of fulfillment.**

Not some distant time in the future, but *now.*

This is the moment when "the kingdom of God" *comes into being.*
Be *present to life!*

Each moment is the only time that is real.
Each moment is when you can experience the wonder of all that is.
In each moment the *sacred* becomes *one* with the *ordinary.*

Awaken* to the *Divine Presence.

Let the endless commentary, the constant loop of
repetitious thoughts in your mind, cease.

Stop.

Be.

***Bask* in the glory of God's love.**

+++

Listen to the song for the day "I Stand in the Light" on the *Mercy Reigns* album.

JANUARY

BECOMING WHOLE 11

Mark 1:45

The man went away and began to publicize the whole matter. He spread the report abroad so that it was impossible for Jesus to enter a town openly. Jesus remained outside in deserted places, and people kept coming to him from everywhere.

Jesus never strove for "superstar" status.
He didn't seek the spotlight.

The gospels show that Jesus never did anything to show off or call attention to *himself.*
In today's scripture, Jesus sternly told the man he had just cured of leprosy *not* to tell anyone, but the man did the *opposite.*

Jesus knew that people would focus on his incredible miracles and would miss the point.
It wasn't about him!
It was about people *being restored to wholeness* through acts of *love, mercy, forgiveness, compassion and justice.*

This was the *kingdom of God!*
Jesus wanted to be a *servant*, not a *superstar.*
The world's philosophy tells us to strive for fame and fortune, which props up a *false self* and leads to *inner emptiness.*

Following Christ means *detaching* from the enticement of power, prestige and possessions. This allows the *true self* to rise, which leads to *inner fullness.*

Which path will *you* choose?

Listen to the song for the day "Let It Be Done to Me" on the *Mercy Reigns* album.

JANUARY

12

GIVE GLORY TO GOD

Psalm 50:23

Those who offer praise as a sacrifice honor me.

It seems that God is more interested in you sacrificing your *ego* than sacrificing any *material* things.

Jesus said, "Go and learn the meaning of the words, 'I desire mercy, not sacrifice'" (Matthew 9:13).

He was echoing what the prophet Hosea had said: "For it is loyalty that I desire, not sacrifice, and knowledge of God rather than burnt offerings" (Hosea 6:6).

When you sacrifice your ego's cravings, you are free to give your *loyalty* to God.

Only then can you offer God your heart.
Then your *true self* is revealed.

When you are being your true self, you are being the unique reflection of God that you were intended to be.

As St. Irenaeus said, "The glory of God is the human person fully alive."
Just as *all creation* gives glory to God through its very *being*, so do *we*.

But it's *only human beings* who seem to have a *choice.*

When we wholeheartedly share our gifts and talents for the betterment and goodness of the world instead of our selfish interests, we are truly *praising our Creator.*

So *be you* with *all your heart.*

Listen to the song for the day "Glorify You with Me" on the *Give Praise and Thanks* album.

BE STILL

Mark 1:35-38

Rising very early before dawn, he left and went off to a deserted place, where he prayed. Simon and those who were with him pursued him and on finding him said, "Everyone is looking for you." He told them, "Let us go on to the nearby villages that I may preach there also. For this purpose have I come."

Follow Jesus' prayer practice.

He often went to a "deserted place" to pray.

When he taught his followers how to pray, he instructed them to "go to your inner room, close the door, and pray to your Father in secret." He also told them to not use many words (Matthew 6:6-7).

It seems important to spend time in relative *silence* with God. This time of *surrender* is exactly the foundation from which Jesus' next steps in ministry *arose*: *contemplation* leads to *action*.

I recommend a regular *meditation* or *centering prayer* practice, before dawn is ideal but not mandatory.

This is *not* a time to think. It is a time to *not think;* a time to *let go* and *listen*.

As St. John of the Cross said, "Silence is God's first language." To which Thomas Keating added, "Everything else is a poor translation."

Listen to the song for the day "Slow Me Down" on the *Mercy Reigns* album.

JANUARY

14 BEHIND THE FAÇADE

1 Samuel 16:7

"Not as man sees does God see, because man sees the appearance but the Lord looks into the heart."

How true!
And yet appearance continues to be the world's criterion for determining a person's worth and identity.
Appearances are *deceiving*.

God's criterion is at the *heart* level.
That is where God sees us as we are, the positives and the negatives together.
God's *seeing* is through the *lens of love*.
Our Loving Creator sees each of us as a *beloved daughter* or *son*.

As for you and me, let us look at ourselves and ask:
Am I trying to uphold an appearance? A *false self*, instead of my *true self* as a *beloved daughter or son of God?*

When we become aware of our *egos in action*, trying to build a false persona and all that goes with it, our egos will finally begin to *diminish*.

It is only then that our *true selves* can begin to *rise*.

Stop for a moment and become *aware* of *your inner self*.
Become *aware* of your *beating heart*.
Become *aware* that with *each* beat you are loved for your *innate worth as a child of God*.
Rest in that awareness.

Be* the Love you *are!

Listen to the song for the day "How Wonderful to Me" on the *Live to Love* album.

GLORIOUS

Psalm 78:4

We do not keep them from our children;
we recount them to the next generation, the praiseworthy deeds of the LORD and his strength,
the wonders that he performed.

It's easy to miss the miracles happening all around us each moment.
It's happening in *nature*, in our *bodies*, in the *earth*, in the *skies*, and in the *grand expanses of the universe.*
But many times we focus on the *human-made delusions* that spring from *egomania.*

Instead of *love* being our motivation, it's *greed* and *fear.*
We must *wake up!*
We need to make it a regular practice to pass along to the next generation "the praiseworthy deeds" of God!
We need to tell them the wonders that God performed!
That means, of course, that we must *pay attention* to those wonders.
This takes a *contemplative approach* to life.
It takes being a *mystic.*
As Richard Rohr puts it, "Mysticism is about the experiential knowledge of God…not just textbook definitions."
Or as the Jesuit theologian Karl Rahner wrote, "The Christian of the future will be a mystic, or he will not exist at all (in *Theological Investigations* XX, 149)."
Mysticism, he wrote, is "a genuine experience of God emerging from the very heart of our existence."

Are you *awake* to the *sacred in your midst?*

A *contemplative prayer practice* will be very helpful if not essential.

Listen to the song for the day "How Magnificent, Wondrous and Glorious" on the *Mercy Reigns* album.

JANUARY

16

Open Minds and Hearts

Mark 2:22

"No one pours new wine into old wineskins. Otherwise, the wine will burst the skins, and both the wine and the skins are ruined. Rather, new wine is poured into fresh wineskins."

Jesus was making the point that sometimes *old containers and structures* need to be *replaced* or at least *revised.*

Many prophets called on the current institutions of their day to change.

One such prophet was Martin Luther King, Jr.

The "dream" he preached about so famously has yet to be realized.

Jesus is still calling us to listen to his words above.
The institutional *Church* should listen to Jesus as well.

Today we have vast new knowledge in the realms of medicine, science, psychology, astronomy, etc.
There have been many advances.
No one would dream of treating an illness with a *first century* treatment.

All this new information and understanding affects and informs our practices today, and that includes religion.

At least, it *should.*

New wine is being poured.

Be open to following the Spirit to new frontiers.

Listen to the song for the day "God Is the Goal" on the *Live to Love* album.

LOVE RULES

Mark 3:2

They watched him closely to see if they might accuse him.

It was the Sabbath and under the religious laws, work was forbidden.

The law's purpose was to help people focus on their relationship with God.

But when Jesus was confronted with the situation of curing a man with a withered hand, he knew that extending God's love would trump following the law.

The Pharisees were blind to this.

Their hearts were hardened.

Sometimes the *rule book* has to be put aside.

Jesus said the greatest commandments were to *love God* and to *love your neighbor as yourself.*

Allow God's love to rule your life.

Open your heart in a new way today!

Listen to the song for the day "Love God" on the *Live to Love* album.

JANUARY

18 GOD IS CALLING

Mark 3:13

He went up the mountain and summoned those whom he wanted and they came to him.

Jesus called his apostles and they followed him.

They left whatever lives they had chosen and ended up doing something *completely different.*

It required letting go of their *self-centered* desires.

Be open to hearing God's voice in your heart.

Jesus is still calling us to follow him.

For *each* of us the call will lead us to a *unique path* in which we use our God-given talents to make this world a better place, to "build the Kingdom of God."

It's never too *early* or too *late* to *listen to your heart* and *follow Jesus.*

It will no doubt require changes in your life and perhaps taking a road less traveled, but you will experience great joy and peace along the path of becoming your *true self.*

Listen to the song for the day "Take the Road Less Traveled" on the *Live to Love* album.

BE PRESENT

Mark 4:18-19

"Those (seeds) sown among thorns are another sort. They are the people who hear the word, but worldly anxiety, the lure of riches, and the craving for other things intrude and choke the word, and it bears no fruit."

We have heard the words of Jesus many times.
The question is: Have the "seeds" (Jesus' words) sprouted and taken root?

Continuing with that metaphor, have we *tended our soil?*

How *fertile* is our soil?

Do we "fertilize" by setting aside time to practice *silent* prayer or to *contemplate* and *reflect* on scripture?

Do we regularly take part in spiritual reading?

Do we *consciously open our awareness* to *see* and to *hear* God through our interactions with people and nature?

Or, do we allow "worldly anxiety, the lure of riches, and the craving for other things" to rule our lives?

Perhaps if we spent more time cultivating our soil, the thorns (all the distractions of the world) would *wither* and our lives would *blossom* in ways we could never have imagined!

Listen to the song for the day "God's Love Is All You Need" on the *Listen to Your Heart* album.

JANUARY

20 GOD'S WILL

Psalm 40:7

Sacrifice or oblation you wished not, but ears open to obedience you gave me.

This scripture is very similar to what the prophet Hosea said that God told him to preach: "For it is loyalty that I desire, not sacrifice, and knowledge of God rather than burnt offerings." (Hosea 6:6).

Jesus quoted it as well: "Go and learn the meaning of the words, 'I desire mercy, not sacrifice.' I did not come to call the righteous but sinners" (Matthew 9:13).

It seems God doesn't need our sacrifices.

That doesn't mean that our sacrifices are *bad* – not if they are actually making us more *loving, compassionate,* and *forgiving.*

When we sacrifice our *egos*, we sacrifice *our* way for *God's* way.

And *God's* way is *always* the *loving, compassionate* and *forgiving* way.

May it be *ours* as well.

Listen to the song for the day "Breathe On Me" on the *Listen to Your Heart* album.

MAKE YOUR MUSIC

JANUARY

21

Psalm 96:1

Sing to the LORD a new song;
sing to the LORD, all the earth.

Each day gives us a *new opportunity* to sing a *new song* to our loving Creator.

Whatever happened *yesterday* is *over* and *gone.*

What will be in the *future* is only *God's* to know.

The only time that is *real* is *now.*

Each *moment* is a *gift*, a true "present." It is where we meet the true Presence of God.

So *be fully present* to that gift.

Live each moment and *be who you are*, channeling God's love and goodness through your unique gifts.

All living things are singing their unique songs in each successive moment.

May *each* of us *join the chorus!*

Listen to the song for the day "Sing a New Song" on the *Live to Love* album.

JANUARY

22 BE OPEN

Psalm 40:2, 4

I waited, waited for the Lord; who bent down and heard my cry, and put a new song in my mouth, a hymn to our God.

This Psalm is very powerful and meaningful to me
because it is very literally true in my life.

I cried out to God. I waited.
Ultimately, I was given a new song in my mouth.

It all happened on a Friday evening of the first week of March in 1997.
That was the start of a transformation that would lead me to begin writing songs about my spiritual journey.

What is it that *you* are crying out to God for at this moment?

Trust. Wait. Be open.

Wait in the sense of being intensely *present*.

This is the *only* time that God can speak to you.
When the time is right according to a much *bigger picture* than we can see, like a loving Father or Mother, God will direct you to something new and amazing.

It's what you are yearning for.

God made you to manifest God's Presence in the world in a way that only *you* can do!

Listen to the song for the day "Show Me…Me" on the *Listen to Your Heart* album.

HAVE FAITH

2 Timothy 1:8

...bear your share of hardship for the gospel with the strength that comes from God.

If you follow Jesus you are called to make the Good News of God's unconditional love, mercy, forgiveness, and compassion the motivations for your life.

Others who are motivated by the pursuit of power, prestige and possessions will clash with you.

Perhaps there is a clash of motivations going on *inside you* as well.

We *all* struggle with the *world's* influences.

St. Paul wrote today's scripture verse while in prison for preaching the gospel.

God doesn't promise a life of no struggles, but *does* promise to give us purpose, fulfillment, inner-peace and strength amidst the struggles.

Open yourself to God's grace by spending some time in silent prayer, scripture reading and any practice that makes you *present* to the *Divine Presence.*

That will require a daily practice of *letting go* of your *ego's* desires, so that *God's* desires might rise in you.

Listen to the song for the day "Turn Off the Noise" on the *Listen to Your Heart* album.

JANUARY

24 INNER VOICE

Psalm 37:4

Find your delight in the Lord who will give you your heart's desire.

We all have a hole in our hearts that we are trying to fill, a *yearning* that we are trying to satisfy.

Are you trying to fill that void with something material or physical?

The *yearning* will only be truly satisfied with a spiritual solution.

God placed that hole in your heart so that *only* God could fill it. God *wants* to fill it but gives us our freedom to *respond.*

When and how do you experience joy?

This is the place where God *loves* experiencing the world through you.

How is God *calling* you to use your *abilities* and *talents* as a *channel* of God's love to the world?

***Listen* to that *inner*-voice and it will *lead* you to your heart's desire.**

Listen to the song for the day "Listen to Your Heart" on the *Listen to Your Heart* album.

PEACE AND JOY

Hebrews 10:34

You even joined in the sufferings of those in prison and joyfully accepted the confiscation of your property, knowing that you had a better and lasting possession.

What are the things that bring you happiness?

Are they *human-made* things that will not last or *spiritual* things that *will*?

What is at the center of your *motivation* for whatever you do? Is it to please your ego or to please *God?*

We tend to treasure material possessions while *God* treasures love, mercy, forgiveness, compassion and justice.

We are actually *spiritual beings* in the *process* of *becoming* the *unique human expression of God's Love*. Many times we get side-tracked into the grasping for power, prestige and possessions.

We will have to *let go* of *all those things* when we die.

Why not start letting them go *now?*

As your attachments *diminish* your true self *emerges*.
It springs from the depths inside you where God (Love) abides at your core.

***Peace* and *joy* are available now, for the *kingdom of God is present.* (Luke 17:21).**

"Be still and know that I am God!" (Psalm 46:11).

Listen to the song for the day "Love Will Always Lead You Home" on the *Mercy Reigns* album.

JANUARY

26 YOU ARE INVITED

Mark 4:26-27

He said, "This is how it is with the kingdom of God; it is as if a man were to scatter seed on the land and would sleep and rise night and day and the seed would sprout and grow, he knows not how."

When Jesus spoke of the "kingdom of God" he was almost never talking about some *distant* reward.
He interchangeably talked about the "kingdom of God" and the "kingdom of heaven," but was almost always talking about the *now.*
That is obvious in today's scripture.

Jesus also said that the kingdom of God, or what we sometimes refer to as the reign of God, is "among you." (Luke 17:21).
This can also be translated as "within you."

Whether we are aware of it or not, the kingdom of God is growing in our very midst.
It is at work in the *very fiber of all that is.*
As St Paul says, "We know that all creation is groaning in labor pains even until now." (Romans 8:22).
All of creation began with Love's spark and will end in a grand finale of Love's masterpiece. It's just a matter of time.

The question is: *Will we take part in it?*
Most of creation has no choice. *We do.*
Each of us can cooperate in the on-going coming of the kingdom of God, a place of love, mercy, forgiveness, justice and compassion. Or, we can choose not to.
Or, we can be completely unaware of it happening.

May we awaken to the reign-of-God-in-progress and *enter the dance!*

Listen to the song for the day "Shall We Sing" on the *Listen to Your Heart* album.

JANUARY

27

SHINE GOD'S LIGHT

Mark 4:21

He said to them, "Is a lamp brought in to be placed under a bushel basket or under a bed, and not to be placed on a lampstand?"

Do you know how *deeply* God loves you?

We are told in scripture that God *is* Love.

Each of us is God's *beloved child.*

This is the truth, the *Good News.*

All that God asks is that you *accept it.*

It's that easy!

Are you keeping the Good News of God's unconditional love, mercy, grace, forgiveness and compassion inside yourself, or are you sharing it with others?

How can you use your gifts and talents to be God's light to the world?

Listen to the song for the day "May I Be Light" on the *Listen to Your Heart* album.

JANUARY

28 GO WITH THE FLOW

Mark 4:24

"The measure with which you measure will be measured out to you…"

What Jesus was saying is the more you *give*, the more you *receive*.

It's the law of the Universe.

It's the law of Love.

It's the way of the Trinitarian God: a *non-stop-Flow* of *giving* and *receiving*.

God creates this way.

All things *blossom* then *wither* in giving themselves in the making of new life.

Jesus demonstrated this *self-emptying* model with his whole life.

As St. Paul described it, "He emptied himself, taking the form of a slave, coming in human likeness; and found human in appearance, he humbled himself, becoming obedient to death, even death on a cross." (Philippians 2:7-8).

This is the path of *kenosis* that we are *all* called to *give-ourselves-over-to*.

Enter the Flow and love *everyone* and *everything*.

Give freely.

Only *then* will you truly be *you*.

Listen to the song for the day "Pour Me Out" on the *Give Praise and Thanks* album.

LOST AND FOUND

JANUARY
29

Matthew 10:39

"Whoever finds his life will lose it, and whoever loses his life for my sake will find it."

Jesus made this statement when telling his followers that in order to choose following him, they must turn from their ego's desires.

The *ego* seeks happiness in p*ower, prestige and possessions*, but such happiness will be *brief* and the desire for more, *endless.*

The result will be never knowing your *true self*, the person God made you to be.

In other words, if you're looking to discover who you are and why you are here by choosing to satisfy your ego, it will lead to *emptiness.*

Power, prestige and possessions *cannot last* and will disappear at death for sure.

Turn from worldly desires as your motivation and instead follow the way of Jesus. You will find your *true self* and *inner peace,* as well.

This will require reading the gospels and spending time with the Lord.

Listen to the song for the day "You'll Lead Me" on the *Listen to Your Heart* album.

JANUARY

30 BUILDING THE KINGDOM OF GOD

Matthew 9:37

Then Jesus said to his disciples, "The harvest is abundant but the laborers are few; so ask the master of the harvest to send out laborers for his harvest."

Each one of us is called to spread the Good News that *all* are loved *unconditionally* by God and that *following Jesus* is the path to *wholeness* (salvation).

There is *nothing* to fear.

Everything that *is*, is a *gift* from God!

We are called to cooperate *with God* in building God's kingdom *here* by *allowing* God to work *through* us.

God has a *dream* for *all of creation.*

God has a dream for *you*, for *everyone* and *everything.*

What will be *your* unique contribution to God's *ongoing* creation?

The answer will be found in sharing your *talents, gifts and inner passions.*

Allow God to send you out in the service of all.

It is the path to *fulfillment, freedom* and your *true self.*

Listen to the song for the day "Salvation" on the *Live to Love* album.

OPEN YOUR HEART

Matthew 11:25

Jesus said in reply, "I give praise to you, Father, Lord of heaven and earth, for although you have hidden these things from the wise and the learned you have revealed them to the childlike."

The "wise" and the "learned" sometimes think *brain power equals superiority.*

But God seems to have a particular fondness for the *simple* and *humble.*

When our *egos* are in control, we are often quite *unaware* of God's Presence.

That's because we are too *full of ourselves.*

If a person is only motivated by his or her ego's insatiable desires to be the center of the universe, that person will never truly become the "real self" that God intended.

Simply *observe* your ego's demands.

This will *begin* the *process* of the ego's *diminishment* and give your *true self* a chance to *emerge.*

Jesus opened himself totally to God's will and allowed God to define him: "This is my beloved son, with whom I am well pleased." (Matthew 3:17).

Each of us* is also God's *beloved child.

For us to know who we *truly are,* we must put a *childlike trust* in our Creator, open our ears, eyes and hearts and then begin to *live the answer!*

Listen to the song for the day "The Way You Are" on the *Mercy Reigns* album.

1 LET GO

Hebrews 10:32, 36

Remember the days past when, after you had been enlightened, you endured a great contest of suffering. You need endurance to do the will of God and receive what he has promised.

Have you been "enlightened?"
Many times we have "aha" moments, but true *enlightenment* is
not just a *momentary inspiration.*
It's *life-changing.*
It's a complete shift in a *paradigm.*
The meaning of *your* existence and *all* existence *shifts.*
The *way you see* your *consciousness* changes.
For me, I have to say that enlightenment is a *process that ever deepens.*
But there was a moment – an *epiphany* – after which my life would never be the same.
I can easily go back to that moment and see that my old life died and *something new was born* in that moment.
But it was *not* easy.
The old ways of life no longer made sense to me.
I had to change a number of behaviors and beliefs.
That brought more than a little pain and anguish: a "great contest of suffering."
Looking back at what I endured, I see that God was leading me to new life.
I am *very grateful!*
You can't *manufacture* enlightenment.
Life delivers it.
If you know in your heart that you are being *called*, let me tell you:
Listen to that *inner yearning.*
Surrender* to it. *Open your heart.
Go where you are led and know that you are being led safely to
wholeness (*salvation*) and your *true self.*

Listen to the song for the day "Take the Road Less Traveled" on the Live to Love album.

TRUST IN A HIGHER POWER

Luke 2:26-30,32

It had been revealed to Simeon by the holy Spirit that he should not see death before he had seen the Messiah of the Lord. He came in the Spirit into the temple; and when the parents brought in the child Jesus to perform the custom of the law in regard to him, he took him into his arms and blessed God, saying: "Now, Master, you may let your servant go in peace, according to your word, for my eyes have seen your salvation, a light for revelation to the Gentiles, and glory for your people Israel."

Simeon must have been a very spiritual man.

He must have *cultivated* a relationship with God by spending time in *quiet* contemplation so as to know the *stirrings* and *movements* of the Holy Spirit.

He also was not stuck in his *preconceived ideas* of God or how God acts.

He was *open* to something new, or he would not have been open to seeing God in the face of a little baby!

Are you taking time to *cultivate* a relationship with God through *quiet reflection* and *contemplation?*

Are you open to God doing something new in *your life?*

Listen to the song for the day "Let It Be Done to Me" on the *Mercy Reigns* album.

3 CHANGE DIRECTION

Mark 6:12

So they went off and preached repentance.

When Jesus sent off the apostles they were *not* sent off to scare people with threats of punishment.

They were sent out to tell the "Good News" of God's love!

They were sent out to tell all people to *repent* – as in, *turn away* from the ways in which you are looking for happiness – and *turn toward* God.

When you *know* that you are loved, your heart will *melt*, and you will *want* to *share* that love with others.

You will *want* others to *turn toward* this God of Unconditional Love.

What is the *motivation* of your *daily living?*
Is it to please *you*, or to please *God?*

Paradoxically, when you live to please *God*, you end up pleasing *yourself*, because God wants *nothing more* than for *you* to be happy and fulfilled!

Listen to the song for the day "God Is the Goal" on the *Live to Love* album.

HELP IS NEAR

Psalm 31:23

Once I said in my anguish, "I am cut off from your sight." Yet you heard my voice, my cry for mercy, when I pleaded with you for help.

Sometimes it takes hitting *rock bottom* before our egos will finally *relinquish control* long enough for us to actually be *present* to the *Divine Presence.*
It is only then that we have a chance to actually *hear* God.

Paradoxically, that is also when we can hear our *true self.*
As Thomas Merton said, "If I find (God), I will find myself, and if I find my true self I will find (God). (*New Seeds of Contemplation*)
For me, I had to become *completely miserable* with my job, and life in general, before my ego would *surrender.*
It happened on a Friday in March of 1997.
That's when I heard in the silence of my heart: "get your guitar" – a guitar I hadn't *touched* in ten years.
I did pick up my guitar that day and ten years later I released my first album of original songs titled *Listen to Your Heart.*
Today I have four albums and two published books.

The music led me on a winding path to youth ministry, chaplaincy, jail ministry and social justice work.
God *does hear us* when we cry out.
God *always hears us*, it's just that many times we are only listening to the constant chatter of our *ego-controlled minds.*
Now is the time to *stop*, take a *deep breath*, be *present*, and *listen.*

You are already *perfectly loved* and *complete.*
Live from *that* place.

Listen to the song for the day "Make Your Way" on the *Mercy Reigns* album.

FEBRUARY

5 LIFE SONG

The Book of Sirach 47:8

With his every deed he offered thanks to God Most High, in words of praise. With his whole being he loved his Maker and daily had his praises sung.

King David was said to have lived much of his life in thanks and praise to God.

Jesus was the perfect example of living in thanksgiving, totally pouring himself out in compassion and love to all those in need.

The word "Eucharist" comes from a Greek word that means "giving thanks."

When Jesus broke the bread, gave it to his followers and said, "Take and eat; this is my body" (Matthew 26:26), he meant for his followers to *become* the *body of Christ.*

You've heard the old adage: "You *are* what you *eat*"?

When we eat the Eucharist, we are meant to *become thanksgiving.*

We take *the-way-of-Jesus* into the world so that the kingdom of God truly comes in the *here and now.*

When we are thankful for all that we've been given, we live in thanks-*giving.* Giving our thanks to others, we sing the praises of our Maker.

Each of our lives becomes a melody adding new harmony to a wondrous Divine Symphony.

Listen to the song for the day "Sing a New Song" on the *Live to Love* album.

LISTEN TO YOUR HEART

FEBRUARY

6

Mark 6:4-5

Jesus said to them, "A prophet is not without honor except in his native place and among his own kin and in his own house." So he was not able to perform any mighty deed there.

You know deep within your heart that you have a *calling*. At least, I hope you do.
If not, *I'm letting you know right now!*
You are here to share the love of God with the world in the *unique* way that only *you* can.
Hopefully, by grace, you are able to respond to the call
or you will never have inner peace.
If you respond, you will have new life.
All it takes is *being present* to life as your *true self.*
That will mean *letting go of all the attachments that are distractions from this path.*
And that will mean *making changes.*
It will *not* be an easy road.
Those closest to you will likely *not respond favorably* to your *changed ways.*
Those in Jesus' home town were first "astonished" by his teaching in the synagogue. But then they remembered how he was before he had left town, how Jesus had been a simple carpenter and the "son of Mary."
Then they "took offense at him." (Mark 6:3).
Let this be a lesson to you: Do not look for approval or validation from someone before you follow the dream in your heart.
When you set off on a new course with enthusiasm,
those close to you will feel their status quo threatened.
Most people do not want to change!
That's okay, *change anyway!*
Listen to your life speak* and *follow your dreams.
It's never too *late* – or *early* – to start!

Listen to the song for the day "Listen to Your Heart" on the *Listen to Your Heart* album.

FEBRUARY

7 BE FREE

Mark 6:7-8

Jesus summoned the Twelve and began to send them out two by two and gave them authority over unclean spirits. He instructed them to take nothing for the journey but a walking stick—no food, no sack, no money in their belts.

How *reckless* to send people out on a journey with *nothing!*

Actually, this is an example of *radical trust.*

It's ridding yourself of all *attachments* so that you can focus on the *one thing.*

Yes, this is *radical.* But Jesus is making a *point*.

Do *you,* as a *follower* of Jesus, *trust* in the *care of God?*

As Jesus put it later in this same gospel passage, "Therefore I tell you, do not worry about your life, what you will eat [or drink], or about your body, what you will wear. Is not life more than food and the body more than clothing? Look at the birds in the sky; they do not sow or reap, they gather nothing into barns, yet your heavenly Father feeds them. Are not you more important than they?" (Matthew 6:25-26).

So why not *let go* of all that *clutter*, all that *stuff* that is *distracting* you from the *one thing:* being *present* to the *Divine Presence.*

This is the only way to be open to *receiving* and *channeling* the love of God in each moment in the unique circumstances of your life.

Listen to the song for the day "Breathe On Me" on the *Listen to Your Heart* album.

GOD CENTERED

Mark 7:24

Jesus entered a house and wanted no one to know about it, but he could not escape notice.

It's very refreshing to realize that Jesus did not want *notoriety.*

He did not strive for the spotlight of *stardom.*

Jesus was always spending time with the rejects, the "nobodies."

His mission was to *heal, free the oppressed, include the outcast* and *restore people to their communities.*

He didn't want *recognition.*

The focus was *not* on *him* as a great healer but on the *other* in need of experiencing God's unconditional love.

Jesus showed us that God wants to *be with us in our brokenness* and wants to *lead us to wholeness.*

In my life, it was God's intimate embrace *during my struggles* that *transformed* me.

The journey *itself* is *intertwined with God* so that as we *live our questions* we *find our answers* in the *process of growing in love.*

As writer and retreat leader Paula D'Arcy said,
"God comes to you disguised as your life."

Listen to the song for the day "Love God" on the *Live to Love* album.

FEBRUARY

9 DETACHMENT

James 1:11

For the sun comes up with its scorching heat and dries up the grass, its flower droops, and the beauty of its appearance vanishes. So will the rich person fade away in the midst of his pursuits.

Be on guard against the pursuit of *power, prestige* and *possessions.*
In and of themselves they are not evil as long as you do not *identify* with them or get *attached* to them.
When used for good they each can be sources of great good.
But when they become *ends in themselves*, when they become our *first priority*, when we *attach* them to our own *identity*, they lead to a *dead end.*
Why would you pursue things that by their very nature will *dry up* and *vanish?*
Pursuing such things will divert you from discovering your *true self* and thereby away from doing your part in building the kingdom of God.

Jesus seemed to enjoy a good party. He said that some criticized him because he "came eating and drinking and they said, 'Look, he is a glutton and a drunkard.'" (Matthew 11:19).
While Jesus *enjoyed* life, he did not become *attached* to any of it, freely *letting go* of all that God gave him.

When you are grounded in a relationship with God – when you find your identity in *being God's beloved* – your motivations will not be self-centered but for the good of all.
Worldly pursuits* will end up producing an *empty life,* while *Godly pursuits* will end up producing an *abundant life.

And the beauty of it all is that God's love is available *now* and *always within you.*

All you have to do is *awaken to the moment* and *fall into Love's endless embrace.*

Listen to the song for the day "Pour Me Out" on the *Give Praise and Thanks* album.

SHADES OF GRAY

Mark 7:8-9

"You disregard God's commandment but cling to human tradition." Jesus went on to say, "How well you have set aside the commandment of God in order to uphold your tradition!"

How many religious rules exclude people from belonging?
This seems to contradict the life of Jesus.

He was quite at home with the people thrown-out by their own religion as well as with a wide variety of "sinners."

The only group Jesus sharply criticized was the Pharisees: the *religious leaders.*
They held the people to strict rules no matter what the situation, not allowing any exception based on compassion and grace.

They saw everything as *black or white* when real life is made up of many *shades of gray.*

Rules are nice to have as a foundation to give us some guidance.
But don't forget that Jesus said the two greatest commandments are to *love God with all your heart, soul and mind* and to *love your neighbor as yourself.* (Matthew 22:38-39).

Love is the *top priority.*
It allowed Jesus to set aside rules quite frequently.
How could anyone miss this?

Rules must be tempered by mercy and forgiveness.

Filter all you see and do through the *lens of love.*

Listen to the song for the day "Mercy Reigns" on the *Mercy Reigns* album.

II CYCLE OF LOVE

Psalm 104:29-30

When you take away their breath, they perish and return to the dust. When you send forth your spirit, they are created and you renew the face of the earth.

We are part of a grand cycle of *dying and rising.*
It's been happening since the universe began with the *big bang,*
estimated to have happened *14 billion years ago.*
We have no idea what was before that!

We see this cycle at work in all things: *birth, growth, decline* and *death.*
It happens *throughout the cosmos.*
Life, somehow, is *animated* or *sparked into being.*
We believe the Animator, the Giver of Life, is God, Who *is* Love *itself.* (1 John 4:8).

Each* of us has a *part* in this cycle and *God* is *intimately involved in all of it.
St. Paul described our *interconnectedness* with God in this way:
"In him we live and move and have our being." (Acts 17:28).

Jesus showed us that life is an exercise in *letting go, dying before dying.*
When we *die* to our egos' *self-centered desires,* our *true selves rise.*
We are called to do what Jesus did, "Who, though he was in the form of God,
did not regard equality with God something to be grasped.
Rather, he emptied himself." (Philippians 2:6-7).

God *empties God-self into us and all things,* and then we and all things *empty ourselves back into God.*

And Jesus also showed us that death is *not* the *end,* but the *beginning* of *new life* that is *eternal.*

Listen to the song for the day "Seasons" on the *Listen to Your Heart* album.

LESSON IN LIFE

Psalm 128:1

Blessed are all who fear the LORD, and who walk in his ways.

My translation of today's scripture would be: "Happy and fulfilled are all those who are full of awe when contemplating God, and who walk in God's ways."

The word "fear" is a *poor* translation.

Stop being afraid of God!

Jesus often told his followers to *not* be afraid.

Jesus described God as a loving Father: "Look at the birds in the sky; they do not sow or reap, they gather nothing into barns, yet your heavenly Father feeds them. Are not you more important than they?" (Matthew 6:26).

Another scripture I often quote is, "God is love." (1 John 4:8).
Further along in that passage it states, "There is no fear in love, but perfect love drives out fear because fear has to do with punishment, and so one who fears is not yet perfect in love. We love because he first loved us." (1 John 4:18-19).

So *fear not!*

Then *walk in the ways of Jesus* who *personified* God in all he *said* and *did.*

First and foremost: *love God and your neighbor as yourself.*

Listen to the song for the day "How Wonderful to Me" on the *Live to Love* album.

FEBRUARY

13 STOP. LOOK. LISTEN.

Mark 8:18

"Do you have eyes and not see, ears and not hear?"

It seems that much of the time, we are on "auto-pilot."
Our eyes and ears are *functioning*, but they aren't really *seeing* and *hearing*.
We find ourselves walking around in a *daze.*
While our eyes and ears are technically seeing and hearing, our minds are nattering away on something *far, far away* from what's right in front of us.
We aren't truly *present* to what *is*.

Jesus' question in today's scripture verse is meant to jolt us awake.
Be present!
There's another layer here.
I will only speak for myself, but I know how many times the rug has been pulled out from under my "certainty" about one thing or another.

To really *see* and *hear* is to be *open* and *humble*.
The mystery of God and the universe, and *our place in it* is still *unfolding.*

Beware of people who give you stock answers of *certainty* in the realm of *mystery.*
If you truly had the answer, there would be no need to take the journey.
I believe God wants you to take your unique journey so that you are *transformed* by the answer you'll find *on the way*.
***Being given easy answers* will *not* transform you.**
Living out tough questions will!

Following Jesus requires the *humility* to admit *we don't know* and the *willingness* and *openness* to be *changed.*

Listen to the song for the day "Changed" on the *Give Praise and Thanks* album.

SAVED

Luke 9:23-24

Jesus said to all, "If anyone wishes to come after me, he must deny himself and take up his cross daily and follow me. For whoever wishes to save his life will lose it, but whoever loses his life for my sake will save it."

This is a *key* teaching of Jesus, but probably is mostly *skimmed-over* out of lack of understanding.

He's giving us the formula for living our lives, for becoming our *true selves.*

To *deny yourself* is to deny your *ego's self-centered desires* so you can truly *be present to yourself* and *those around you.*

To *take up your cross* is to then carry *whatever struggles you might encounter in following the way of Jesus.*

Living for the greater Good of all* will *not* endear you to those playing the *world's game.

It will make you *radically different* in the eyes of today's culture which tells you to grab and amass more and more possessions, to satisfy your ego's every whim and desire, and avoid struggles while numbing your vulnerabilities.

The paradox is this: If we follow our *culture's* path we end up with lots of *material stuff* that all eventually *disappears* and we never actually know our *true selves.*

But if we follow Jesus and *let go* of our ego's insatiable desires we end up finding the *true meaning* of our existence.

That is *truly* salvation!

Listen to the song for the day "Breathe On Me" on the *Listen to Your Heart* album.

FEBRUARY

15 MASKS OFF

Mark 8:35

"For whoever wishes to save his life will lose it, but whoever loses his life for my sake and that of the gospel will save it."

Jesus often taught through *paradox*, defined as "a seemingly contradictory statement that may nonetheless be true."

When you *save* your life you actually *lose* it. But when you *lose* your life for the sake of spreading Jesus' message, you actually *save* your life.
How so?

Although I wouldn't have consciously admitted it, there was a time when I was a radio news anchor that I craved a certain amount of fame and attention. But eventually, I became miserable.
"My" life was largely formed by my *ego*. I had built up what Thomas Merton would have called my *false self*.

When I finally started following a deep, spiritual yearning in my heart, I started to feel a sense of both excitement and dread! I had to *let go* of 20 years of what I had worked hard to become.
It felt like *dying*, but it was actually a *new birth*.
It was through my *ego-crushing*, *faltering* steps away from my former life that I found *more life* in ministry than I *ever thought was possible*.

Jesus knows what he's talking about!
What is the deep, spiritual yearning inside of *you* asking *you* to walk away from so you can be led to *your* true self?

Listen to the song for the day "Take the Road Less Traveled" on the *Live to Love* album.

CHECK YOUR MOTIVATION

FEBRUARY **16**

Matthew 7:7

"Ask and it will be given to you; seek and you will find; knock and the door will be opened to you."

It seems to me that many people approach God as more like a
genie or *Santa Claus* figure, than a *loving Creator.*
God is clearly *not* some "magic-granter-of-wishes."
We clearly see that asking for any *whim* we have in mind is usually *not* granted.

So what do we make of today's scripture verse?
If God *is* love then wouldn't God want us to be happy?
I say *yes.*

But what is *true, lasting* happiness?
The granting of wishes to satisfy our egos may bring happiness, but
it will be superficial and fleeting.
True happiness is at the "soul" level. I'm thinking that God wants you and me
to *know* love and to be *transformed* by love so that we can *be more loving.*
Now *that* would be *happiness!*

Unfortunately, for that to happen usually requires some painful lessons.
Each of us must learn that our egos are *not* the center of the universe.
Each of us is part of a larger whole.
We are required to act in "oneness" with all others and all creation or
we will essentially be dysfunctional at the soul level.
We are part of a great cosmic and divine dance.
So, with that in mind, for *what* do I ask? *What* do I seek? On *what door* do I knock?
Is my motivation *love*, or *selfish gain?*

If we ask from this vantage point, we will be in the *process of receiving*
and finding exactly what we need.

Listen to the song for the day "Shall We Sing" on the *Listen to Your Heart* album.

FEBRUARY

17 GLORY BE

Psalm 29:1-2

Give to the LORD, you sons and daughters of God, give to the LORD glory and might; Give to the LORD the glory due his name.

Who is *God?*
We believe that God is the Creator of all things.
We also believe that God *is* Love. (1 John 4:8).
Love is still *creating.*

We were spawned by this Love, this Ground of Being.
So how might each of us give glory to this Infinite Love, this Infinite *Beingness?*

By being *ourselves. That's* how.
Be *you.*

You are a *unique manifestation* of this *Divine Love*, your *quirks* and *all.*
Only *you* can be this manifestation of the Holy, the Transcendent.
You and you *alone.*

So don't try to be anything but *you.*
Be *present* to your *deepest desires* and express your uniqueness as your creative contribution to the *unfolding expression of Divine Love.*
It's not about *attaining worthiness!*

You are worthy *now.*
Each moment, you are a *beloved* and *cherished* child of God.
When you are being *you* each *precious moment,* you are *giving glory to God.*

Listen to the song for the day "Glorify You with Me" on the *Give Praise and Thanks* album.

GOD'S WILL

Matthew 6:8-10

"Your Father knows what you need before you ask him. This is how you are to pray: Our Father in heaven, hallowed be your name, your kingdom come, your will be done, on earth as in heaven."

A toddler wants all kinds of stuff, but a loving parent knows what the toddler truly *needs*.

***How much more* is this so with our Loving Creator?**

You are the beloved child of the Maker of the Universe!

Jesus said that the will of God was that His kingdom would come "on earth as in heaven."

The question is, am I more interested in building *my* kingdom or *God's?*

What we truly *need* is *God's* kingdom.

How will God's kingdom come about "on earth" if not through the cooperation of you and me?

Loving God, how do you want to do this through me?

Listen to the song for the day "Listen to Your Heart" on the *Listen to Your Heart* album.

FEBRUARY

19 SWEET SURRENDER

Psalm 23:1

The LORD is my shepherd; there is nothing I lack.

When I am *attached* to material things, I'm in chains.

My concerns are for things that are *temporary.*

When I am *not* attached to material things, I'm *free.*

My hands and heart are open to things that *last.*

I'm able to let go of the masks that I have accumulated trying to be what I am not and trying to conform to a culture that *is immersed in the illusion of a happiness based on passing things.*

When I release those masks, my *true self* can emerge.

I'm free to *be present* to what actually *is.*

I am *immersed* in the *sacred.*

I am part of the miracle of this *one life.*

God is *everywhere.*

I am *held* and *sustained* by Love.

I *lack* nothing.

I am free to *be me* and to *reach out in oneness* to *everyone* and *everything.*

Listen to the song for the day "I Surrender" on the *Live to Love* album.

IN THE NAME OF LOVE

Mark 9:38

John said to him, "Teacher, we saw someone driving out demons in your name, and we tried to prevent him because he does not follow us."

You've got to *love* the apostles as they all give *us* hope!

They are an imperfect bunch *just like us*, but that is *just fine* with Jesus.

Notice how John doesn't like the fact that someone is doing good works in the name of Jesus because the guy isn't in the "in" group, which is *John's* group of *course.* This is the *ego* speaking.

John is concerned about the power and prestige he has for being in the elite group of apostles.

Jesus tells John *not to prevent* the other man from doing his good works.

Perhaps following Jesus just may lead us to a *different path* than others will *appreciate* or *accept.*

But the Spirit is *free* and creative.

Do we sometimes *judge* others as "wrong" who might be doing God's work in ways that are *different* from ours?

Listen to the song for the day "All Are One" on the *Mercy Reigns* album.

21 COMPASSION CALLS

Mark 9:43

"If your hand causes you to sin, cut it off. It is better for you to enter into life maimed than with two hands to go into Gehenna, into the unquenchable fire."

Jesus was not being *literal* about *cutting off your hand!*

He was using hyperbole – *exaggeration* – to make his point.

Whatever is enticing you to make a *selfish, non-life-giving* choice, that influence needs to be *removed.*

If not, you are basically throwing your "true self" away into a garbage dump (which is what Gehenna was, a place where garbage was constantly being burned).

By choosing to satisfy your ego, or *small self*, you will never discover the *true self* that God is calling you to be.

That would truly be a *waste!*

The "you" that God made you to be can only be *realized* and *actualized* if you surrender the insatiable demands of your ego for self-gratification and use your gifts and talents to make the world a more *loving, compassionate* and *just* place.

Listen to the song for the day "Show Me...Me" on the *Listen to Your Heart* album.

FEBRUARY

LET LOVE LEAD YOU

22

Mark 9:23-24

Jesus said to him, "'If you can!' Everything is possible to one who has faith." Then the boy's father cried out, "I do believe, help my unbelief!"

A desperate father's final hope was that maybe, just maybe,
Jesus could cure his son from a long illness.
Maybe? It's Jesus, for crying out loud!
Of course, we read these words in hindsight, after reading the stories in the gospels.
We have faith that Jesus was a healer.
Or *do we?*
I must admit, I have prayed over many people. Some have recovered, but none in such a dramatic, instantaneous way.
People close to me have died despite my prayers.
So I find myself relating to this man who cried out, "I do believe, help my unbelief!"
I truly have no doubt in Jesus being a healer and that the healing power of Christ is still pulsing through the universe.
But what I don't know is the *big picture.*
I don't know why many die while others are cured. I do know that
God is love (1 John 4:8) and I have experienced that Love even when members of a family have gathered round a dying loved one to pray only to see that person slip away.
I also believe that that loved one is not dead, but *transformed*, and is *deliriously happy* in that transformation.
I'm convinced of this after reading many accounts of amazing *Near Death Experiences* and having spoken to several who have had an *NDE.*
All I can say is this: Faith is not about being given easy answers. It is about *living through the questions* and believing that *Love will always triumph.*

Poet Rainer Maria Rilke put it this way: "Be patient toward all that is unsolved in your heart and try to love the questions themselves, like locked rooms and like books that are now written in a very foreign tongue. Do not now seek the answers, which cannot be given you because you would not be able to live them. And the point is, to live everything. Live the questions now. Perhaps you will then gradually, without noticing it, live along some distant day into the answer."

Listen to the song for the day "Love Will Always Lead You Home" on the *Mercy Reigns* album.

FEBRUARY

23

NURTURE YOUR TRUE SELF

Jeremiah 17:7-8

Blessed is the man who trusts in the Lord, whose hope is the Lord. He is like a tree planted beside the waters that stretches out its roots to the stream.

God plants seeds in our hearts.

They are God's dreams for us.

However, our egos generally have more self-centered dreams.
God's seeds are many times ignored.
They wither.

They become buried under mounds of materialism, consumerism and elitism promoted by our culture.

If God's seeds are watered and nourished they will grow into a tree with deep roots that stretch to the never-ending stream which is God.

Does that describe *your* life?
Are you living God's dream for you?

Turn now from all that stifles your spiritual growth and turn toward your true nourishment: God.

Stop.
Rest.
Listen.
Open your heart.
Be still.
Be.

Listen to the song for the day "Slow Me Down" on the *Mercy Reigns* album.

ALLOW

Sirach 2:4-6

Accept whatever happens to you; in periods of humiliation be patient. For in fire gold is tested, and the chosen, in the crucible of humiliation. Trust in God, and he will help you; make your ways straight and hope in him.

When we don't accept what *is*, we *create suffering for ourselves.*
This does *not* mean we cannot work to *change a situation* that we don't like or is *unjust.*
But we *first* must *accept the present moment.*

Simply be *present* to what *is.*
That's it.
No mental commentary.

This current moment may be one of *transition* when life is telling you it's *time to make a change.*
But taking *offense,* mentally *rebelling* or *ranting* are all signs that your *ego is in charge.*
Let go of that!
Simply observe what your mind is doing, going on *endless commentaries* and *diatribes.*
Situations change.

Remember: This, *too,* will pass.

Allow the cauldron of life's current situation to lead you to the change that will *free* you.

Trust that a Great Love is evolving *all that is* on an arc towards *Goodness* and *Wholeness.*

Listen to the song for the day "I Will Give You Rest" on the *Live to Love* album.

FEBRUARY

25 LISTEN TO YOUR HEART

Matthew 23:11-12

"The greatest among you must be your servant. Whoever exalts himself will be humbled; but whoever humbles himself will be exalted."

This is about as *counter-culture* as you get.

Instead of *material wealth* being the measuring stick for success as it is by the *world's standards*, Jesus says our measuring stick should be whether we *serve others.*
And the more *humbly* we serve, the more *exalted* we are in the eyes of *God.*

All of creation pours itself out in being whatever it is.
A bird is *all in* as a bird. A dog is *all in* as a dog. A flower is *all in* as a flower. But each of *us* has a *choice.*

Will I be *all in* as I pursue my *ego's* desires, or *all in* as I pursue my *true self's* desires?
To know the difference I must be awake.
I must see my ego for what it *is* and for what it *is not.*
It is necessary to give me some structure as I start out in life, but it will never lead me to my *true self.*

It takes *letting go* of my *ego's desires* for me to discover *God's desires for me.*
When my selfish desires *diminish*, then I will be open to the needs of *others.*

It is then that I will discover my *true self.*

It is then that I will know true *joy* and *peace.*

Listen to the song for the day "Glorify You with Me" on the *Give Praise and Thanks* album.

LET IT BE DONE TO ME

FEBRUARY

26

Sirach 5:1-2

Do not rely on your wealth, or say,
"I have the power." Do not rely on your strength
in following the desires of your heart.

When we are able to let our egos' control over our lives *diminish*, there's a chance for our *true selves* to actually *emerge*.
We will also then be *in touch* with a *Higher Power*.

St. Paul put it this way: "For when I am weak, then I am strong."
(2 Corinthians 12:10).
When he was able to surrender his *stubborn will*, he had experienced that a *Higher Power* could take over.

John the Baptist had a similar "letting go" experience when Jesus came on the scene.
That's when John knew it was time for him to step aside:
"He must increase; I must decrease." (John 3:30).
Mary also knew when it was time to jettison *her* plans when she replied to the angel,
"I am the handmaid of the Lord. May it be done to me
according to your word." (Luke 1:38).
Jesus emptied all of his desires in deference to God when he said,
"Not my will but yours be done." (Luke 22:42).

When we *let go* of our *egos'* desires, we give our *true self's* desires a chance to be *realized*.

This *letting-go* takes *practice*.

A *meditation* or *contemplative prayer practice* is *essential*.

It is your path to *freedom*.

Listen to the song for the day "You'll Lead Me" on the *Listen to Your Heart* album.

FEBRUARY

27 LET LOVE FLOW

Mark 10:29-30

Jesus said, "Amen, I say to you, there is no one who has given up house or brothers or sisters or mother or father or children or lands for my sake and for the sake of the gospel who will not receive a hundred times more now in this present age."

Jesus gives us another lesson today in *letting go* of *attachments.*
When we let go of our attachments to *all* things, even our families, to enter into the Presence of the *unrestricted Flow of God's Love* we experience deep peace.
It is from this place that we are able to cooperate in the *channeling* of this love to all.
We will be basking in Grace.
Our culture encourages the *opposite:* grab as much as you can for yourself. This is consumerism. The *more* stuff we have, the *more likely* we will become *attached* to something that will direct us off course.
Jesus calls us to turn away ("repent") from this way of trying to attain happiness.
He says instead of *taking*, try *giving.*
As long as you believe your possessions or status *define* you, Jesus said, you will never know who you truly are.
You must *disassociate* yourself from those things.
This is not *renouncing*, but not *identifying* with them.
It is only when you *let go* of the things you've been *grasping* that your hands are free to *give.*
Paradoxically, it is then that your hands are free to *receive* what God wants to give you.
There is a *free-flowing circle of giving and receiving.*
It is only in giving yourself away in the service of others that you finally find your *true self*, your true *calling.*

That is worth a hundred times more than any possession you could ever grasp!

Listen to the song for the day "Pour Me Out" on the *Give Praise and Thanks* album.

Matthew 16:15

Jesus said to them,
"But who do you say that I am?"

That is the question.

If Jesus is indeed "the way and the truth and the life," (John 14:6), then what does that mean to each of us?

If Jesus has "the words of eternal life," (John 6:68), then wouldn't it make sense to listen to him?

Jesus said, "I am the light of the world. Whoever follows me will not walk in darkness, but will have the light of life." (John 8:12).

Wouldn't the path that he would lead us on be the one that would lead us to *true* fulfillment, inner peace and joy?

Jesus asks the question to you today: "Who do ***you*** say I am?"

Listen to the song for the day "I Stand in the Light" on the *Mercy Reigns* album.

MARCH

I DYING TO LIVE

2 Corinthians 6:2

Behold, now is a very acceptable time;
behold, now is the day of salvation.

This is a time of *new beginnings.*
New life brought by spring is just around the corner.

We are surrounded by God's *blueprint for life* through the plants, trees, insects and all creatures as well as the changing seasons.
They are all in a *continuous cycle* of *dying* and *rising.*

Our lives are made up of a series of *little deaths* to the *small self* (ego) and then *risings* when we're *made new through the experience of the struggle*, the *letting go* so that a Great Love can *transform* us and the *true self* can *emerge.*
Jesus showed us that even the *final death* is *not* the *end* at all,
but the *ultimate new beginning.*

When will it be time for *your* new beginning, *your* step into being transformed into the *unique expression* of God's love that *only you* can be to the world?
Now, of course.
It's the only time that is *real.*
It's the time and place where God *is present.*
It's the time to *begin your healing* and your *road to wholeness* (salvation).

Rise from the ashes!

Are you ready to start anew?

"A clean heart create for me, God; renew in me a steadfast spirit." (Psalm 51:12).

Listen to the song for the day "Take the Road Less Traveled" on the *Live to Love* album.

PROJECT LOVE

2 Corinthians 5:20

We are ambassadors for Christ, as if God were appealing through us.

There is a *Goodness* at work, a *Benevolent Flow* that is *evolving* all that *is* toward a *Grand Wholeness.*

Sometimes it's hard to see this due to all the evil things that are done, but that doesn't mean that it's not happening.

Jesus spoke of this in the parables of the mustard seed and the yeast. (Matthew 13:31-33).

We many times are not noticing the overwhelming amount of good that is *covertly* and *not so covertly* being done.

We are all called to be *part* of this *Flow of Good*, using our gifts and talents to be agents of love.

In other words, we are "ambassadors for Christ, as if God were appealing through us." St. Paul also put it this way: "We know that all things work for good for those who love God, who are called according to his purpose." (Romans 8:28).

It is not for us to see the end result, but to humbly take part in the *Process.*

This takes much *self-emptying* and *presence.*

Listen to the song for the day "Pour Me Out" on the *Give Praise and Thanks* album.

MARCH

3

BUILDING THE KINGDOM OF GOD

Matthew 21:43

"Therefore, I say to you, the kingdom of God will be taken away from you and given to a people that will produce its fruit."

Are you producing more kindness, compassion, goodwill and generosity with your life?
The Pharisees were definitely *not.*
Jesus was again criticizing them for strictly enforcing
religious *rules* with no regard to *love.*

The *kingdom of God*, or the *reign* of God, is a *state of being* that we begin to enter into when we are *consciously present to the flow of God's unconditional love.*
This is "being in the will" of God.
When we are taking part in the flow of God's Trinitarian love (an *eternal flow of selfless giving and receiving*) we are taking part in *building the kingdom of God.*

But each of us has a choice of whether we want to build *God's* kingdom or *my* kingdom.
When my *ego* or *false self* is in charge, I am about building *my* kingdom, trying to satisfy my self-centered desires.

When I am about building *God's* kingdom, I am *dying to my false self* (ego) and am *allowing Christ to live more fully in me.*
Then, I am using my gifts and talents for God's purposes in the service of others.

When I do this, it's not so much *me* doing it, as *God* doing it *through* me.

And when this happens, paradoxically, I am being my *true self.*

Then I will enjoy the fruits of my work, fruits that
will truly satisfy my deepest yearning.

Listen to the song for the day "Listen to Your Heart" on the *Listen to Your Heart* album.

THIS IS THE MOMENT

Deuteronomy 30:15

See, I have today set before you life and good, death and evil.

Moses told the people that they would find "life and good" if they followed the commandments.

This was a good *first* step.

The commandments are solid laws of what *not* to do, so as to be *living right.*

When Jesus came along, though, he said it's not so much about not doing what is wrong, but *doing what is good and life-giving.*

He said it really comes down to *love:* Love God and your neighbor as yourself.
And that means loving your neighbor *as if they were you!*
Because when you get down to it, they *are* you.

We are all part of the One *Body of Christ.*

But we have a *choice.*

We can do what is *good* and have *life*, or we can do what is *evil* and have *death.*

When we do good we *take part in the life of God* which leads to an *abundant life.*
But when we do evil, we take part in *delusion* that leads to an *empty life.*

Each moment* provides yet another *choice.

Listen to the song for the day "You'll Lead Me" on the *Listen to Your Heart* album.

MARCH

5 TEAM EFFORT

Isaiah 65:17-18

Lo, I am about to create new heavens and a new earth; The things of the past shall not be remembered or come to mind. Instead, there shall always be rejoicing and happiness in what I create."

God is always *loving* and *creating.*

The hurts and the pains of the past are shadows.

They are *gone.*

God has transformed all the struggles into goodness.

That's what God does: redeems, restores and transforms.

Where there is pain and suffering, God is there to be a *Loving Presence* and to inspire *compassion.*

Those who are open to this Loving Presence are able to mirror that love to those in need.

So in *each* moment, God is about the work of *renewing* all things.

Are we open to being channels of God's loving creativity?

How are you using your gifts and talents to be a part of building God's kingdom?

Listen to the song for the day "Shall We Sing" on the *Listen to Your Heart* album.

LOVE REQUIRES ACTION

Mark 12:32-34

The scribe said to Jesus, "Well said, teacher. You are right in saying, '(God) is One and there is no other than he.' And 'to love him with all your heart, with all your understanding, with all your strength, and to love your neighbor as yourself' is worth more than all burnt offerings and sacrifices." And when Jesus saw that he answered with understanding, he said to him, "You are not far from the kingdom of God."

The scribe had just asked Jesus to tell him the greatest commandment.
Jesus had answered that it was to *love God with all your heart, soul, mind and strength.*
And then Jesus added that the second greatest commandment was
to *love your neighbor as yourself.*
Jesus is also quoted in Matthew 25 as saying, "whatever you did for
the least of my brothers and sisters, you did for me."
And what is it he asks us to do?
"For I was hungry and you gave me food, I was thirsty and you gave me drink,
a stranger and you welcomed me, naked and you clothed me, ill and you cared for me,
in prison and you visited me." (Matthew 25:35-36).
All those people are our neighbors.
That means *everyone.*
Love is not just a concept. It requires *action.*
So when we love others *as though they are us,* we love *Jesus.*
That's because *we are all one in God.*
As St. Paul said, "In (God) we live and move and have our being." (Acts 17:28).
The scribe told Jesus that loving God and others is more important than any sacrifice or
offering you can make to God.
That's because when we join in the Trinitarian *Flow of Love,* an *out-pouring of Love that has no end,* we are truly "not far from the kingdom of God."

Listen to the song for the day "All Are One" on the *Mercy Reigns* album.

MARCH

7

MAIN MOTIVATION

Psalm 106:19-20

At Horeb they fashioned a calf, worshiped a metal statue. They exchanged their glorious God for the image of a grass-eating bull.

When we hear what God's people did after God had faithfully freed them from oppression through the leadership of Moses, we shake our heads.

How could they actually worship a statue of a bull?

And yet, what *golden idol* takes *center-stage* in *our* lives?
Instead of a statue of a bull, is it our various media devices?
Is it our computers and the internet?
What about our fancy cars or houses?
Is it money, power, prestige, alcohol, sex, etc.?
Is our golden idol nationalism or perhaps the military?
Or could it be sports?
Is our "church" a metal and cement structure called a stadium and do we glorify and worship the team on the field?

Jesus turned away from all the false gods and gave himself totally to the One God in the service of all.

Love* took *center stage.

May that be so for each of us.

Set yourself apart from all the distractions and listen for the Voice of Love in your heart directing you to your true self.

Listen to the song for the day "Turn Off the Noise" on the *Listen to Your Heart* album.

CONTEMPLATION

MARCH **8**

Matthew 6:7-8

"In praying, do not babble like the pagans, who think that they will be heard because of their many words. Do not be like them. Your Father knows what you need before you ask him."

This is a rather profound statement by Jesus about prayer.

His followers had just asked him to teach them how to pray.

The first thing Jesus said was that they should go to their inner room, close the door and pray to God in secret. (Matthew 6:6).

Given that he said that God *already knows what you need,* why not just simply *commune* with this *Divine Presence* who *is* Love? (1 John 4:8).

If you first *emptied yourself* (Philippians 2:7), then perhaps you would have space to receive the peace of God that surpasses all understanding. (Philippians 4:7).

***Go to your inner room,* the place where God resides deep inside you.**

Set aside time for a contemplative practice such as meditation or Centering Prayer.

Listen in the silence.

Listen to the song for the day "Slow Me Down" on the *Mercy Reigns* album.

MARCH

9

NEW LIFE IN PROGRESS

Psalm 51:12

A clean heart create for me, God;
renew within me a steadfast spirit.

Renewal and *growth* require *change.*

This means *letting go* of something that is no longer *life-giving.*

It means *moving on.*

It's like the change of seasons when dead leaves *fall* to provide nutrients for new sprouts to *grow.*
Death to *life.*
Spring is coming.

"See, I am doing something new! Now it springs forth, do you not perceive it? In the wilderness I make a way, in the wasteland, rivers." (Isaiah 43:19).
We are in the *Flow* of the *paschal mystery* of *dying and rising*, of constant *renewal.*

But we must be *willing to let go* and *let God.*
"Behold, I make all things new." (Revelation 21:5).
This is what is happening quite naturally *all around us.*
Love with a capital "L" is at work!

Why not consciously enter into this pattern of renewal now?
Human beings have the option to *ignore* this pattern, but eventually *life* will make it *inevitable.*

Freely choosing to go with the Flow leads to the *discovery of your true self* and *true life.*
The opposite is to live in *delusion* and *death.*
What is *your* choice?

Listen to the song for the day "Make Your Way" on the *Mercy Reigns* album.

DIVINE GUIDANCE

MARCH

10

Deuteronomy 4:1

"Now, Israel, hear the statutes and decrees which I am teaching you to observe, that you may live, and may enter in and take possession of the land which the Lord, the God of your fathers, is giving you."

God gives us laws and commandments to guide us as spiritual children.

All children need rules and regulations to give them firm foundations and boundaries, or their lives become chaos.

They are *enticed* to *indulge* in every whim and self-centered desire.

God wants to lead us to the Promised Land, the place of abundance where we become whole, the unique expression of God that God *intended.*

The rules and regulations give us a secure launching point for a deeper spiritual journey into discovery of our true selves.

Do not mistake the rules and regulations for the journey!

Ask yourself: *What are the whims and self-centered desires enticing me? What is distracting me from the narrow path that Christ is calling me to follow?*

Listen to the song for the day "I Want to Follow You" on the *Listen to Your Heart* album.

MARCH

II JOURNEY TO WHOLENESS

Matthew 7:9-11

"Which one of you would hand his son a stone when he asks for a loaf of bread, or a snake when he asks for a fish? If you then, who are wicked, know how to give good gifts to your children, how much more will your heavenly Father give good things to those who ask him."

If a child asked to have a gallon of ice cream for breakfast, lunch and dinner, what loving parent would say *yes?*

Just so, could it be that what we think we want God to give us might actually not be what's *good* for us?

We may really *want* something, but is what we want really to satisfy a *self-centered desire?* Or is it something that will be *life-giving* to *us* and *others?*

If God is *like* a loving parent, we must trust that such a God would give each of us what we *need* so that each of us can fully become the *unique* person that we were intended to be.

This is what God wants for *you*, to become *whole* and your *true self.*

Ask the Holy Spirit to give you the desire to ask God for what you truly *need.*

Listen to the song for the day "Let It Be Done to Me" on the *Mercy Reigns* album.

NOT MY WILL, BUT YOURS

MARCH

12

John 5:30

"I cannot do anything on my own; I judge as I hear, and my judgment is just, because I do not seek my own will but the will of the one who sent me."

A while back I had a bizarre dream.

I was among a few people taking part in some type of class outside in which we were taking turns reading what God was saying to us in all the surrounding scenery.

I remember I was simply reading the scenery as if words were somehow communicated in each thing.

I don't remember much about this but I do remember that I was reading a frayed rope and I awoke with these words still clear in my mind: *"But in the moment do not be thinking of yourself..."* The rest trailed away.

In centering prayer we simply sit in silence and surrender each moment, allowing our egos to *fade away.*

It is the practice of "dying to yourself" and allowing God's will to become clearer.

Jesus was the master of this *letting go* as a *way of life* but we all need plenty of *practice.*

How about starting in *this moment?*

Listen to the song for the day "Breathe On Me" on the *Listen to Your Heart* album.

MARCH

13 ALWAYS AND FOREVER

John 8:29

"The one who sent me is with me.
He has not left me alone, because
I always do what is pleasing to him."

Jesus knew who he was.

He came to know this through his close relationship with God.

This was something no doubt modeled to him by his mother who would reflect on things in her heart. (Luke 2:19).

Jesus also spent time in reflection, cultivating his relationship with God through quiet prayer alone.

He allowed God to name him and define him.

The relationship was *intimate.*

"This is my beloved Son, with whom I am well pleased." (Matthew 3:17).

Set aside some special one-on-one time with God.

Get to know the One who cherishes *you* like a *son* or *daughter.*

Listen to the song for the day "I Will Give You Rest" on the *Live to Love* album.

VOCATION

Matthew 20:26

"Whoever wishes to be great among you shall be your servant."

Jesus throws our culture's ideology *upside down.*

Society says that the sign of *success* or *greatness* is when you are *being served.*

When you're wealthy, people work for you.

People *serve you.*

You've *made it.*

But *not so* in the *kingdom of God.*

Jesus tells us that in God's eyes the *greatest* is the *one who serves.*

Allow his words to *settle in your soul.*

Look *deep* inside.

What is your *deepest gladness* and how are you being called to *experience* it in *serving others?*

For me, my soul soars when I play guitar and sing as a ministry to others, whether at retreats, visiting shut-ins in their homes, in nursing homes, or inmates in jail.

What about *you?*

Listen to the song for the day "Glorify You with Me" on the *Give Praise and Thanks* album.

MARCH

15 ATTUNED TO THE NOW

Matthew 1:20

The angel of the Lord appeared to him in a dream and said, "Joseph, son of David, do not be afraid to take Mary your wife into your home. For it is through the holy Spirit that this child has been conceived in her."

God is in the business of transforming apparent *obstacles* into *opportunities.*

If you have *faith*, amazing things *will happen.*
But you may be taken *way out of your comfort zone.*

This scripture depicts radical acceptance to what is.
Joseph accepts Mary when all conventional wisdom says to reject her.

This gives us an example of a deep connection with God, being open to receiving a message from the Divine Source, a message that was *life-changing.*

Are you open to hearing and seeing messages from God?

Are you paying attention to your dreams?

Are you expecting a life-changing message that will lead you to wholeness and peace?

The messages may very well *not* be dramatic, but rather, *subtle.*

You will need to *cultivate* your *spiritual receptivity.*

Are you setting aside quiet time for contemplative prayer or meditation?
Or are you immersing yourself further and further into the *noise* of the world?

Listen to the song for the day "Turn Off the Noise" on the *Listen to Your Heart* album.

John 8:24

"For if you do not believe that I AM, you will die in your sins."

Jesus invites us to go deeper than a superficial understanding.

When Moses asked for God's name, God said, "I am who I am." (Exodus 3:14).

God is "Being" itself.

In today's scripture verse, Jesus said he is *one with God.*

Earlier Jesus had said that if we know *him* we know *God.*

Jesus is at one with our Creator who is always in the *now*, always *present* to us.

So for us to be present to God, *we* must be *present* to *what is.*

That requires *letting go* of our *attachments* to the *things of this world*, all the things that entice our egos into thinking that they will bring us lasting happiness. They are actually distractions that will lead us to a *self-centered dead end.*

When we turn away from what is Life-Giving, we might as well be *dead.*

Jesus showed us that by following his example of lovingly serving others we find the path to life.

Listen to the song for the day "I Want to Follow You" on the *Listen to Your Heart* album.

MARCH

17 HEART'S DESIRE

Jeremiah 17:5

Thus says the LORD: Cursed is the man who trusts in human beings, who makes flesh his strength, whose heart turns away from the LORD.

Life is not about trying to please *others.*

It's about trying to please God.
And if you please God, you are pleasing the *real you.*

This is the place where you find your *inner-most-self*, or your *true self.*
That can only happen by *following your heart.*
That's where God has planted your deepest desires.
It's the place where your true self *springs forth.*

You are a *unique manifestation* of the Divine.
How will you *express* that divinity in the world?

Trying to satisfy all the yearnings of your body will *not* bring you deep happiness.
What is your *heart's desire?*

To know takes a lot of *letting go*, a lot of *practice* at *setting aside thoughts and physical desires* so that your *true self can emerge.*

A meditative or contemplative practice *helps immensely*.

Follow your *deepest soul yearnings* and, if you aren't sure what they are, start by simply following your *interests.*

Allow life to *unfold* and perhaps one day *live into the answer* you've been *yearning* for.

Listen to the song for the day "Listen to Your Heart" on the *Listen to Your Heart* album.

LOVE LEADS TO ACTION

John 8:31-32

"If you remain in my word, you will truly be my disciples, and you will know the truth, and the truth will set you free."

Remaining in Jesus' word is *more* than *knowing* or *believing.*

It's *living* his word.

It's *being* his word.

There are probably many paths to this way of life.
But one way is to actually get to *know* Jesus.
Making a practice of reading the gospels and pondering his words is a great start.
But just *reading* his words and *knowing* them is a "head" thing.
Jesus is talking about a "heart" thing.
Information* in your head will not lead to *transformation of your heart.
Try sitting in peace and quiet and dwelling on Jesus' words.
Allow them to sink into your heart space.
"Remain in my word."
Be.
Allow.

When we do this, the Holy Spirit is eager to reveal the truth and *set you free.*
And in that freedom you will be led to a *changed life* where *Jesus'* mission and *your* mission will be *one and the same:*
"The Spirit of the Lord is upon me, because he has anointed me to bring glad tidings to the poor. He has sent me to proclaim liberty to captives and recovery of sight to the blind, to let the oppressed go free, and to proclaim a year acceptable to the Lord." (Luke 4:18-19).

Listen to the song for the day "Make Me a Channel" on the *Listen to Your Heart* album.

MARCH

19 GIVING TO RECEIVE

John 8:54

Jesus answered, "If I glorify myself, my glory is worth nothing; but it is my Father who glorifies me…"

Life is all about *relationship.*

All **of the** ***universe – all creation*** **– is in** ***relationship.***

Science is proving this.

Love **is at the core of it all.**

There is a *flow* of this Love from *God to Jesus* and then from *Jesus out to all,* and therefore *back to God.*

Jesus is the fullness of this Love.

He gave us the perfect example of how to live.

Jesus *emptied* his *own* desires and *opened* himself to *God's* desires, thereby allowing God's Love to flow *through* him *to* others.

Jesus knew that any "glory" that came his way was due to *God*, not his *ego.*

The only way your ***true self*** **can shine through is if your ego** ***gets out of the way.***

That will require a contemplative practice of *letting go.*

The old adage is true:
"Let go. Let God."

Listen to the song for the day "I Surrender" on the ***Live to Love*** **album.**

LISTEN

MARCH

20

Jeremiah 7:23, 25-26

Listen to my voice; then I will be your God and you shall be my people. From the day that your fathers left the land of Egypt even to this day, I have sent you untiringly all my servants the prophets. Yet they have not obeyed me nor paid heed.

God's consistent message is to *listen,* because God *is speaking.*
God is speaking in each of our hearts a tender message of unconditional love, a message that tells us who we are.
Each* of us is *God's beloved.

Unfortunately, most of us are not hearing the message because we have only been taught verbal prayer and nothing about *silent, listening* prayer.

That's despite Jesus himself stating, "When you pray, go to your inner room, close the door, and pray to your Father in secret. And your Father who sees in secret will repay you. In praying, do not babble like the pagans, who think that they will be heard because of their many words. Do not be like them. Your Father knows what you need before you ask him (Matthew 6:6-8)."

God has spoken for thousands of years through the prophets, as well, delivering message after message that we must turn away from our ego's insatiable desires for power, prestige and wealth – and *turn back* to the God who calls us to love and serve *all* as *one.*

But those in power have consistently *thrown out* the prophets.
The prophets are *still being thrown out* and God is *still speaking!*

Set aside time to go into the spiritual desert so you can listen to God's *silent voice.*

Listen to the song for the day "Listen to Your Heart" on the *Listen to Your Heart* album.

MARCH

21 HOLY LONGING

Psalm 42:2-3

As the deer longs for streams of water, so my soul longs for you, O God. My being thirsts for God, the living God.

Each of us has a *primal yearning* inside, a yearning that *longs* to be *satisfied.*

Why do we often try to *numb* that yearning, *cover it up*, or try to satisfy it with *material* or *physical* things?

The yearning is on the "soul" level.

It's a *spiritual longing.*

The *deepest* part of you is yearning for *God.*

It's a yearning only *God* can satisfy.

How do you experience God?

Is it in music, silence, art, nature or something else?

Maybe all of those!

***Seek* God in *all* those places and *allow* your Loving Creator to *nourish* you.**

God *yearns* to do just *that.*

It's the path to *wholeness* and your *true self.*

Listen to the song for the day "God Is" on the *Give Praise and Thanks* album.

BLIND FAITH

Luke 1:37

"For nothing will be impossible with God."

Do you believe that?

It's what the angel Gabriel said to Mary after she questioned how she could conceive the Son of God.

And her reply was: *"May it be done to me according to your word."*

What amazing plans does your Loving Creator have in mind for you to help transform this world into the Kingdom of God, the compassionate place God intended?

Back in 1997, I *heard a voice in my heart* that asked me to pick up a guitar that I had abandoned for *over ten years.*

How could such a crazy idea be the answer to changing my miserable life?

Picking up that guitar that day led to four original music albums, a Master's degree in religious and pastoral studies and my becoming a youth minister and then a chaplain. It also brought me amazing experiences in Guatemala, Assisi, and others *too numerous to mention!*

What dream is God trying to awaken in *your* heart?

Open your heart and surrender to the One who *loved you into existence!*

Listen to the song for the day "Let It Be Done to Me" on the *Mercy Reigns* album.

MARCH

23 GRACE HAPPENS

Psalm 25:4-5

Make known to me your ways, LORD; teach me your paths. Guide me by your fidelity and teach me, for you are God my savior.

We all want *answers.*
Lord, please just show me the right way to go!
But this is *not* what usually happens.
We seldom get a clear answer from God.
We usually don't see how a *Benevolence* helped guide us until we look back in hindsight.
I think that's because God wants each of us to *live into the answer.*
The whole point of our existence is to *grow*, to *learn*, to *experience love* and be *changed* by it.
That's tough work! You can't just jump from *question* to *answer.*

If someone gave you the answer, it would erase the growth you were supposed to experience on your *journey.*

It's like the story of the caterpillar that was turning into a butterfly but was struggling to escape from its cocoon. A little boy thought he'd help by getting a scissors and cutting the cocoon to make it easier for the butterfly to get out. Unfortunately, the butterfly dropped to the ground. It had a swollen body and shriveled wings. It would never be able to fly. What the boy didn't understand is that the butterfly needed the struggle to escape the cocoon.
That was the only way it could *build strength* in its wings so that it would be able to fly.

God's ways are not *our* ways.
The important thing is to trust that there is a *Great Love drawing us forward.*
Be attentive to that Higher Power.
Go with the Flow of Love.

Listen to the song for the day "Love Will Always Lead You Home" on the *Mercy Reigns* album.

LET IT SHINE

Isaiah 42:6-7

I, the Lord, have called you for the victory of justice, I have grasped you by the hand; I formed you, and set you as a covenant of the people, a light for the nations, to open the eyes of the blind, to bring out prisoners from confinement, and from the dungeon, those who live in darkness.

These words written in the Book of Isaiah about 700 years before
Jesus of Nazareth was born foretell of his ministry.
Jesus would be the *servant* Messiah, not a *militaristic* one.
He would show us who God is by *being himself.*
"If you know me, then you will also know my Father." (John 14:7).

And who is God? God is love. (1 John 4:8).
Love has no boundaries.
This Love was (and *is*) a light to all nations.
This Love opened (and *still opens*) the eyes of the blind.
And this Love freed (and *still frees*) the oppressed.
When you are *present* to others *in love, light shines,*
eyes are opened* and *people are freed.

This Love is Eternal Light and that Light is inside each of us. As Thomas Merton wrote in *Conjectures of a Guilty Bystander,* "It is like a pure diamond, blazing with the invisible light of heaven. It is in everybody, and if we could see it we would see these billions of points of light coming together in the face and blaze of a sun that would make all the darkness and cruelty of life vanish completely."

Allow God's love to *stir up* the flame already within you and then *let it shine!*

Listen to the song for the day "May I Be Light" on the *Listen to Your Heart* album.

MARCH

25 JUST BE YOU

Psalm 147:12

Glorify the LORD, Jerusalem.

How do we "glorify" God?

By being our *true selves.*

Each of us is a *unique* and *beautiful child of God, just as we are.*

Under all the *masks* we have put on, beyond all the *titles* bestowed on us by society, or *labels* pasted on us by others, lies the *pure* and *beloved soul* that God crafted.

So allow it to come forth.

***Let go* of all the *false trappings* that you have let define you.**

They are all the masks our egos have made to satisfy our childhood programs for happiness based on security, power and esteem.

Look at all living things in creation as they are simply *being themselves fully and completely.*

Do the same with joy!

When you do, you will be reflecting the glory of God in the way that *only you can!*

Listen to the song for the day "Glorify You with Me" on the *Give Praise and Thanks* album.

MARCH

REJUVENATION 26

Psalm 16:11

You will show me the path to life, abounding joy in your presence, the delights at your right hand forever.

It's that nagging *perpetual* question: What is my *purpose?*

What is God's *will* for *me?*

Finding the answer is the way of *contemplation.*

It takes *being present* to God (who *is* Presence) and *listening* in the depths of your heart.

Then it takes *action*, taking steps in the direction that you *sense* God is leading you.

It might not be the *popular* path.

It may be a *lonely* path leading you away from what loved ones want for you or what your ego wants.

It may cause anxiety and anguish, but you will also experience inner peace and excitement!

This path will lead you to your *true self* and to *God.*

As Thomas Merton wrote in *New Seeds of Contemplation*, "Not to accept and love and do God's will is to refuse the fullness of my existence."

Where is God leading *you?*

Listen and then take a step in that direction today.

Listen to the song for the day "Take the Road Less Traveled" on the *Live to Love* album.

MARCH

27 SACRED SYMPHONY

Psalm 105:1-2

Give thanks to the Lord, invoke his name; make known among the peoples his deeds! Sing praise, play music; proclaim all his wondrous deeds!

There is *much* to be *thankful* about.
Contemplate *this*: We are all beloved children of God and are destined for eternal life.

God is with us and has showed us the *extreme* nature of Divine Love in the life of Jesus.
Jesus said if we knew *him* that we would know *God.* (John 14:7).

And what do we know of Jesus?
He reached out to all those who were suffering and excluded.
He reached out to those who were regarded as "sinners."
And finally, he endured the worst injustice possible and
then while dying on the cross *forgave all!*

This is who God *is!*
Now we are called to be the body of Christ to the world.
How will we do this?
For me it means, in part, to literally *sing* and *play* music.

What do *you* enjoy doing?
What talent or trait have you been given that when you express it, you experience pure joy?

Perhaps God is asking you to use that gift as an expression of God's love.

When we do this the glory of God is revealed and the kingdom of God breaks into the present!

Listen to the song for the day "Shall We Sing" on the *Listen to Your Heart* album.

TRUE GREATNESS

Matthew 18:1-4

At that time the disciples approached Jesus and said, "Who is the greatest in the kingdom of heaven?" He called a child over, placed it in their midst, and said, "Amen, I say to you, unless you turn and become like children, you will not enter the kingdom of heaven. Whoever humbles himself like this child is the greatest in the kingdom of heaven.

Our culture says the one who *wins,* who comes out on *top*, is the one who is *exulted.*
The person who attains the *most power, prestige* and *possessions* receives the *glory.*
That person is the *greatest.*

Jesus, however, says the *opposite.*
He says the one who is *humble*, who reaches out to help those in need and *joins* those at the *bottom*, that person is the *greatest* in the *kingdom of heaven.*
Jesus praises the one who *trusts* and *depends* on God like a child depends on a parent.
There is certainly nothing wrong with receiving praise from an achievement.
The question is, what is your *motivation?*
Are you responding to the call of *God* or the call of your *ego?*
Which kingdom are you serving, *God's* or your *own?*
Are you building your *own* kingdom or are you *humbling* yourself and allowing God to lead you in helping to build *God's* kingdom?
This is a great question to ask yourself each day.
I know, for me, it is very humbling to see my *mixed motivations!*

The more you humble yourself and allow your ego's desires to diminish, the more God's desires can grow in you and the clearer your calling will become.

Listen to the song for the day "Breathe On Me" on the *Listen to Your Heart* album.

MARCH

29 LISTEN TO YOUR HEART

Matthew 22:36-39

"Teacher, which commandment in the law is the greatest?" He said to him, "You shall love the Lord, your God, with all your heart, with all your soul, and with all your mind. This is the greatest and the first commandment. The second is like it: You shall love your neighbor as yourself."

We have all kinds of *rules* and *rituals* in religion.
When Jesus was asked to boil it down to one thing, he said:
Love God and your neighbor as yourself.
That's the *bottom line.*
Everyone has an inborn desire to be happy.
The trouble is, we get so many mixed messages.
Religion gives us a list of practices and guidelines.
Our culture gives us an endless list of ways to be happy that can satisfy us *briefly*, but each time we are left *empty* and *yearning* for something more.
Jesus shows us the way in two simple commandments.
But how *hard* it is to accomplish!
Our *egos* are constantly telling us to satisfy our every desire while *Jesus* tells us to *let go* of those desires and to set *love of God* and *others as ourselves* as our *top* priority.
Trying to satisfy your ego is like trying to satisfy a *false self* that will *never* be satisfied.
Jesus' way awakens you to your *true self.*
Inner peace and happiness are *by-products* of the process.
Which choice will *you* make: *your ego's* desires or *God's?*
One necessary practice to help discover God's desires for you is *contemplative prayer.*
Try setting aside 15 to 20 minutes to simply sit in silence and allow your thoughts to dissipate.
God's primary language is *silence.*

Listen to the song for the day "Turn Off the Noise" on the *Listen to Your Heart* album.

BELOVED CHILD

Matthew 16:24-26

Then Jesus said to his disciples, "Whoever wishes to come after me must deny himself, take up his cross, and follow me. For whoever wishes to save his life will lose it, but whoever loses his life for my sake will find it. What profit would there be for one to gain the whole world and forfeit his life? Or what can one give in exchange for his life?"

It's a *paradox.*
When you *let go* of what you *thought* your life was about, you *find* what your life is *truly* about.
When you *let go* of *self-centered desires*, it *feels like dying.*

When you surrender your *ego's* insatiable desires for power, prestige and possessions, while asking for God to show you God's desires *for* you, you will be on the path of uncovering your *true self.*
This is the path of letting go of all the layers of "stuff" that you thought defined you.

After you strip away all the "masks" you were wearing, what remains is the *beloved child of God* that *you are.*
Then you are free to use your gifts and talents to help those in need.
Those who do not share your desire to lift the ones who have fallen through the cracks or the ones on the fringes will try to block your path.

You will be called to respond to your persecutors with *love*, just as Jesus did.
In letting go of what your *false* self *wanted,* you will find what your *true* self *needed.*
What could be *more important* than *that?*

Listen to the song for the day "Pour Me Out" on the *Give Praise and Thanks* album.

MARCH

31 CUTTING ATTACHMENTS

Matthew 19:20-22

The young man said to him, "All of these (the Ten Commandments) I have observed. What do I still lack?" Jesus said to him, "If you wish to be perfect, go, sell what you have and give to (the) poor, and you will have treasure in heaven. Then come, follow me." When the young man heard this statement, he went away sad, for he had many possessions.

The rich young man wanted to be *perfect*, which is *impossible!*

He *falsely* believed that it was up to *him* to be *good enough* for God's acceptance, when God loves us *as we are, in* our *imperfection.*

That is what *saves* us.

The man was on his own *personal salvation project* (as Thomas Merton would've called it).

Observing the Ten Commandments is a great idea to keep us in line, to give us boundaries so that we can have a strong moral foundation.

But there isn't a person who can keep them to the *letter*.

The rich young man was very concerned about what he needed to *do* to "gain eternal life." He didn't understand that we are all *imperfect* and cannot possibly do *anything* to *earn* our way into heaven.

That is a *free gift!*

What Jesus calls each of us to do in response to God's unconditional love is to *love God with all our hearts and to love our neighbor as ourselves.*

This is the path to wholeness and becoming our *true selves.*

It is not through *our* doing, but through *God's.*

We receive God's *un-earned* transforming grace and forgiveness, so we can *pass it on.*

Jesus could read the young man's heart and see that his possessions were *attachments* and his *top priority.* His attachments prevented him from being open to receiving a free gift.

What are *your* attachments?

What do you need to *let go* of so that you can become your *true self?*

Listen to the song for the day "You'll Lead Me" on the *Listen to Your Heart* album.

Now Here

Psalm 46:2

God is our refuge and our strength, an ever-present help in distress.

The key words here are "ever-present."

God is always in the *now*, at least in our *human experience.*

We, too, must be *present* if we are to experience God as our *refuge, strength* and *help in distress.*

How often are we actually *present?*

How often are our minds *running a mile-a-minute, rehashing* and *rehashing* one topic or another?

Most of us, I'm afraid, are *attached* and *obsessed* with those thoughts, actually believing that we *are* those thoughts.

Stop for a second and *observe* those thoughts.

***Who* is the *observer* of your thoughts?**

The *real you*, that's *who!*

Let go of those *endless streams* of thoughts and actually *experience presence.*

Rest* in the *Presence* of the *One* who *always* loves you and will *never stop.

Reflect that Presence to the world!

Listen to the song for the day "I Will Give You Rest" on the *Live to Love* album.

2 YOUR CALLING

John 5:44

"How can you believe, when you accept praise from one another and do not seek the praise that comes from the only God?"

***Whose* praise are *you* seeking?**

Whose praise *really matters?*

Many of us are *people pleasers.*

We were conditioned to head down that road from our earliest childhood.

When did you – or have you ever – asked yourself: "What does *God* want from me?"

We have been *loved into existence* by Love *itself* so that we can be a *channel of love* to the world.

When you are doing that, you are pleasing God.

Because that's when you are in touch with your *true self.*

As Thomas Merton wrote in *New Seeds of Contemplation,* "If I find Him (God), I will find myself, and if I find my true self I will find Him (God)."

If you are looking for a way to be compassion to the world, follow the example of Jesus or his closest follower Mary Magdalene.

If and when we do this, God's praise is *resounding* in our souls.

Listen to the song for the day "I Want to Follow You" on the *Listen to Your Heart* album.

ETERNAL NOW

John 3:16-17

For God so loved the world that he gave his only Son, so that everyone who believes in him might not perish but might have eternal life. For God did not send his Son into the world to condemn the world, but that the world might be saved through him.

God became like us in Jesus and showed us *how to be human.*
Jesus showed us how to *live* and how to *die.*
He showed us how to be "whole."

If we follow his way we find true life right *here* and *now.*
It's the way of dying to our ego's selfish desires so that our true self can rise.
When we surrender our *self-centered pursuits* we naturally begin using our gifts and talents in the service of *others' needs.*

Pursuing our own egocentric desires leads to an *endless* quest for *more* which always leads to a *dead-end.*

But when we let go of our attachments to possessions, prestige and power, we paradoxically receive all that we need.

Unencumbered by these attachments, we find freedom, peace and joy.

In other words, we find abundant life that is both *now* and *eternal.*

That, my friend, is how we are *saved* through Jesus.

Turn to Jesus. *Follow* him and discover *true life* that *never ends.*

Listen to the song for the day "Come to Jesus" on the *Live to Love* album.

APRIL

4 PAY ATTENTION

Luke 24:32

Then they said to each other, "Were not our hearts burning within us while he spoke to us on the way and opened the scriptures to us?"

I truly believe God is speaking to us all the time, but we are not paying attention.

When driving, how often are we in such deep thought about something that we can't remember anything about the last five or ten minutes?

How often have we stared blankly at what's in front of us only to be amazed by some spectacle, like a beautiful sunset or starry sky, that we would have totally missed had someone not jostled us from our daze and pointed it out to us?

How often have we had our minds made up and were completely closed to miraculous possibilities?

The two disciples on the way to Emmaus finally recognized Jesus, but only in retrospect could they recognize the "burning" in their hearts when Jesus had "opened up the scriptures" to them.

Wake up!

God is speaking to us in many ways if we'd only pay attention.

Start listening and looking for the Divine Presence.

Be ready for your heart to be moved.

Listen to the song for the day "Listen to Your Heart" on the *Listen to Your Heart* album.

APRIL

READY AND OPEN

5

Luke 1:38

Mary said, "Behold, I am the handmaid of the Lord. May it be done to me according to your word."

Mary gives us the perfect example of being *open* and *present.*

She is *open* to *receiving a divine message.*

She is open to *accepting* what *is,* even if it's something *totally different than she planned.*

She is *open* to *setting aside* her own *ego* and *its desires* and to allowing God to do something with her life that she could *never have dreamed on her own.*

That takes *humility.*

That takes *presence.*

That takes knowing that you are part of *something bigger than yourself.*

Are we following Mary's example?

If we do, God just might do something amazing with our lives as well.

Listen to the song for the day "Let It Be Done to Me" on the *Mercy Reigns* album.

APRIL

6 CALLED TO LOVE

Genesis 17:3-4

Abram fell face down and God said to him:
For my part, here is my covenant with you:
you are to become the father of a multitude of nations.

God makes a covenant with *each* of us.
God will always do *God's* part.
We just have to go along with it.

God will never stop loving us.
Each of us is God's beloved daughter or son.

Following God involves learning to love as God loves and then loving God and neighbor as ourselves.
Now that's hard!
Love God, neighbor (meaning *everyone*), and myself.

I don't know about you, but loving myself is sometimes the biggest challenge.
We all do things of which we are ashamed, but God loves us just the same.
We are asked to do the same, using our gifts and talents as channels of that love.

God calls each of us in unique ways.
Abram, who became Abraham, was called at an old age to a new project.
He did indeed become "the father of a multitude of nations" after first humbling himself before God and basically saying, "May Your will be done."

What is God calling *you* to do, in *this place*, in *this moment* of time, to channel God's love?

Listen to the song for the day "The Way You Are" on the *Mercy Reigns* album.

BORN TO LOVE

Isaiah 49:1

The Lord called me from birth, from my mother's womb he gave me my name.

Each **of us is very special in the eyes of our Creator.**

The Prophet Isaiah said that God knew us intimately in the womb.

And hundreds of years later, St. Paul wrote that we were all known by God well before that:
"Blessed be the God and Father of our Lord Jesus Christ, who has blessed us in Christ with every spiritual blessing in the heavens, as he chose us in him, before the foundation of the world, to be holy and without blemish before him. In love he destined us for adoption to himself through Jesus Christ, in accord with the favor of his will, for the praise of the glory of his grace that he granted us in the beloved." (Ephesians 1:3-6).

You might want to read that *several times* and let it *sink in.*

It says we were chosen *in* Christ *before the world began!*

How many people live in the *illusion* of *separation* from God when God is actually as close to us as our breath.

St. Paul said this in Acts 17:28, "For 'In him we live and move and have our being.'"

We are all *intimately involved* with God's creation *in progress.*

Listen to the Divine Voice inside you leading you on a journey of love.

Don't miss taking part in the epic adventure unfolding in *each* moment!

Listen to the song for the day "God Is" on the *Give Praise and Thanks* album.

APRIL

8 BE HEALERS

Acts 4:29-30

"And now, Lord, take note of their threats, and enable your servants to speak your word with all boldness, as you stretch forth [your] hand to heal, and signs and wonders are done through the name of your holy servant Jesus."

Peter and the followers of Jesus were impassioned by the Holy Spirit to spread the words of Jesus and to allow his healing and love to be channeled through them, even to those who were threatening them.

Jesus said to build the kingdom of God *here and now* through love, mercy, forgiveness, compassion and justice.

He also said to love our enemies.
How is *that* possible?
Only through God's *grace!*

As Jesus said, "No one can see the kingdom of God without being born from above." (John 3:3).
In other words, you have to be willing to throw-out your old way of thinking and allow the mind of Christ to be born in you.

It takes *transformation.*
You have to take on a whole new way of thinking!
You and I are a part of a much bigger picture.
We are part of a bigger plan.
The path we are on is one of *faith* and *grace*, not *merit.*

What you have received, *pass it on!*

Listen to the song for the day "Mercy Reigns" on the *Mercy Reigns* album.

Isaiah 50:4-5

Morning after morning he wakens my ear to hear as disciples do; The Lord GOD opened my ear; I did not refuse, did not turn away.

To hear God speak, you must be *listening.*
You must be *attentive.*
This simply means you must be *present.*

Once, while on retreat, I heard a reading from the gospel of John where Jesus said: "Before Abraham came to be, I AM." (John 8:58).

When the priest finished his homily, I was dissatisfied with his summation that Jesus was simply proclaiming that he was God.

In the silence that followed, I heard birds singing outside the church with seeming delight.
And it was then that I received a *sudden revelation* in my heart.
I understood that the birds were preaching Jesus' *deeper message* with each joyful chirp: *"I am! I am! I am!"*
In an instant, I understood that just as the *birds* are a part of the "I AM-ness" of God – *so am I, so are you* and *everyone else.*

My heart leaped for joy and I felt deep gratitude to be a part of the *oneness* of God's amazing creation.

Take some time to really *be present.*

Let go. Listen and be glad!

Listen to the song for the day "How Magnificent, Wondrous and Glorious" on the *Mercy Reigns* album.

APRIL

10 LISTEN

John 6:44-45

"No one can come to me unless the Father who sent me draw him, and I will raise him on the last day. It is written in the prophets: 'They shall all be taught by God.' Everyone who listens to my Father and learns from him comes to me."

We're all *yearning* for *something.*

Unfortunately, many times we end up trying to *satisfy* that yearning with *material things.*

That will *not* work because the *origin* of our deep yearning is *God.*

The yearning can only be satisfied on a *spiritual* level.

God is *drawing* us, *calling each of us to wholeness.*

To be *whole* you need to be your *true self.*

This requires *letting go* of things that are preventing you from being your true self so that God can give you what you truly need.

Try setting aside quiet time to simply *be present* to the *Divine Presence.*

Listen to the *silent whisper* in your heart, that *internal yearning* inviting you to *be you.*

You are being *drawn* by God, your Divine Teacher, to follow the path of Christ.

It will lead you to *service* and *new life.*

Listen to the song for the day "Turn Off the Noise" on the *Listen to Your Heart* album.

MERCY REIGNS

Acts 9:17

"Saul, my brother, the Lord has sent me, Jesus who appeared to you on the way by which you came, that you may regain your sight and be filled with the holy Spirit."

When Saul was blinded by a flash of light on the way to Damascus, he was heading there to persecute Christians (he was "breathing murderous threats"). He had been responsible for dragging Christians from their homes to be imprisoned and many certainly were killed.
This* is the man that *Jesus chose* as his *instrument of love, mercy, grace, forgiveness and compassion!

God's ways are clearly *not* the ways of *humans!*
God sees *each* of us as a *precious daughter* or *son, no matter what we've done.*
God sees our *infinitely good core.*

God knows that many of us are experiencing *inattentional blindness*, when we are oblivious to something in plain sight, like our oneness with all humanity.
So in the case of Saul, the risen Jesus spoke to a man named Ananias and told him to go to Saul and lay hands on him so that he might regain his sight.

We read the words of Ananias in today's scripture verse above.
What followed was the transformation of Saul into the one who would become known as St. Paul.
Instead of *punishment* and *retribution*, Christ responded to Saul with *mercy* and *compassion.*

This is what *changes hearts.*

How might *each of us* respond in the *same way* to someone in our lives?

Listen to the song for the day "Mercy Reigns" on the *Mercy Reigns* album.

APRIL

12 PROPHETS NEEDED

Acts 7:52

"Which of the prophets did your ancestors not persecute?"

The prophets got plenty of praise after they were long dead.

While they were alive they generally got persecuted by those who were in power, whether by those in government or religious leaders.

The prophets were always calling attention to the ways that the people of God were failing to make their top priority to serve God.

The prophets had to be prayerful to listen to the inner voice of God and then they had to be brave in speaking out to those in power – both government and religious leaders – in the name of compassion, fairness and justice.

For the prophet Stephen, it cost him his life.

Following God's will is not always easy but it is *everyone's* calling!

This is the only way to true freedom and to becoming your *true self.*

Who are *today's* prophets?

They are likely the ones being persecuted and thrown out by those holding the power.

God is still calling prophets to stand for those being treated unjustly and unfairly.

Maybe God is calling *you?*

Listen to the song for the day "Singing My Song" on the *Live to Love* album.

BE FREE

APRIL 13

John 10:9

"I am the gate. Whoever enters through me will be saved, and will come in and go out and find pasture."

When you read the word "saved" above, substitute the words "made whole."
When we follow Jesus in *the way he lived and died,*
we are on the path of *becoming whole.*

This is the path of *letting go of our ego's desires* so that our *true self can bloom.*
It is the *path of love.*

When we *love,* we are all that we were made to be.

Then, we are truly *free.*

Then we will "have life and have it more abundantly," as Jesus put it (John 10:10).

In the "Our Father" prayer, Jesus said that we should pray for
God's kingdom to *come*, meaning *into the present.*

When Jesus is our *gate*, we determine what we *do* and *say* by following his way.

If we do this we are promised true freedom and inner peace.

When we live in the presence of God who is *always present,*
is not the kingdom of God *at hand?*

Easier *said* than *done!*

Let's do it.

Listen to the song for the day "Slow Me Down" on the *Mercy Reigns* album.

APRIL

14 GROUP EFFORT

Acts 9:10

There was a disciple in Damascus named Ananias, and the Lord said to him in a vision, "Ananias." He answered, "Here I am, Lord."

God has a plan to bring *all* things to a grand completion.

The kingdom of God will come about *on earth as it is in heaven.*
But it can only happen "on earth" with the *cooperation* of *human beings.*

Ananias was certainly a man of great spiritual depth whose prayer life consisted of being silently attentive to the Spirit.
Whatever way that he sensed God's voice, it was clear to him that he must go to a certain house and lay his hands on Saul so that Saul might regain his sight.

Saul was the great persecutor of Christians who, through the grace of God and the cooperation of followers like Ananias, was transformed into one of the greatest followers of Christ: St. Paul.

(What if Ananias had said, "No. Saul doesn't deserve healing?" Merit obviously has *nothing* to do with God's grace. Thank God!)

Who in *your* life needs the transforming grace and healing of God's unconditional love?

Perhaps God is trying to send *you.*

Are you listening?

Listen to the song for the day "Shall We Sing" on the *Listen to Your Heart* album.

BECOMING WHOLE

Acts 4:8-10

Then Peter, filled with the holy Spirit, answered them, "Leaders of the people and elders; If we are being examined today about a good deed done to a cripple, namely, by what means he was saved, then all of you and all the people of Israel should know that it was in the name of Jesus Christ the Nazorean whom you crucified, whom God raised from the dead; in his name this man stands before you healed.

This is a very telling comment by the Apostle Peter.
He equates the physical healing of a crippled man to his being "saved."
God wants each of us to be *restored, redeemed,* made "whole."
That would be *physically, mentally, emotionally and spiritually* whole.

Any such healing or restoration is done by God alone.
However, God does use us as *instruments* in the healing of others *if we* cooperate.
Our part might be through our role as a doctor, nurse, chaplain, mother, father, teacher, brother, sister, priest, minister, writer, singer, mechanic, CEO, etc.

No matter what your calling is, God can use *you* in the healing process.
Peter knew it was not *he* but *Jesus* who had healed the crippled man.

Sometimes restoration and wholeness are not so instantaneous.
Sometimes it's a process that can take *years.*

But have no doubt, you are in the *process of becoming whole.*

Listen to the song for the day "Make Me a Channel" on the *Listen to Your Heart* album.

APRIL

16 POUR ME OUT

John 3:35-36

The Father loves the Son and has given everything over to him. Whoever believes in the Son has eternal life, but whoever disobeys the Son will not see life.

God pours out *everything* to Jesus.
In turn, Jesus pours out *everything* back to God.
In this *everlasting flow* of Love and Goodness we find the Holy Spirit *in action*.

We* are invited *into this flow.
Unfortunately, many remain stuck in a Christianity of only
beliefs, rules and regulations – all "head" stuff.
They never move on to the actions that naturally flow from a *transformed* heart.
Information is not *transformation*.

We have a lot of *information about* Jesus and many of us *admire* Jesus and are *fans* of Jesus, but how many of us *follow* him?
That's really what he asked us to do: to *follow* him.

Jesus was the *ultimate model* for how we should live our lives.
He showed us how to be human.
He modeled how to *let go* of things that are impermanent – not to renounce them – but simply to *not be attached* so that we would be *free* to live as our *true selves*, as the *unique reflections* of God that we were *intended to be*.

So if we *believe* all Jesus told us then we must *follow* as well.
When we obey, in other words, *follow his ways,* we *enter into the flow of the Spirit.*
Then we have eternal life, not just one day in a future heaven, but also *now*.
You will begin to experience God's dream for you in the *present.*
The kingdom of God is at hand – *both* now *and* forever.

Listen to the song for the day "Pour Me Out" on the *Mercy Reigns* album.

LOVE CONNECTION

John 15:5

"I am the vine, you are the branches. Whoever remains in me and I in him will bear much fruit, because without me you can do nothing."

Jesus said that he is the vine and that God is the vine grower.
Each one of us is like a branch from that vine whose source is Love. ("God is love" – 1 John 4:8).
All of creation is connected to that vine, but we may not be *conscious* of it.
When we are conscious of this *divine connection* and *live* in that awareness,
we are truly living in the will of God.

It is *letting go into the flow* of unconditional love and acceptance.
However, our egos do not like this!
Our egos want to take over and make our lives "all about me," *my* will, *my* plan.
Then we are not consciously connected to the vine.

My own "private salvation project" (as Thomas Merton called it) will not lead to a joyful life (branches with *fruit*) but to emptiness (withered branches).
Don't forget that Jesus also said that God would prune the branches that bear fruit.
That means that there will be some painful struggles that will lead to bearing even more fruit if we remain consciously connected to the vine.
How?
By being present!
This takes practice.
Take time to simply "be."
Set aside time for silence (contemplative prayer) and meditation.
Give your mind a rest.
Simply observe without judgment.
Allow yourself to bask in God's unconditional love and acceptance.
Be, and *be free.*

Listen to the song for the day "Breathe On Me" on the *Listen to Your Heart* album.

APRIL

18 BE A BEACON

Luke 8:16

"No one who lights a lamp conceals it with a vessel or sets it under a bed; rather, he places it on a lampstand so that those who enter may see the light."

It's easy to tell people to shine their light, but it can seem hard to be a light when in the midst of struggles and difficulties.
It's also hard to be a light when the people around you don't seem very receptive, or even downright *antagonistic*.
Those people are struggling as well.

Remember, it is *not* about *you* being *perfect* before you can shine your light.
It is *not* about *you* being *worthy* enough to shine your light.
It is *not* about getting anyone's *approval* to shine your light.
It's not really *your light* anyway.
It's the light of *God* inside you.
That Light is *always* there at your core.
God works with you *where you are.*

***In our imperfection and struggles,* every time we turn to the mercy and unconditional love of God in the *present moment,* we are more able to reflect that Divine Light to others.**
Sometimes we can lack confidence that we'll be able to say or do the right thing in tough situations.
But, to paraphrase part of a prayer Mother Teresa often quoted: "Do it anyway."
It's not our job to change people's minds or hearts, that's up to a *Greater Power.*

Our job is to allow the light of Unconditional Love to shine forth from our core through the use of our varied gifts and talents.
Bask in the Light of the Love that made you.
It shines on you, in you, and through you *right now, just as you are.*

Listen to the song for the day "The Way You Are" on the *Mercy Reigns* album.

BEING YOU

John 3:3

Jesus answered and said to him, "Amen, amen, I say to you, no one can see the kingdom of God without being born from above."

The kingdom of God begins in the *here* and *now* to those who are *awake*.
As Jesus put it, "For behold, the kingdom of God is among you." (Luke 17:21).

It takes a *new mind* to see this kingdom, this realm of God's goodness.
St. Paul said, "Do not conform yourselves to this age but be transformed by the renewal of your mind, that you may discern what is the will of God, what is good and pleasing and perfect." (Romans 12:2).

It takes being *transformed*, or being *reborn*.
Usually this happens when we experience *grace*, unconditional love, and forgiveness when we *least* deserve it.

Or it can happen through an experience of Great Compassion during a time of deep suffering or love.

We must first die to our *old selves*, our *ego-created false selves*, before we can *rise* to our *true lives* in the Spirit.

That is how St. Paul could say, "I live, no longer I, but Christ lives in me." (Galatians 2:20).

Trust that there is a Love *beyond* Love.

Rest in the presence of that *Divine Presence* and be *free*.

Listen to the song for the day "Changed" on the *Give Praise and Thanks* album.

APRIL

20 DETACHMENT

Acts 4:32

The community of believers was of one heart and mind, and no one claimed that any of his possessions was his own, but they had everything in common.

The followers of Jesus were transformed.
They had been *changed.*

They were *not attached* to their possessions but willingly shared all they had so that no one was in need.

It was not about amassing wealth.
It was not about consuming and taking.

It was about giving and receiving.

It was about loving God and loving your neighbor.

This is about as *counter-cultural* a message as possible!

The truth is, the more attached we are to power, prestige and possessions, the more in *bondage* we are.

***Letting go* of these things gives us the freedom to know what is truly important in life.**

How can I take this message to heart?

What do *I* need to *let go of?*

How can I live in this way?

Listen to the song for the day "Glorify You with Me" on the *Give Praise and Thanks* album.

SINGLE HEARTED

APRIL
21

John 14:23

Jesus answered and said to him, "Whoever loves me will keep my word, and my Father will love him, and we will come to him and make our dwelling with him."

With Jesus, "love" certainly is the *key*.

He said the two greatest Commandments were to love God with your whole heart, soul and mind and to love your neighbor as yourself. (Matthew 22:37-39).

And in today's scripture verse, Jesus says that *love* is what *binds* you to his *word* and to *God*.

If we love Jesus then we will *follow* his ways.
If we do that, then Jesus says that he and God will make a dwelling with us.
How personal and intimate is that?

In truth, God is always dwelling within us but for us to *experience* this, our egos must loosen their attachments to things that won't last.
Then we are free to experience the inner joy of lasting peace *beyond understanding*.

There are many ways to experience the deep, intimate love of God: through creation, relationships, music, art, a child's smile, etc.

One of the surest ways to experience God's love is by *living-out* the words of Jesus.

When you do this, you will not only experience inner peace and joy but you will also discover your *true self*.

Listen to the song for the day "How Wonderful to Me" on the *Live to Love* album.

APRIL

22 KINGDOM BUILDER

Acts 14:22

They strengthened the spirits of the disciples and exhorted them to persevere in the faith, saying, "It is necessary for us to undergo many hardships to enter the kingdom of God."

Struggles and persecutions are promised us in our human experience.
But if we walk in faith with Jesus they will always lead to *new life.*
It's the path Jesus showed us.

In today's scripture passage, Paul had just been stoned and
dragged out of a city for preaching about the risen Christ.
He somehow survived.

Rough treatment for someone doing God's work!

Notice how the disciples didn't plan retaliation.
They didn't form a militia for a counter-attack.

They simply moved on with the same message of
unconditional love, mercy, forgiveness and compassion.
That* is *transformation!

For this is the only way the kingdom of God will break into the *present!*

They learned well from Jesus and his path to the cross.

Have *we?*

Listen to the song for the day "Salvation" on the *Live to Love* album.

BE THE CHANGE

Matthew 13:54-55

Jesus came to his native place and taught the people in their synagogue. They were astonished and said, "Where did this man get such wisdom and mighty deeds? Is he not the carpenter's son?

Isn't it true that sometimes the people *closest* to us can be
the *biggest stumbling blocks to our growth?*
Perhaps they feel threatened by the way we've *changed*
and that *they* may have to *change* as well?

Many people *do not want to change.*
They can end up standing in the way of us reaching our full potential.
Sometimes they can also refuse to let go of the past mistakes
we've made or shortcomings we had.
The people who remembered Jesus as a boy could *not* accept the inspiring
young man he had become.
"Jesus advanced [in] wisdom and age and favor before God and man." (Luke 2:52).
He had changed in a *big* way.

When you follow Jesus, your life *will change.* That's a *guarantee.*
And that will make others around you uncomfortable because
they may have to confront their unwillingness to change.
If that happens to you, know that you are in good company.
Jesus was rejected by those who knew him while he was growing up.

Following Jesus is *not* easy but it will lead you to *inner peace* as well as your *true self.*
As a follower, remember to respond to those who reject you
as Jesus did – with *love* and *compassion.*
Perhaps your response will be *the encounter with Christ* that *they* need.

Listen to the song for the day "I Want to Follow You" on
the *Listen to Your Heart* album.

APRIL

24 ABUNDANT LIFE

Matthew 19:29

"And everyone who has given up houses or brothers or sisters or father or mother or children or lands for the sake of my name will receive a hundred times more, and will inherit eternal life."

This statement by Jesus is all about *attachments.*
We know that he's *not* asking us to *discard* our families.

What he is saying *is* that when you make *serving God your top priority* you will have to set aside *all other desires.*

When you are living *in the flow of God's desires for you* then you begin to experience the *kingdom of God* right *now* in the *present.*
You are then already inheriting *eternal life.*

The key to understanding this is to know that for Jesus the "kingdom of God" or "kingdom of heaven" which he interchangeably uses (see Matthew 19:23-24) is available *now* to those who live a life of love, mercy, forgiveness and compassion, when you are *present* to the needs of the *other.*

In the Our Father, Jesus instructs us to pray, "Thy kingdom come, Thy will be done on earth as it is in heaven."
How else can God's kingdom *come on earth,* unless we cooperate?
Jesus also promised that those who *give up all,* they will receive *"a hundred times more."*

When you are *living your calling in the service of a Greater Good* you will be *rich* indeed.

Listen to the song for the day "Shall We Sing" on the *Listen to Your Heart* album.

CALLED TO WHOLENESS

APRIL **25**

1 Thessalonians 4:7-8

For God did not call us to impurity but to holiness. Therefore, whoever disregards this, disregards not a human being but God, who also gives his holy Spirit to you.

Sometimes we get hung-up on the word "holiness."
It can bring to mind a very *pious, stiff,* and *arrogant* image.
Jesus was definitely *not* that way!

He is quoted as saying that he was criticized for enjoying food and drink – "The Son of Man came eating and drinking and they said, 'Look, he is a glutton and a drunkard, a friend of tax collectors and sinners.'" (Matthew 11:19).
Jesus was the guy who turned the water into wine!
He was definitely a *joy* to be with, not some *holier-than-thou bore.*

So when we think of the word *holiness*, it might be helpful to think instead of *wholeness.*
When you are in the flow of God's goodness and are being present to this Goodness *and* to *others*, when you are being a *channel* of that goodness and love, you are becoming *whole* and *holy.*

What are the things you are involved in that really aren't helping you be the *fullness* of your *unique* self?
If you take a few moments and sit with this question, an *inner voice* (the Holy Spirit) will help you in the most *loving* way.

God does *not* want to *accuse* you or make you *miserable*, but *uplift* you and give you *joy* and *peace.*

Listen to the song for the day "Show Me...Me" on the *Listen to Your Heart* album.

APRIL

26 QUIET CLARITY

Luke 4:42-43

At daybreak, Jesus left and went to a deserted place. The crowds went looking for him, and when they came to him, they tried to prevent him from leaving them. But he said to them, "To the other towns also I must proclaim the good news of the kingdom of God, because for this purpose I have been sent."

If we are to *follow* Jesus, then we must look at his *example.*

First off, Jesus went off to a deserted place to pray.

Do we carve out some time in silence to be with God?

Secondly, through his prayer with God, Jesus knew his purpose.

He already had quoted the prophet Isaiah (61:1) in announcing his mission: To bring glad tidings to the poor, to proclaim liberty to the captives and let the oppressed go free. (Luke 4:18).

Jesus accomplishes this through forgiveness, mercy and compassion.

That's the Good News and it's what brings about the kingdom of God.

As followers of Jesus, *we must also be about this task.*

Your ego-created false self will likely not want to go along with this!

Only by *letting go* of this *false self* will you discover your *true self.*

Listen to the song for the day "Slow Me Down" on the *Mercy Reigns* album.

APRIL

LET LOVE LEAD YOU

27

Luke 5:11

When they brought their boats to the shore, they left everything and followed him.

What would it take to make you *totally change* the direction of your life in an *instant*?

Jesus had just told three fishermen to cast their nets again after they had caught nothing all night.

When Peter, James and John lowered their nets this time, they caught so many fish that their nets were tearing.

Peter's reaction was, "Depart from me, Lord, for I am a sinful man."

It's as though he felt he didn't *deserve* such a *miracle of generosity*.
Isn't that how *we* are?

We look at our *imperfections* and the *selfish choices* we have made and feel that we aren't *worthy* of God's love.

And yet Jesus seems to say that our *worthiness* or *achievements* have nothing to do with God's response to us.

God's response is out of *unconditional* love for us.

It's the kind of love that, if we opened ourselves to it, might move us to change our lives and drop all the trivial pursuits for happiness that will *never* satisfy our souls.

Following Jesus is the way to living as your *true self*.

The way is not easy, but Love will carry you to the life you were *meant* to live.

Listen to the song for the day "You'll Lead Me" on the *Listen to Your Heart* album.

APRIL

28 LET LOVE SPEAK

Ephesians 4:1-3

I, then, a prisoner for the Lord, urge you to live in a manner worthy of the call you have received, with all humility and gentleness, with patience, bearing with one another through love, striving to preserve the unity of the spirit through the bond of peace.

What a different world it would be if we *lived* these words from the apostle Paul.

He followed Christ by spreading the Good News of God's *unconditional love, mercy, forgiveness* and *compassion.*
After all, that is what *Jesus* did.

When attacked and persecuted, Jesus responded in love, giving the *ultimate example* of unconditional love when he forgave all his persecutors from the cross.

They weren't even asking for forgiveness!

Such Love is what *transformed* Paul, sparking a radical change in his life from persecutor of Christians to a devoted *follower* of Christ.

He, too, had to *bear with patience* the attacks against him.

There is a bigger picture, a bigger vision: God's dream for creation.
Each* of us is *included.

Each of us has received a *call* to share God's love using our unique gifts and talents.
Great joy* awaits you if you *follow the call.

Each moment is a new *opportunity.*

Listen to the song for the day "Let It Be Done to Me" on the *Mercy Reigns* album.

APRIL

29

MAKE ME A CHANNEL OF YOUR PEACE

Luke 6:42

"How can you say to your brother, 'Brother, let me remove that splinter in your eye,' when you do not even notice the wooden beam in your own eye? You hypocrite! Remove the wooden beam from your eye first."

The outcome of being a Christian is that through following Christ, *I* am changed, that *I* am transformed by God, *not* that I change *someone else.*

It is *not* about my *worthiness* or my *achievement* but about coming to know the grace and *unconditional love* of God *in my brokenness.*

In the light of such Grace, *I am changed!*

Jesus never seems angry with those who are struggling in their behavior, but is quite emphatic that he doesn't approve of those who are trying to find fault in others.

Instead of trying to change *someone else*, what if each of us focused on *ourselves* and asked God to open our hearts so that each of us could be more *loving, merciful, forgiving and compassionate?*

Perhaps then each of us could be transformed into the unique channels of God's compassion that we were created to be for *this* time and *this* place.

It is then that the kingdom of God can truly "come on earth as it is in heaven."

Listen to the song for the day "Make Me a Channel" on the *Listen to Your Heart* album.

APRIL

30 REASON TO REJOICE

Psalm 96:1-2

Sing to the Lord a new song; sing to the Lord, all the earth. Sing to the Lord, bless his name; announce his salvation day after day.

Ever listen to the birds whistling and chirping in the early morning?

It's as if when they awaken they instinctively joyfully sing!

With each chirp they proclaim their "is-ness" – they are *alive!*

They are *complete.*

They are *wholly themselves*, in *this* moment, the only time that is *real.*

Each *moment* is a *gift.*
Each *breath* is a *gift.*
Each *experience of our senses* is a *gift.*

All these gifts come from God who *loved all things into existence.*

Each of us is meant to be a *unique* reflection of our loving Creator.

Accept this Love that is *freely given without condition.*

Live in this acceptance.

It will be your *salvation.*

Your life will become a *new song* in praise of God!

Listen to the song for the day "Sing a New Song" on the *Live to Love* album.

MAY

I

LET GO AND LIVE

Acts 5:19-20

But during the night, the angel of the Lord opened the doors of the prison, led them out, and said, "Go and take your place in the temple area, and tell the people everything about this life."

The followers of Jesus faced persecution just like he did.

Jesus preached publicly for the inclusion of all people.

All are *equal* in the kingdom of God.

He was a threat to any power structure that *excluded, separated* or *oppressed* people.

Jesus was killed for standing up to those *governmental* and *religious* powers.

Thanks to the resurrection, his followers knew that death does not have the final say – *Love* does.

Death is a *transition* to *new life.*

Jesus showed us that this "dying to self" is a *daily process* leading to the kingdom of God *now*, not just in the future as some final reward.

Following Jesus *was* and *is* a *way of life.*

We are called to *live this life* and, just like his disciples, to "tell people everything about this life."

Listen to the song for the day "Pour Me Out" on the *Give Praise and Thanks* album.

MAY

2 GIVE THANKS

Psalm 34:2

I will bless the LORD at all times; his praise shall be always in my mouth.

There is reason to rejoice because "God is love." (1 John 4:8).
Therefore, we come from Love and will return to Love.

As St. Paul stated: "In him we were also chosen, destined in accord with the purpose of the One who accomplishes all things according to the intention of his will, so that we might exist for the praise of his glory. (Ephesians 1:11-12).

Sometimes we let the situations of this world overwhelm us and we lose sight of the Big Picture.
Any struggle that we are going through we will eventually understand as something that is helping us grow in love.

St Paul also stated; "We know that all things work for good for those who love God, who are called according to his purpose." (Romans 8:28).

So I exhort you to keep in mind that you are a *spiritual* being having a *human* experience.

I was so impressed during a jail ministry outing when I was waiting with the other volunteers in the lobby before going to our assigned cell blocks. A man ministering for another church group was saying softly over and over to himself in a very sincere fashion, *"Hallelujah, thank you, Jesus!"*

He was truly filled with thanksgiving that he was able to be there early on a Sunday morning to bring the Good News to those in need.

May praise always be in *my* mouth and in *yours* as well!

Listen to the song for the day "Give Praise and Thanks" on the *Give Praise and Thanks* album.

LOVE WINS

Acts 7:59–8:1

As they were stoning Stephen, he called out, "Lord Jesus, receive my spirit." Then he fell to his knees and cried out in a loud voice, "Lord, do not hold this sin against them"; and when he said this, he fell asleep. Now Saul was consenting to his execution.

Stephen, known as the first Christian martyr, would appear to have been a "loser" in the eyes of the *world,* but *not* in the eyes of *God.*

When we respond to hate with *love* – just like Jesus did – *transformation* is just around the corner.

We believe that Stephen's violent death did not mean his end.
We believe that it was simply a transition to *new life*.
Thanks to Jesus' example, Stephen was confident that death did not have the final say.

Just as Jesus sparked transformation in his followers through the way he lived, died and rose, Stephen's way of living and dying brought transformation as well.
His example likely began a transformation in a man named Saul who "was consenting" to the execution.
Saul, who persecuted Christians and was at least complicit in the killing of Christians, would one day be known as St. Paul – perhaps the greatest evangelist in history.

That's what can happen when hate is met with *love*.
May God's unconditional love transform us.
May our hearts be changed so that we are willing and able to respond to our persecutors with love.

Listen to the song for the day "Salvation" on the *Live to Love* album.

MAY

4 DO YOUR PART

Acts 13:2

While they were worshiping the Lord and fasting, the holy Spirit said, “Set apart for me Barnabas and Saul for the work to which I have called them.”

What is God calling *you* to do?

You are a unique expression of God who is meant to be a unique expression of God’s love to the world.

What is *your* part in building the kingdom of God?

Quite honestly, you probably can’t come up with the answer by way of your *mind.*

It’s more of a *heart* thing than a *thinking* thing.

How can you *hear* the Holy Spirit calling you to your next step on the journey?

Just like anything, it takes *practice.*

If you want to get better at anything you have to invest some of your time.

You have to sit *still* and *listen.*

Let the thinking mind be *quiet.*

Be *present* to God in the *silence.*

What is God saying to you in the patterns of your life?

Listen to the song for the day “Listen to Your Heart” on the *Listen to Your Heart* album.

BE OPEN

Acts 4:31

As they prayed, the place where they were gathered shook, and they were all filled with the holy Spirit and continued to speak the word of God with boldness.

Sometimes we get signs that seem to be *definite responses* from God to our prayers – *amazing* signs.

And sometimes we get more *subtle* responses.

We may get signs that we simply *miss* because we are *not paying attention*, not spending any time in *quiet* prayer, or are too distracted by the noise and busyness of our daily lives.

Or perhaps what we get in response from God is *silence.*

Could it be that some of God's most eloquent responses are spoken in a rich *silence* that needs to *sink* in and saturate our *open* and *surrendered* hearts?

As St. John of the Cross said, "Silence is God's first language."

To which Fr. Thomas Keating added: "Everything else is a poor translation."

What "word of God" are you being asked to speak and live with "boldness?"

Listen to the song for the day "Turn Off the Noise" on the *Listen to Your Heart* album.

MAY

6

GO MAKE A DIFFERENCE

John 14:5-6

Thomas said to him, "Master, we do not know where you are going; how can we know the way?" Jesus said to him, "I am the way and the truth and the life."

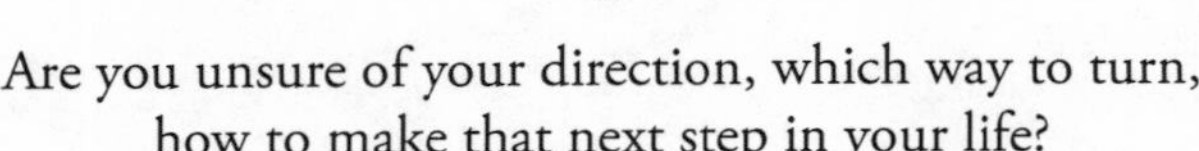

Are you unsure of your direction, which way to turn,
how to make that next step in your life?

Jesus gave us the *template* of *how to live.*

Believing what he said is one thing, but that's just *mind* stuff.

A *belief* in your brain *doesn't make any real difference.*

You can *believe* all kinds of stuff and still be a nasty person.

Jesus asked us to *follow* him.
Following Jesus requires *carrying out* what he said and did.

This is *heart* stuff.

This is the path to *transformation* and *true life.*

This is how the kingdom of God actually *comes* – as in,
"Your kingdom come, your will be done, on earth as in heaven." (Matthew 6:10).

Jesus went to great lengths to show us that the *path* to *life* included *dying* –
dying to selfish desires, dying to all the trivial pursuits aimed
at attaining things that won't last.

This is the *kenotic path* that leads us to being our true selves:
beloved children of God.

Listen to the song for the day "I Want to Follow You" on the *Listen to Your Heart* album.

MAY

BE TRANSFORMED

7

Acts 9:1-2

Saul, still breathing murderous threats against the disciples of the Lord, went to the high priest and asked him for letters to the synagogues in Damascus, that, if he should find any men or women who belonged to the Way, he might bring them back to Jerusalem in chains.

The man named Saul brought fear into the heart of any follower of Jesus. **He would have been looked upon much the same as we look upon a terrorist today.** Saul did *reign terror down* upon the followers of "the Way," as the first Christians were known.

So who did God select as a very special spokesman for following the way of Christ? ***Saul!***

Clearly, God does not choose us based on our own *merit!*
As you may have heard, God does not call the *qualified.* God qualifies the *called.* Or, as Saul went on to say after his conversion when he became known as Paul, "God chose the foolish of the world to shame the wise, and God chose the weak of the world to shame the strong, and God chose the lowly and despised of the world, those who count for nothing, to reduce to nothing those who are something, so that no human being might boast before God." (1 Corinthians 1:27-29).

So perhaps we should not be so quick to judge someone as "unredeemable."
Everyone* – including *you* and *me* – can *change.

Do not judge others, but allow God's unconditional Love to change hearts, including yours and mine.

Listen to the song for the day "Changed" on the *Give Praise and Thanks* album.

MAY

8 SOUL FOOD

John 6:27

"Do not work for food that perishes but for the food that endures for eternal life, which the Son of Man will give you."

Jesus tells us that there is more important nourishment than the food that fuels the body.

There is spiritual nourishment that fuels the *soul.*

The body, though important and in need of the proper nourishment, will eventually wither and die.

The soul will not die, but go on.

What do you do to nourish your soul?

The earliest movement that was following Jesus was called "the Way" because Jesus had shown them *the way of life.*
It was a way that led to abundant life *now*, a life full of promise, peace and happiness.

That doesn't mean it was idyllic – no – *far from it.*
There was adversity from those who didn't like this "Way" that called for all people to be accepted, treated fairly and loved.

It was a *Way of freedom from attachments to things that didn't last and offered no true fulfillment.*

If you want food that *endures*, feast on the words of Jesus.

Mull over them.

Let them *ruminate* in your heart and lead you to your *true life.*

Listen to the song for the day "Breathe On Me" on the *Listen to Your Heart* album.

LIFE-CHANGING

Acts 5:40-41

After recalling the apostles, they had them flogged, ordered them to stop speaking in the name of Jesus, and dismissed them. So they left the presence of the Sanhedrin, rejoicing that they had been found worthy to suffer dishonor for the sake of the name.

It was only a *short time* before this that these *same followers* of Jesus were *cowering* inside, *hiding out* in fear that they would meet the same horrible demise as their teacher.

What could have *changed* these men into bold proclaimers of the Good News of Jesus?

What could have made them so willing to be harshly treated and eventually even *give their lives* in order to spread their Master's teachings?

***They each had a deep experience of the risen Christ*, the revelation that he indeed was alive, that death has no sting.**

They had been *transformed.*

Do you *long* to live for a cause that you could die for? A cause that is bigger and *more meaningful* than anything this world could offer?

Christ is calling *you.*

It's never *too early* or *too late* to *answer* the call.

Let the* adventure *begin!

Listen to the song for the day "Mercy Reigns" on the *Mercy Reigns* album.

MAY

10 EVERYTHING BELONGS

John 10:16

"I have other sheep that do not belong to this fold. These also I must lead, and they will hear my voice, and there will be one flock, one shepherd."

We all start out in life believing that *we* are at the *center* of the universe.
It's all about *me.*

Sadly, some people never seem to get beyond this *delusional* perspective.

The ego feeds on being *separate* from others, inflating its own *self-importance*, always judging who is *right* and who is *wrong*.

Of course, the ego always judges itself to be *right!*
The ego wants me to believe that I am on the winning side, that I am in the "in" group. That would mean that *someone else* is *not.*

When we *exclude* we are clearly *not* being Christian.

Jesus *reached out* to all the *outcasts.*

He insisted that *all* will be *one* flock and that he will be the one shepherd.

This is what the kingdom of God is about, *diverse* yet *one.*

For this to happen, *egos* have to *diminish.*

As John the Baptist said, "Jesus must increase; I must decrease." (John 3:30).

Ask yourself: "How can *I* change to be more *merciful* and *accepting* that *everything* and *everyone belongs?*

Listen to the song for the day "All Are One" on the *Mercy Reigns* album.

DEATH TO LIFE

John 16:20

"Amen, amen, I say to you, you will weep and mourn, while the world rejoices; you will grieve, but your grief will become joy."

Jesus knew his followers would *grieve* when he was killed, but he also knew that they would *rejoice* after his resurrection.
Such it is in life when we lose something or someone or even as we slowly lose the *false image* of ourselves.
Our egos are more concerned about an image reflected by our *power, prestige* and *possessions.*

If we *awaken* from the *delusion* of this image we realize that these things will *not last.*
We realize that in order to grow the *egocentric version* of ourselves must *die* so that our *true selves* can *rise.*
This reminds us of one of the key teachings of Jesus:
"Unless a grain of wheat falls to the ground and dies, it remains just a grain of wheat; but if it dies, it produces much fruit." (John 12:24).
Your *true self* "produces much fruit" because it reflects the *unique image of God* that you were meant to reflect.

Observe your ego and its self-centered ways.
Do not fight or repress it, as it is *not* your "bad" self, but your "false" self.
Your ego can help you immensely once you utilize it as your friend.
Simply observe it and see it for what it is and its *control* over you will begin to *fade.*
The decline of the false self is difficult.
You may feel like *weeping and mourning*.

As Jesus showed us, something old must end for something new and beautiful to start!
Your grief will also become joy as you live as your *true self.*

Listen to the song for the day "Take the Road Less Traveled" on the *Live to Love* album.

MAY

12 VOCATION

Acts 20:22, 24

"But now, compelled by the Spirit, I am going to Jerusalem. What will happen to me there I do not know. Yet I consider life of no importance to me, if only I may finish my course and the ministry that I received from the Lord Jesus, to bear witness to the gospel of God's grace."

What is the Spirit compelling *you* to do?
Is there a growing desire in your heart to do something positive, something loving, something in the name of Goodness?
Are you aware of a passion inside you that is *yearning* to be expressed for the betterment of the world?
Are you in *tune* with this Spirit?

Take time to *listen* in silence with the ears of your heart.

Paul realized that Christ was calling him to share the good news of God's grace, God's *free* and *unmerited* love and acceptance of *all* people.
He had experienced that grace when he was a persecutor of Christians.
It *changed* him.

That same Grace loves and accepts *you* – *just as you are!*

You are being called to share it as well.

How will you do it?

What is *your* ministry?

Listen to the song for the day "The Way You Are" on the *Mercy Reigns* album.

HARMONIZE

MAY 13

John 17:16,18

"They do not belong to the world any more than I belong to the world. As you sent me into the world, so I sent them into the world."

Ever get the feeling that you just don't *fit* in?

Are you trying hard to fit into the *world's* idea of *normal, acceptable* or *"cool?"*

Some people have fallen so far into this trap that they have wrapped themselves in many layers of *illusion.*

They have accumulated many *masks.*

Such a person is quite unaware of his or her "true self."

How *sad!*

We are *not meant* to mirror the *world,* but to mirror *God to the world.*

You and I are unique expressions of God (Love) who are meant to be the *one* and *only* you and me in order to channel Love to the world.

How else will God's "kingdom come on earth as in heaven." (Matthew 6:10)?

What is your part in this *evolving expression* of Love?

Listen to the song for the day "Make Me a Channel" on the *Listen to Your Heart* album.

MAY

14 SLOW DOWN

John 6:45,47

"Everyone who listens to my Father and learns from him comes to me. Amen, amen, I say to you, whoever believes has eternal life."

Listening to God takes *effort* and *letting go.*

It means devoting some time to simply *being present.*

Most of the time, we *aren't.*

Our brains are *constantly* at work either mulling over things that have *already happened* to us or worrying about things in the *future*.

Past and *future* are *not real*, they exist only in our *minds*.

The only time that is *real* is *now*.

Spend ten to twenty minutes in *silence* to be *present* to the Great Presence, the Loving Source of all things.

***Listen* with the ears of your heart.**

Read the words of Jesus and *follow* his example.

Notice that Jesus says "whoever believes *has* eternal life" (*"has,"* not *"will have"*).

When you are living in the *presence* of God, eternal life *is at hand.*

It is only through this Presence that your true self can *emerge*.

Listen to the song for the day "Slow Me Down" on the *Mercy Reigns* album.

MISSIONED

John 15:16

It was not you who chose me, but I who chose you and appointed you to go and bear fruit that will remain.

***Each* one of us is *chosen* by our Creator out of Love.**

We *come* from Love and will *return* to Love.

We are *eternal souls* meant to, in the words of William Blake, *"learn to bear the beams of love"* here on Earth.

That means we are meant to "bear fruit that will remain."

We are here for a *purpose*, that through our cooperation God's kingdom would "come on earth as it is in heaven." (Matthew 6:10).

We are meant to be *channels of God's love.*

For this to happen, we need to *find* our calling and to *live* it.

This is the only way to actually *be* your *true self.*

You have been *chosen.*

In order to respond, you need to *listen, discern* and *develop your talents* so you can be the *uniquely fashioned you* that shines the light of God's love *now* and *always.*

If you do this, your life will become a great and wondrous *adventure!*

Listen to the song for the day "May I Be Light" on the *Listen to Your Heart* album.

MAY

16 GREATEST COMMANDMENT

John 15:12-13

"This is my commandment: love one another as I love you. No one has greater love than this, to lay down one's life for one's friends."

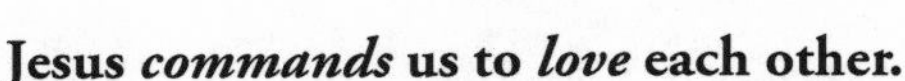

Jesus *commands* us to *love* each other.

It seems that in the Church we make many things *non-negotiable* that Jesus *never talked about.*

However, we seem to let this *clear command* slide.

He *commanded* us to love each other – and our *enemies* as well!

A *command* is *non-negotiable.*

Jesus showed us *how* to love, *all the way to the cross.*

He showed us how to love when being hated.

He gave us the most extreme example, not as an *end* in itself, but as a *model.*

Jesus tells us to *do the same.*

This is the path we *must* follow.

It's the path to *wholeness, oneness* in God and becoming our *true selves.*

In other words, it's the path to *salvation.*

Listen to the song for the day "Salvation" on the *Live to Love* album.

FOLLOW THE CALL

MAY

17

Acts 20:24

"Yet I consider life of no importance to me, if only I may finish my course and the ministry that I received from the Lord Jesus, to bear witness to the gospel of God's grace."

At the time Paul said these words he was in such communion with his calling that even though he sensed his physical death was looming, he was at *peace* with the *mystery* ahead.

He knew in the deepest way that true joy and peace could only come through carrying out his calling *moment by moment.*

He realized that the *world's ways* of attaining happiness would all eventually lead to *emptiness.*

It was only in his ego's "self-emptying" through carrying out of his calling that he would be *filled* and *made whole.*

We are all called to "bear witness to the gospel of God's grace" or, in other words, *to bear witness to the Good News of God's freely given love and forgiveness.*

How do we do this with the talents, abilities, and deep passions we've received from our loving Creator?

That is our *ministry,* and when we *live it,* the *kingdom of God is at hand.*

How are ***you*** called to *bear witness to the gospel of God's grace* with *your* life?

Listen to the song for the day "Pour Me Out" on the *Give Praise and Thanks* album.

MAY

18 LIVE

Psalm 145:10

All your works give you thanks,
O Lord, and your faithful bless you.

All of God's creation is living fully in the moment, just "being" to the fullest extent.

Every bug, every bird, every flower, every tree, every animal is just *being itself* with every fiber of its being.

No cat is thinking, "I wish I was a *dog.*"

No flower is thinking, "I'd rather be a *tree.*"

They are "all in."

They are completely content at being what they are to the fullest degree.

In doing so, they are *giving thanks* and *praise* to their Creator.

The question is, are *we* doing the *same?*

Is *each* of us being the *unique* person that God created to the *fullest measure?*

Set aside time each day to simply *be present* to the *Divine Presence.*

Rest in that Presence.

Experience God's unconditional love and acceptance.

Then respond by sharing your gifts and talents for the good of someone else.

Your acts will be acts of praise to God and reason to be *very thankful.*

Listen to the song for the day "Glorify You with Me" on the *Give Praise and Thanks* album.

ABIDING PEACE

John 15:4

"Remain in me, as I remain in you. Just as a branch cannot bear fruit on its own unless it remains on the vine, so neither can you unless you remain in me."

Jesus says that God is the vine grower, he is the vine, and we are the branches.

How can we make sure that our lives will "bear fruit"?

Jesus says by *remaining in him.*

How do we do this?

By getting to know him through reading his words in the gospels and meditating on them.

By following his example of *letting go* of our ego's desires and serving those in need.

By being his hands and his feet, allowing Jesus to live through us.

In the prayer known as the *Our Father*, Jesus instructed us to pray these words to God: "Your will be done." (Which, of course, means not *my* will be done!)

By *consciously being connected* to Jesus as a branch is to the vine, we are promised *life to the full.*

We will find our *true selves.*

"I came so that they might have life and have it more abundantly." (John 10:10).

Listen to the song for the day "How Wonderful to Me" on the *Live to Love* album.

MAY

20 PATH TO JOY

John 15:10-11

"If you keep my commandments, you will remain in my love, just as I have kept my Father's commandments and remain in his love. I have told you this so that my joy might be in you and your joy might be complete."

We know that God's love is *unconditional*, so just because we slip up on keeping the commandments doesn't mean that God *withholds* that love.

It does mean that we may move away from the *flow* of God's love.

It would be like singing in a great chorus but purposely singing out of tune.

When we are keeping the commandments, we are in the flow of God's love and are singing a beautiful harmony in the great chorus.

When we remain in God's love, our hearts are *transformed* and we naturally want to spread that love to others.

We are participating in a *circle of giving and receiving love*, the very *life of the Trinity*.

Contemplate for a moment how God loves you unconditionally.

Allow that to settle into your heart.

***Feel* the *joy* that Jesus wants *you* to experience and then *share* it with *someone else*.**

Listen to the song for the day "Shall We Sing" on the *Listen to Your Heart* album.

UNIVERSAL PATTERN

MAY 21

John 16:21

"When a woman is in labor, she is in anguish because her hour has arrived; but when she has given birth to a child, she no longer remembers the pain because of her joy that a child has been born into the world."

There is a pattern in life all around us.

It is the pattern of *dying* and *rising*.

Franciscan priest Richard Rohr in his book *Falling Upward* writes:
"Reality, creation, nature itself, what I call the "First Body of Christ," has no choice in the matter of necessary suffering. It lives the message without saying yes or no to it. The "Second Body of Christ," the formal church, always has the freedom to say yes or no. That freedom allows it to say no much of the time, especially to any talk of dying, stumbling, admitting mistakes, or falling. Yet God seems ready and willing to wait for, and to empower, free will and a free "yes." Love only happens in the realm of freedom."

A woman's *"yes"* in giving birth to her child is a beautiful example of following Christ's example of *dying to yourself.*

New life follows.

In that loving act there is transformation.

May we all say "yes" to God's invitation to *"dying"* to our *false selves* so that our *true* selves can be born.

Listen to the song for the day "Seasons" on the *Listen to Your Heart* album.

MAY

22 SHARE THE LOVE

Psalm 57:9-10

Awake, my soul; awake, lyre and harp! I will wake the dawn. I will praise you among the peoples, Lord; I will chant your praise among the nations.

For me these verses took on a *literal* meaning.
It wasn't until my *soul* was *awakened* that I started writing and singing songs of praise to God.

My soul was awakened when my misery rose to such a level that my ego was forced to *surrender.*
It could no longer prop up the *false self* it had created.
My *true self* was hidden under layers of masks.
My "soul pain" had finally *overwhelmed* my ego's resistance.

Is your soul *awake?*
Are you being your *true self?*

This requires listening to the gentle nudges of God in your heart.
To do so, practice *being present* to the *Divine Presence.*
Otherwise, the *noise of the world* and your mind's *non-stop commentaries* will enslave you.

I once heard this wonderful piece of advice from the late spiritual author and speaker Dr. Wayne Dyer: "Don't die with your music still inside you."

What is *your* "music" that is meant to be shared with others?

What unique gifts do *you* have to offer the world from your *awakened soul?*

Go forth glorifying God with your life!

Listen to the song for the day "Singing My Song" on the *Live to Love* album.

FOUNTAINS OF GOD

MAY 23

Psalm 87:7

So singers and dancers:
"All my springs are in you."

God is the *Ultimate Creator.*

Everything that exists is the work of God's *creativity.*

And that creation is *ongoing!*

The Universe is *still* expanding and the artistry is *astounding.*

Just look at the *stunning photos* that the Hubble Space Telescope has taken.

We are all children of this ineffable Creator who scripture says *is* Love.

We are all *spawned* in Love's *creative flow.*

God's "springs" are in each of us.
***We* are meant to *create* as well.**

Some create as singers, others as dancers, artists, writers, chefs, landscapers, etc.

When you share your talents, you are sharing *love* with the world.

You are accepting God's invitation to the *Great Dance.*

When you do this, you are being your *true self*
and a *unique reflection* of your Creator.

Whatever you do to create, the universe celebrates your contribution!

Listen to the song for the day "How Magnificent, Wondrous and Glorious" on the *Mercy Reigns* album.

MAY

24 LIVE YOUR LIFE

John 15:8

"By this is my Father glorified, that you bear much fruit and become my disciples."

Before saying today's scripture verse, Jesus said that he is the vine, God is the vine grower, and we are the branches.

Sometimes using *metaphor* is the only way to communicate such spiritual truths.

It is impossible for us to truly sever ourselves from the vine, but we can be completely *unconscious* of our connection.

When we *let go* of our ego's need to *control* and open ourselves to our *eternal connection* with the *Source of Life* (God or *Love itself*) we can then live as our true selves.

The lives we were *created to live* can then *flourish.*

We will then "bear much fruit" indeed and will be able to walk the path that Jesus modeled.

This will truly *give glory to God!*

Your life will be a *song of praise!*

Listen to the song for the day "Lift Up Our Voices" on the *Give Praise and Thanks a*lbum.

OBSTACLES TO LIFE

Mark 10:21

Jesus, looking at him, loved him and said to him, "You are lacking in one thing. Go, sell what you have, and give to the poor and you will have treasure in heaven; then come, follow me."

***Eternal life* in the Christian tradition can be tasted *now* for those who are truly *in the flow* of God's will.**
The rich man in today's scripture passage wanted to know what he must *do* to "inherit eternal life."
He was *doing* all the right things – following all the commandments and religious rules – but he knew *something* was *missing.*

Jesus knew that the man's *disorienting dilemma* was that he was *attached* to his *many possessions.*
That *attachment* blocked him *being present* to the *flow of God's goodness.*
It prevented him from knowing God's call and becoming his *true self.*
Notice that Jesus "loved him" while calling him to make a major change.
***Love* was Jesus' motivation, *not* chastisement.**
Possessions in and of themselves can be good if we are good stewards and generous with them. Renouncing them is *not* a requirement.

However, it is difficult to have many possessions and not be attached to them, obsessed with *protecting* and *increasing* them.
We mistakenly believe that power, prestige and possessions will bring us happiness.
Maybe they *will* briefly, but all those things will eventually *disintegrate.*
The source of *lasting happiness* is *letting go of all that will not last.*
What is left is the Presence of God alone.
Material possessions will fade away, but God's love will *never* end.
What* or *who* is blocking you from the free flow of God's love and being your *true self?

Listen to the song for the day "Come to Jesus" on the *Live to Love* album.

MAY

26 AWAKEN

Luke 9:18-20

“Who do the crowds say that I am?” They said in reply, “John the Baptist; others, Elijah; still others, ‘One of the ancient prophets has arisen.’” Then Jesus said to them, “But who do you say that I am?”

Ah! *That* is the question!

At some point (if it hasn’t happened already) you will hear Jesus ask that question directly to *you*: “Who do you say I am?”

If Jesus is “the way, the truth and the life” as he said (John 14:6), then what implications does that have on *your* life?

If you are struggling, or if there seems to be something missing, a void inside, or if you are trying to make meaning of your life: look to Jesus’ words in the gospels for direction.

The one thing Jesus asks of us is to *follow* him.

That is what it means to be a “Christian.”

Following him will require *letting go* of many things that are blocking you from being your *true self.*

This will no doubt require making tough changes.
But you will find a new peace in the midst of your struggle.

It will be in the *process* of following Jesus that you will find *yourself.*

And in *each moment* of that journey, you will experience ever deepening joy and peace.

Listen to the song for the day “I Want to Follow You” on the *Listen to Your Heart* album.

REIGN OF GOD

MAY

27

1 Peter 4:10

As each one has received a gift, use it to serve one another as good stewards of God's varied grace.

As our Creator gives each of us special talents and abilities, we are meant to use them for the purpose of *love* and *goodness.*
What a wonderful world we would have if only everyone took this to heart!

For those who are Christians, they are supposed to be *following* Jesus, which requires serving others.

The natural inclination is to serve *ourselves. Each* of us is looking out at the world as if we are the *center* of the universe.
What's in it for ***me****?*

At some point our egocentric "it's-all-about-me" world comes crashing down.
It may be due to illness or a great loss.
Many times it is only *in our brokenness* when we are able to *experience* the unconditional love, mercy, forgiveness and compassion of God.

It is a total *gift*, freely given to us *without any merit of our own.*
We know we did nothing to deserve it!

Feel* this Unconditional Love for you in *this moment.
Let it *wash* over you.

Now, what is your gift or talent – freely given to you by God – that you can use to extend that *same* compassion to someone in need?

Listen to the song for the day "There Is Three" on the *Mercy Reigns* album.

MAY

28 MAKE ME A CHANNEL OF YOUR LOVE

Acts 17:24-25

"The God who made the world and all that is in it, the Lord of heaven and earth, does not dwell in sanctuaries made by human hands, nor is he served by human hands because he needs anything. Rather it is he who gives everyone life and breath and everything."

We cannot put God in a box.

We cannot *contain* or *define* the Creator, the Infinite and Loving Source of *all* that *is*.

God gives freely expecting *nothing* in return.

All that we have and all that surrounds us is pure *gift*.

What about those who are being unjustly treated in the world?

It is *our* responsibility to be God's instrument in bringing them the Good News of God's *unconditional* Love.

God's love is a *free* gift to *everyone* and *everything!*

It is not based on merit!

How can I be a channel of that Love with my life?

Listen to the song for the day "Make Me a Channel" on the *Listen to Your Heart* album.

CALLED

Ephesians 1:17-18

"May the God of our Lord Jesus Christ, the Father of glory, give you a spirit of wisdom and revelation resulting in knowledge of him. May the eyes of [your] hearts be enlightened, that you may know what is the hope that belongs to his call."

This was the prayer of St. Paul for *everyone.*

May we all pray for *a spirit of wisdom and revelation resulting in the knowledge of God.*

And *may the eyes of our hearts be enlightened, that we may know what is the hope that belongs to God's call.*

Are you *seeking God* in your *daily life?*

The sacred is *everywhere.*

You are a part of it!

What is *your* call?

The *finding* is *in the seeking.*

Seek God *always* and you *will find!*

Listen to the song for the day "Show Me…Me" on the *Listen to Your Heart* album.

MAY

30 LET IT BE DONE TO ME

Luke 1:46-47

"My soul proclaims the greatness of the Lord;
my spirit rejoices in God my savior."

Mary's statement *resonates* in my heart.

When I am *in the flow* of the will of God, my *inner-most-being exults.*

No matter what struggles are in my life, there seems to be an inner *calm*, a certain "yes" that pervades my interior.

There are really no words to describe it accurately.

It is at the level of mystery.

When I am operating in the will of God, I am saying *yes* to this great Mystery at work in me.

My egocentric desires are neutralized.

When I am in this state of being, I am my *true self.*

It's not so much that I have done anything, it is more like *it is being done to me!*

I wish I could say this is my state all the time but it is *far from it.*

I must continually return to *letting go* and *being present.*

May we all surrender to God's desires for us and, like Mary, say, "May it be done to me according to your word." (Luke 1:38).

Listen to the song for the day "Let It Be Done to Me" on the *Mercy Reigns* album.

MAY

SELF-EMPTY 31

Romans 12:12-14

Rejoice in hope, endure in affliction, persevere in prayer. Contribute to the needs of the holy ones, exercise hospitality. Bless those who persecute [you], bless and do not curse them.

When it comes to *rejoicing in hope, enduring in affliction* and *persevering in prayer* – that's a *tall order* but many are able to *understand* it and put it into *practice.*
When it comes to the rest of St. Paul's statement above,
I think you'll find *plenty of opposition.*
Questions come up: "Are the holy ones *deserving* of my *contribution to their needs?*
What if they are slackers?
What's with this *exercise hospitality* stuff?"
Really? I'm supposed to help *those* people?

When it comes to *blessing those who persecute you*, you'd be *hard pressed* to find examples of people who practice that.
Actually, this one doesn't compute to our basic *binary* brain function which says:
Being *good* gets you a *reward*; being *bad* gets you *punished.*
Period.
Not so* with *Jesus* and *not so* with *St. Paul.
It took being *transformed* by *forgiveness* and *grace* for
Paul to get to this place of *radical love.*
Make no mistake, *this* is what Christians are *called* to do—*all of it.*

If you need inspiration, gaze at Jesus hanging on the cross.
Gaze at *love poured out* to demonstrate the extreme
example of *responding to evil* with *love.*
His demonstration was done on behalf of those who were *totally unworthy.*
He calls *us* to *do the same.*
Allow this knowledge to marinate in your heart.

Listen to the song for the day "Radically Okay" on the *Mercy Reigns* album.

JUNE

1 SHINE

Psalm 112:1, 4

Happy those who fear the Lord, who greatly delight in God's commands. They shine through the darkness, a light for the upright; they are gracious, merciful, and just.

We are all looking for happiness,
but happiness is *not* something you *search* for and *find*.

It is a by-product of the spiritual journey through which you come to know Love and share Love.

Only then can you actually live as your "true self."

Fear of the Lord is *not* being *afraid* of God but being in *awe* of such an unconditionally loving Creator so that in each moment you delight in being truly present to God in yourself, in others and in all of creation.

Be present to the One who loves you unconditionally, the Source of all life.

Let go of your rambling thoughts and constant judgments and simply allow the Divine Presence to fill you.

It's only then that you will begin to reflect the same compassionate Light to the world.

Awaken to your part in God's unfolding love story.

Jesus gives us the ultimate example.

Follow him!

Listen to the song for the day "I Want to Follow You" on the *Listen to Your Heart* album.

PRAISE BE

Psalm 90:14

Fill us at daybreak with your love,
that all our days we may sing for joy.

**When you awaken each morning, why not acknowledge
your gratefulness at being alive?**

Consciously take a breath.

**It's a new day with *endless* possibilities of *seeing, hearing,* and *feeling*
the blessings God is *pouring out* to us without cost.**

Listen to the sound of birds greeting the dawn.

**It's as if they were awakened from their sleep by the voice of their Creator saying,
"You are loved. Be what you are!"**

They respond in the fullness of their being praising God
with the beautiful voices they've been given.

God is saying the same thing to us: *"You are loved! Be what you are!"*

How will you respond with the fullness of your being?

**Listen to the song for the day "Glorify You with Me" on
the *Give Praise and Thanks* album.**

JUNE

3 WINDING ROAD

Psalm 25:4-5

Make known to me your ways, Lord; teach me your paths. Guide me in your truth and teach me, for you are God my savior.

There is no *predetermined path* set for us.

God gives each of us *free will* to do as we please.

How *else* would we be able to experience *unconditional love* if we didn't have the ability to choose to *accept* it or *reject* it?

But the Creator of all things wants to *partner with you* in the grand love story that is unfolding throughout the universe.

We all have a part to play.

Each of us can choose, *over* and *over*, whether or not we want to *take part* in the dance.

God yearns to be with you in each moment of your life to encourage and to inspire; to celebrate with you in joys and to comfort you in sorrows and to lift you in your struggles.

Allow a Love "that surpasses all understanding" (Ephesians 3:19) to lead you.

Listen to the song for the day "You'll Lead Me" on the *Listen to Your Heart* album.

MAKE A CHANGE

Luke 15:7

I tell you, in just the same way there will be more joy in heaven over one sinner who repents than over ninety-nine righteous people who have no need of repentance.

We all need to *repent*, which simply means to *change the direction* we are headed.

When our egos are in control we have no need for God.

We are on a *never-ending* path of *self-satisfaction.*

The yearning we feel inside is not truly for anything *material* or *physical.*

It's a *spiritual* yearning for *wholeness.*

When we turn *from* our egos and *toward* God we allow our Loving Source to lead us to our *soul's* satisfaction.

It's the path to finding your *true self* – the complete you that you were meant to be.

It's a daily and even *moment by moment* process.

All those in heaven are rooting for us to simply *be* what we are meant to be!

Listen to the song for the day "Take the Road Less Traveled" on the *Live to Love* album.

JUNE

5

GRAND PLAN

Psalm 119:166

I look for your salvation, Lord,
and I fulfill your commands.

When I think of the word "*salvation*" I know it's something that God *grants*, not something we *accomplish.*

But God calls us to *cooperate!*

God calls us into *relationship.*

It is *through* that relationship that we come to know *who we are.*

Salvation is "wholeness."

God wants nothing more than for *each of us* to become *whole*, a completed work of art, the unique *me* that God had in mind.

As St. Paul says, "I am confident of this, that the one who began a good work in you will continue to complete it until the day of Christ Jesus." (Philippians 1:6).

So may you *look* for your salvation.

May you *yearn* for your wholeness and completion as the unique creation God intended.

May you *surrender* your ego*centric* desires so that Christ can *live* more *fully* in you.

For when you *die* to your *false self*, the *paradox* is that you *discover* your *true self* as Christ *grows in you.*

Listen to the song for the day "Show Me...Me" on the *Listen to Your Heart* album.

ENTER THE WONDER

Psalm 98:4

Shout with joy to the Lord, all the earth;
break into song; sing praise.

From subatomic particles, to the atom, to the earth and the moon and all the planets and galaxies, creation is still unfolding and expanding.

How could there *not* be a wondrous Creator behind such magnificence?

The same Loving Source Who holds all this together, breathes life into the tiniest insect; a budding flower; a playful puppy; a smiling child – and you!

Trees reach for the skies. Birds sing with reckless abandon.
Dogs play like there is no tomorrow.

To them, there *is* no tomorrow, only the *eternal now,* receiving the gift of life and celebrating it.

Think about that.

Be present.

Be you.

Sing *your* song!

Listen to the song for the day "How Magnificent, Wondrous and Glorious" on the *Mercy Reigns* album.

JUNE

7 ILLUMINE

Matthew 5:15-16

"Nor do they light a lamp and then put it under a bushel basket; it is set on a lampstand where it gives light to all in the house. Just so, your light must shine before others, that they may see your good deeds and glorify your heavenly Father."

Each of us is a *reflection* of our Creator.
Scripture tells us that humankind is made in *God's image.* (Genesis 1:27).
It also tells us that "God is light" (1 John 1:5) and "God is love." (1 John 4:8).

So when we are *reflecting Love* through our *unique human form* we are *shining a light.*
Jesus said that each of us has a light.
This light – or reflection of God – is meant to be shared in the darkness of the world.

We do this by *channeling God's unconditional love* which helps build the *kingdom of God*, or *realm of God*, *here* and *now.*

Allow God's light to shine in you.
What are your gifts and talents?
What do you enjoy doing?
***Live* these questions and see what *answers* develop.**

Pay attention to your ego's desires for power, prestige and possessions, things that can never truly satisfy.
Observe this and allow those desires to *dissipate.*

Jesus said, "Blessed are the poor in spirit, for theirs is the kingdom of heaven." (Matthew 5:3).
That means *now* and *forever.*

Listen to the song for the day "May I Be Light" on the *Listen to Your Heart* album.

JUNE

FREE 8

2 Corinthians 3:17-18

Now the Lord is the Spirit, and where the Spirit of the Lord is, there is freedom. All of us, gazing with unveiled face on the glory of the Lord, are being transformed into the same image from glory to glory, as from the Lord who is the Spirit.

The Spirit of God is *alive.*

That Spirit is in the *fabric* of the *flow of life.*

When we are able to *let go* and let this Flow take us we have experiences that *we could never have imagined.*

It happened and continues to happen in my life.

When I allow the Flow to direct me, my life changes for the better.

When we are in this space of the Spirit we are truly *free.*

We are being the *unique masterpiece* that God always intended.

This is what it's like to be saved by Grace.

***Stop* and listen to the *gentle voice* of the Spirit directing your heart to freedom.**

Listen to the song for the day "Changed" on the *Give Praise and Thanks* album.

JUNE

9 RESURRECTION

2 Corinthians 4:8-10

We are afflicted in every way, but not constrained; perplexed, but not driven to despair; persecuted, but not abandoned; struck down, but not destroyed; always carrying about in the body the dying of Jesus, so that the life of Jesus may also be manifested in our body.

St. Paul got the underlying message of Jesus and the Paschal Mystery.

The *blueprint* Jesus left us is that *death leads to life.*

It wasn't just his physical death and the resurrection.

He showed us that this *dying-and-rising pattern* happens *all through our lives.*

We are constantly met with *afflictions* and *persecutions.*

They are like *little deaths* if you will.

When we go *through* each struggle *trusting* that *Love is leading us* we find we are being *transformed* with *new life.*

It's like the caterpillar struggling in the cocoon to free itself and finding at the end of the struggle it has wings and can fly.

Trust that whatever struggle you are going through now, it's going to be integral to your discovery of an *ever-deepening* way – *your true self.*

Listen to the song for the day "Pour Me Out" on the *Live to Love* album.

IT'S NOT ABOUT ME

JUNE
10

Philippians 2:5-7

Have among yourselves the same attitude that is also yours in Christ Jesus, Who, though he was in the form of God, did not regard equality with God something to be grasped. Rather, he emptied himself.

Jesus did not *exult* himself in his Divinity, but *emptied* himself in all that is human so that he could show us the way to true happiness and wholeness in a life of *self-giving.*

He did not hoard the immense love of God
but allowed it to pour forth *through* him to *all.*

Do we take his example and empty ourselves, letting go of our egocentric desires so that our true selves can emerge to serve our fellow sisters and brothers?

Or do our *egos* have control of our lives causing us to grasp for more and more stuff and to live more and more in the delusion that our egos are at the center of the universe?

The truth is, the more I "die to myself" (ego)
the more Christ's life (my true self) comes to life.

How am I being called to detach from power, prestige and possessions *(false self)*
so that I am free to be me *(true self)?*

Listen to the song for the day "Make Your Way" on the *Mercy Reigns* album.

JUNE

11 BIG PICTURE

Matthew 5:43-45

"You have heard that it was said, 'You shall love your neighbor and hate your enemy.' But I say to you, love your enemies, and pray for those who persecute you, that you may be children of your heavenly Father, for he makes his sun rise on the bad and the good, and causes rain to fall on the just and the unjust."

Jesus tells us we *must do* what goes against *every fiber of our being.*
I mean, is he *serious* about *loving our enemies?*
Yes, that's what he said!

When was the last time you heard someone preach on that scripture?
Not often to *never.*
When it comes to loving our enemies, let's face it: *We don't.*
It just doesn't make sense to our logical, dualistic minds.

It's only when we are *transformed* by *receiving* mercy when we don't *deserve* it
that we seem to be able to grant the same mercy to others.
Jesus invites us to step beyond the egoic consciousness that *divides* and *separates.*
God's sunshine and rain falls on all people.

Are we open to working on forgiving and loving the people who hurt us?
Are we praying for the conversion of terrorists?
Are we praying for the *grace* to be able to have a *change of heart?*
Instead of trying to change someone else, Jesus asks *each of us to change.*
Such *transformation* will only happen through a *relationship* with God.
It takes *grace.*
It's not easy following Jesus, but following him
changes *each* of us and the *world* as well.

Listen to the song for the day "Mercy Reigns" on the *Mercy Reigns* album.

DISCERNING GOD'S WILL

JUNE

12

Matthew 6:10

"Your kingdom come, your will be done, on earth as in heaven."

Before this passage, Jesus gives his followers a lesson on how to pray by telling them to "go to your inner room" and to refrain from using many words because God "knows what you need before you ask."

Today's scripture comes from what follows and is known as "The Lord's Prayer."

Jesus says we should pray that *God's* kingdom will *come,* that it be made real in the *here and now on earth.*

We're told to pray that *God's* will be done – not *our* will.

May we have the grace to ask God to direct us in building God's kingdom through the circumstances of each of our lives by using the time, talents and gifts we've been given.

God wants to work *with* us in those circumstances.

As author and retreat leader Paula D'Arcy says,
"God comes to you disguised as your life."

What is your life saying to you?

Listen to the song for the day "Listen to Your Heart" on the *Listen to Your Heart* album.

JUNE

13 INFINITE WORTH

Matthew 6:21

"For where your treasure is,
there also will your heart be."

When we think of the word "treasure" we usually think of *material things.*

If this meaning does not change for us, it sets in motion a *never-ending* quest of *amassing more and more things.*

Is that where *your* heart is?

The actual *greatest treasure* of all is *love.*

To *love* and to *experience love* – *that* is the *most valuable treasure.*

God challenges us to a *never-ending quest* of *experiencing what it is to love* and *to be loved.*

May your heart be *filled* with *this treasure* and then may you *freely share* it.

Through this experience, may you know who you truly are: *Love.*

Listen to the song for the day "The Way You Are" on the *Mercy Reigns* album.

JUNE 14

GOD CENTERED

Psalm 119:36-37

Direct my heart toward your decrees and away from unjust gain. Avert my eyes from what is worthless; by your way give me life.

Who is at the *center* of my existence?
Is it *God*, or is it *me*?

The truth is that God *is* at the center of our existence,
but we have a *choice* to live from that truth or not.
If my *ego* remains in charge, I am living out of the *delusion* that *everything revolves around me and my desires.*
When God is at the center of my life then my main motivation is "love" since God is love. (1 John 4:8).
My ego must *surrender* control.
Our egos seldom *willingly* "let go and let God." It usually happens through great love or great suffering.

The other way is to *practice* letting go.
Regular contemplative prayer or meditation is needed.
Another help is to follow Jesus who said he was "the way, the truth and the life."
Jesus demonstrates the path of "letting go" in his ministry and death.
This path leads to resurrection and new life.

Jesus said that the greatest two commandments are to *love God with your whole heart, mind and soul* and to *love your neighbor as yourself.* (Matthew 22:37-39).

If *love* is at the center of my motivation then I can *turn away from unjust gain* and *avert my eyes from what is worthless.*

Then, I truly have life to the full.

Listen to the song for the day "God Is the Goal" on the *Live to Love* album.

JUNE

15 DYING TO LIVE

Matthew 7:21

“Not everyone who says to me, ‘Lord, Lord,’ will enter the kingdom of heaven, but only the one who does the will of my Father in heaven.”

When you look at Jesus’ statement through the *lens* of a “reward-punishment” scenario, it brings fear.

That scenario is a *false* one.

When Jesus talked about the *kingdom of heaven*, he often used the phrase, “kingdom of God.”

He was generally talking about the *present.*

When you are doing the *will of God*, you are *already experiencing* the *awakening* of the kingdom of God.

It’s in *dying to ourselves* and our *self-centered, ego-centered* desires that Christ can fill us and we can *become* what God intended us to be.

There was a time in my adult life when I had no idea I would be writing songs and books, would have a music ministry along with four original albums, would be a youth minister, then a chaplain – all while having countless other amazing experiences.

When we *surrender* our will, *God’s* will takes over.

It’s not so much us *doing* God’s will as God’s will *being done to us.*

As Mary said, “May it *be done* to me according to your word.” (Luke 1:38).

Listen to the song for the day “Let It Be Done to Me” on the *Mercy Reigns* album.

SEND ME

Isaiah 49:6

I will make you a light to the nations, that my salvation may reach to the ends of the earth.

We are all literally *loved into existence.*

God breathes life into us and names us.

Each of us is a *unique beloved son or daughter of God.*

We each have a unique *purpose* and *design* to *reflect* the Light of God into the world.

Our Loving Maker wants everything in creation to be *transformed* into the fullness of its being, including *you.*

How can we allow God to use our lives to help nurture, encourage and love others as well as all creation?

***Following Jesus* is a great start.**

He said that he was "the way and the truth and the life." (John 14:6).

He shows us the path to *wholeness* (salvation) both *now* and *forever!*

Listen to the song for the day "How Wonderful to Me" on the *Live to Love* album.

JUNE

17 BORN AGAIN

Luke 1:80

"The child grew and became strong in spirit, and he was in the desert until the day of his manifestation to Israel."

Today's passage comes from the account of the birth of John the Baptist.

Many believed John was destined to do something great, but he spent years in the desert before realizing his "call."

Each moment was part of the "birthing process" of his *true self.*

It's easy to feel impatient because we, too, feel like we are in a "desert" sometimes, wandering, not sure where it's leading.

It's a *struggle.*

Many succumb to *numbing* their yearnings with various addictions.

If we remain faithful – persevere, and keep returning to God after taking two steps forward and one step back, one day we will be able review what has transpired and see the transforming work God did in our lives.

What will be *your* "manifestation" to the world?

Letting go of your ego and entering the desert is the only way for your true self to emerge.

How is this happening in your life?

Listen to the song for the day "Love Will Always Lead You Home" on the *Mercy Reigns* album.

JUNE

PURPOSE 18

Isaiah 49:1

The Lord called me from birth, from my mother's womb he gave me my name.

God calls us into being as an expression of God-self.

It is not *my* story but *God's* story being told *through me* and *through all of creation.*

God calls each of us to be a unique expression of the Divine in the world.

The Word became flesh in Jesus.

How is the Word – Christ – *becoming flesh in you*?

How is the love of Christ to be expressed to the world through *your* gifts and talents?

Follow Jesus and *listen* in your heart to God's *silent voice.*

Listen to the song for the day "Show Me…Me" on the *Listen to Your Heart* album.

JUNE

19 IMPORTANCE OF PRAYER

Matthew 7:17

"Just so, every good tree bears good fruit, and a rotten tree bears bad fruit."

A *good* tree that bears *good* fruit will have strong roots in fertile soil.

A strong family life provides good soil for us to grow in.

However, our parents are not perfect.

Every mom and dad has been affected by the *positive* and *negative* influences of *their* parents and the environment in which they were raised.

We do, however, have a *perfect parent* in God.

The closer we get to God through prayer, the *deeper* our roots grow in fertile soil and the more good fruit we will bear.

Is your life bearing the fruits of *love, mercy, forgiveness and compassion* to the world?

What kind of prayer life do you have?

Set aside time for silence in the Divine Presence each day.

Listen to the song for the day "Turn Off the Noise" on the *Listen to Your Heart* album.

LESS IS MORE

Matthew 7:14

"How narrow the gate and constricted the road that leads to life. And those who find it are few."

Our culture promotes the idea that the ideal "life" is having lots of *power, prestige and possessions.*

It says grab for *more* and *more,* when in truth that only leads to *bondage to stuff* and an *insatiable craving for more.*

Is that *life?*

Power, prestige and possessions are not *innately bad*, but it's very difficult not to get *attached* to any of it.

Jesus knew that all we *really need* is *God.*
Where do we find God? In the *present* moment.
Since God *is* love (1 John 4:8), all we really need is *presence* and *love.*

I'm not talking about the Eros *romantic* kind of love, I'm talking about the agape *pour-yourself-out, self-emptying* kind.
When you *let go* of your *ego's* desires and allow *God* to *fill* you, you may feel like you're on a "constricted road" but it will *paradoxically* lead you to an *abundant life.*
It will lead you to being the "you" that God uniquely created – your *true self.*

Is your life bringing you *peace, joy* and *inner contentment*, or something *else?*
If you knew your life would end tomorrow,
what *things* would you realize are *meaningless* today?

What would you gladly *let go of,* so that you could *truly live?*

Listen to the song for the day "Make Your Way" on the *Mercy Reigns* album.

JUNE

21

LIFE SONG

Psalm 105:2

Sing praise, play music;
proclaim all his wondrous deeds!

Today's scripture verse resonates with my soul.

I share my music during visits with shut-ins, the sick, inmates, and occasional concerts and church services.

I want to share God's "wondrous deeds" through the songs I've been blessed with, as well as in my writings and reflections.

I desire to express God's amazing *unconditional* love for *you* and *all of creation.* That's because I first experienced that love *myself.*

When I was at my *lowest*, I heard a Divine message in my heart to pick up my guitar which I had abandoned years earlier. I now have four albums of inspirational music.

The desire to write more meaningful songs led me back to college and eventually to leave my former career in radio news and begin a *new life in ministry.*

The Creator of the universe is yearning to work through you and your gifts and talents as well.

How are *you* being called to *proclaim God's wondrous deeds* in *your life?*

First, know that God loves you *unconditionally.*
Believe it.

Allow this Unconditional Love to lead you *one step at a time.*

You are a unique expression of God's love to the world.

Listen to the song of the day "Sing a New Song" on the *Live to Love* album.

GREAT ADVENTURE

JUNE

22

Matthew 16:15

"But who do you say that I am?"

This is a *pivotal* question that Jesus asked his followers, and one that he asks *each* of us.

It's a *life-changing* question – at least, it should be.
I remember over 20 years ago how that question suddenly struck me *personally*.
I knew I had to honestly answer the question.
I had to re-examine everything I had been taught and look again at all that Jesus was credited with saying in the gospels.

I looked at the changed lives of the apostles who claimed the crucified Jesus was not stopped by death. I realized that Jesus showed us all how to *live* and how to *die,* and that God's love was *unconditional* and *forever.*

I realized that he asked me not just to *believe* in him, but to *follow* him.
This is the difference between what I call *Churchianity* and *Christianity.*
Just going to a church does not make you a follower of Christ.
That requires actually *reflecting* Christ to the world in *all you do.*

I realized that just as I had received the unconditional love, mercy and forgiveness of God, I had to *share* it with others and especially "the least of these." (Matthew 25).

My life did *indeed* start to change and it has been a wild, adventurous, fulfilling ride ever since.

It hasn't come without great struggles and conflict with a world that follows a different path, but I wouldn't trade it for anything!

So, who do *YOU* say that Jesus is?

Listen to the song of the day "I Want to Follow You" on the *Listen to Your* Heart album.

JUNE

23

LOVE CHANGES EVERYTHING

Luke 5:11

When they brought their boats to the shore,
they left everything and followed him.

What would it take to make you *totally change* the direction of your life in an *instant?*

Jesus had just told three fishermen to cast their nets again after they had caught nothing all night.

When Peter, James and John lowered their nets this time, they caught so many fish that their nets were tearing.

Peter's reaction was, "Depart from me, Lord, for I am a sinful man."

It's as though he felt he didn't *deserve* such a *miracle of generosity.*

Isn't that how *we* are?

We look at our *imperfections* and the *selfish choices* we have made and feel that we aren't *worthy* of God's love.

Yet Jesus seems to say that our *worthiness* or *achievements* have *nothing* to do with God's response to us.

God's response is out of *unconditional* Love for us.

It's the kind of love that, if we open ourselves to it, can move us to change our lives and drop all the trivial pursuits for happiness that will *never* satisfy our souls.

Jesus is calling you.
He'll lead you to the life you were *meant* to live.

Listen to the song of the day "God's Love Is all You Need" on the *Listen to Your Heart* album.

DOWNSIZING

Psalm 149:4

For the Lord takes delight in his people,
honors the poor with victory.

While the consumeristic culture urges us to *add more* to our lives – to amass *more and more* wealth, power and prestige – the inner Spirit urges us to do the *opposite*.

The spiritual journey is a constant *subtraction*, a *taking away* of things that vie for our attention, so that in the end there is nothing separating us from God.

This is why some people at life's end have no trouble passing quietly into eternal life, while many others fight in bitter anguish.

This is why the poor, or those who have no *attachment* to material possessions, power or prestige (the *poor in spirit*) are many times further along in their spiritual journeys.

They have had no other option but to turn to God for help in their struggles.

What is blocking *your* path from the victory of oneness with God?

Listen to the song of the day "Glorify You with Me" on the *Give Praise and Thanks* album.

JUNE

25 TAKE PART

Romans 8:28

We know that all things work for good for those who love God, who are called according to his purpose.

Life is a long road.

There *have been, are,* and *will be* twists and turns and potholes in that road.

But God has a plan to fulfill a grand purpose in creation.

It is beyond our understanding, but it will be something beautiful.

All of creation is *becoming* one in Christ.

It's way beyond our capacity to grasp.

But *each* of us has a part to play.

God is calling each of us to be our unique selves in this amazing love story.

As long as we stay focused on loving God, getting back up when we fall, and then, with each step, simply focusing on doing the next *loving thing*, I know that something good and wonderful is in the making.

Listen to the song of the day "Shall We Sing" on the *Listen to Your Heart* album.

KENOSIS

Philippians 2:6-7

Who, though he was in the form of God, did not regard equality with God something to be grasped. Rather, he emptied himself, taking the form of a slave, coming in human likeness.

Before his *conversion*, St. Paul was Saul, a brutal persecutor of Christians.

He thought he was right.

He was *convinced* that he was doing God's work.

Then, he had a mystical encounter with the risen and already ascended Christ and was thoroughly changed.

He became a *follower* of Christ, *pouring out* mercy, forgiveness and compassion.

Jesus gave *everything* he had – all of himself – to *all* people to show us the *unconditional* Love of God.

We are asked to do the same.

It is only in *emptying ourselves* that we can make space for God to fill us and we can *discover* who we are!

Listen to the song of the day "Pour Me Out" on the *Give Praise and Thanks* album.

JUNE

27 PEACEMAKERS NEEDED

Luke 9:52-55

Jesus sent messengers ahead of him. On the way they entered a Samaritan village to prepare for his reception there, but they would not welcome him because the destination of his journey was Jerusalem. When the disciples James and John saw this they asked, "Lord, do you want us to call down fire from heaven to consume them?" Jesus turned and rebuked them.

Years of differences between the Jews and Samaritans resulted in the Samaritans shunning the messengers Jesus had sent ahead. In response, two of Jesus' followers asked him if they could call on God to destroy the Samaritans in retaliation.

Isn't that the *usual* human reaction? – to attack someone who has wrongly treated us?

You know, get *revenge?*

It's been going on for years and years and years and years.

Jesus' answer to his disciples' question was a stern "no."

We even see this type of behavior today in politics on a *less violent* scale, where if you disagree with another's position, you *trash* them and *ridicule* them with words.

What would happen if we instead responded to persecution, derision and disagreements in a *non-violent* manner but with a *commitment to justice?* And what if, at the *same time*, we responded with *love* and *compassion?*

It has almost *never* been tried, except for a few notable exceptions such as Jesus, Martin Luther King and Gandhi.

All three paid with their lives, but they also spawned peaceful movements that changed the world and continue to do so.

Violent responses *beget* violent responses. The cycle goes *on and on* with no end.

We need more leaders with the vision of Jesus.

That takes ***both*** courage ***and*** compassion – a combination that *transforms* lives.

Listen to the song of the day "Make Me a Channel" on the *Listen to Your Heart* album.

JUNE

28

NOW IS THE TIME

Luke 9:61-62

Another said, "I will follow you, Lord, but first let me say farewell to my family at home." Jesus answered him, "No one who sets a hand to the plow and looks to what was left behind is fit for the kingdom of God."

If a farmer turned to look back at what he had plowed, he would not be focused on where he was pushing the plow and would get off line.

This is a great lesson about staying focused on what's happening now, in this moment.
Now **is the only time that is** ***real.***
It's when God is truly *present.*
It's when the kingdom of God can truly be ***at hand.***

The past is over.
Hand over your past mistakes to God.

Forgiveness is *freely given.*
God will help you use those mistakes to become your true self and to empathize with someone else going through the same things.

If we're not paying attention to the Divine Presence in each moment of our lives, we'll miss God's direction.

Without that connection, how would we become our *true selves?*

We would also miss the peace and joy that God wants to give us.

Listen to the song of the day "You'll Lead Me" on the ***Listen to Your Heart*** **album.**

JUNE

29 BE NOT AFRAID

Psalm 130:1-2

Out of the depths I call to you, Lord;
Lord, here my cry!

Do you experience a *deep yearning*, an *insatiable craving* for something *more*, something to fill a deep *void* inside?

You cannot satisfy that craving with *anything* of *this world.*
Many fall into the trap of thinking that if they just had more of *this* or *that* then they'd be satisfied: Just a little more *money*, just the *right relationship*, just a little more *control* or *prestige.*

Not so!
St. Paul said, "All creation is groaning in labor pains." (Romans 8:22).
We *all* share in creation's "labor pains" as we are *drawn* by a *Great Compassion* to the *fullness* of God's plan.

St. Paul went on to say that "we do not know how to pray as we ought, but the Spirit itself intercedes with inexpressible groanings." (Romans 8:26).
St. Paul says the groanings we are experiencing are the *Holy Spirit* interceding for us according to God's will.

God is *luring you, lovingly drawing* you, leading you to *wholeness, healing and completion.*

The pain comes from *refusing* to *change*, from *clinging* to things that won't last that we have to *let go* of to be able to *move on.*

So relax.
Let go.
Love is *drawing* you and in *love* there is *no fear.*

Listen to the song of the day "Heal Me" on the *Live to Love* album.

THE TRUE YOU

Galatians 5:1

For freedom Christ set us free; so stand firm and do not submit again to the yoke of slavery.

So many people think that by following Jesus they will be *restricted* from doing a lot of fun things, that somehow their "freedom" will be *limited.*

Instead, as St. Paul writes to encourage the Galatians (and us), following Christ will actually *keep us from getting entangled* and *snared* by *desires* and *compulsions* that would *enslave* us, *not* free us.

Each of us is yearning for something to complete us.

The hole in our hearts will not be filled by anything other than what God can give.

By following Jesus we are actually being *freed* to joyfully become the person we were *made to be.*

Listen to the song of the day "Come to Jesus" on the *Live to Love* album.

JULY

1 SET FREE

Matthew 8:19-20

A scribe approached and said to him, "Teacher, I will follow you wherever you go." Jesus answered him, "Foxes have dens and birds of the sky have nests, but the Son of Man has nowhere to rest his head."

Jesus must have been quite an impressive speaker and also must have had a certain charisma that drew people to him. So following him was probably something very attractive, *until he told you the deal.* **When you *follow Jesus* you have to *let go* of your *attachments* to *everything that the world says is important.***

Now, that doesn't mean you have to *renounce* those things. Jesus apparently enjoyed himself. "The Son of Man came eating and drinking and they said, 'Look, he is a glutton and a drunkard, a friend of tax collectors and sinners.'" (Matthew 11:19). **But he didn't *cling* to any material thing. Jesus made it clear that you can't serve both God and money. (Matthew 6:24).**

With each passing year I see the folly in following the ways of the world and the fulfillment of following Jesus. **The pursuit of power, prestige and possessions leads to a dead end.** It will all disappear when we make the great transition at the end of our earthly lives.

The fulfillment of *following Jesus* and *growing in love* will *never end.* The key is to *start dying* to those dead-end trappings *now.*

Following Jesus will lead you out of your comfort zone and to *letting go of things that don't matter.*

It may *feel* like *dying*, but it will paradoxically lead you to a place of *joy, wholeness* and *new life.*

Listen to the song of the day "Show Me...Me" on the *Listen to Your Heart* album.

TRUE FAITH

John 20:27-29

Then he said to Thomas, "Put your finger here and see my hands, and bring your hand and put it into my side, and do not be unbelieving, but believe." Thomas answered and said to him, "My Lord and my God!" Jesus said to him, "Have you come to believe because you have seen me? Blessed are those who have not seen and have believed."

Who is not like Thomas at times?

How often do we say, "Show me the proof!"?

Since we don't have the advantage of seeing the risen Christ in the flesh, we must ponder and struggle to come to grips with what is said to have happened.

Whatever it was, it *so changed* the apostles that they went from *hiding* in *fear* to *boldly proclaiming* the Good News that death is not the end and that Jesus lives.

Most of them were martyred for their proclamations.

Do we have the *same* kind of *passion* for following in the steps of Christ?

Being a Christian means more than just *believing.* It means *following!*

It's in the *following* that we find our *true selves* and our part in God's *on-going* creation.

Listen to the song of the day "Changed" on the *Give Praise and Thanks* album.

JULY

3 GOD CALLS THE ORDINARY

Amos 7:14-15

Amos answered Amaziah, "I was no prophet, nor have I belonged to a company of prophets; I was a shepherd and a dresser of sycamores. The Lord took me from following the flock, and said to me, Go, prophesy to my people Israel."

God is calling *each* of us.
No one is *exempt.*
No one is *left out.*

We are all called in some way to use our gifts and talents to build the kingdom of God. Or, in other words, to make the world a more loving, merciful, forgiving and compassionate place.

The sooner we *tap into* our *inner source* – God's voice within us – the sooner we will be on the path to becoming who we are called to be: our *true selves.*

Many people need to become something else first, something that is usually the product of their egos.

This could be called the *false self.*
It's not a "bad" self, just not the "true" self.

Jesus calls each of us to "repent" or to *change the direction in which we are seeking happiness.*
That will lead us to a road less traveled.

Nothing is more insecure but at the same time *totally fulfilling* as being on that road where we will not only discover God but *why we're here* in the process.

Listen to the song of the day "Take the Road Less Traveled" on the *Live to Love* album.

HAVE FAITH

JULY

4

Matthew 9:2

And there people brought to him a paralytic lying on a stretcher. When Jesus saw their faith, he said to the paralytic, "Courage, child, your sins are forgiven."

The paralyzed man's friends refused to allow him to be excluded.
They literally *tore off* the ceiling to get him to Jesus.
They *believed* that Jesus could heal him physically.

Faith *that* strong is *powerful!*

Jesus told the paralytic to have "courage" and then said, "Your sins are forgiven."

Jesus, who did eventually *physically* heal the paralytic, was more concerned that the man was *spiritually* healed and *made whole.*

Jesus wanted him to know in a *palpable* way that *he was always in the flow of God's grace.*

Jesus wanted him *restored to his community* as well.

What has *you* "paralyzed" inside?

Is it a *complex* you have? – a *fear*, shame, or an addiction?
– a belief that you somehow *don't measure up?*

Whatever it is that is holding you back from living freely as the beloved child of God that you *are* – holding you back from living as the *unique expression* of God's love to the world that you *are* – allow Jesus to *free* you.

Listen to the song of the day "Salvation" on the *Live to Love* album.

JULY

5

GRACE IS FREE

Matthew 10:7

"As you go, make this proclamation: 'The kingdom of heaven is at hand.' Cure the sick, raise the dead, cleanse lepers, drive out demons. Without cost you have received; without cost you are to give."

Jesus was clearly *not* preaching a message of how to safely be evacuated to a future heaven.
Your life is *not* about a "personal salvation project" as Thomas Merton called it.
That would make it all about *me* somehow *earning* a *future reward* by what I *do* – or by what I say I *believe* – and not about any *transformational journey*.

It would miss my responsibility for loving and caring for my neighbor (and *God and myself*) in the *here and now.*
Jesus told his followers that the number one priority was to *love God and your neighbor as yourself.*
He instructed them to preach that 'the kingdom of heaven is at hand' by healing and helping others return to *wholeness.*
The kingdom of heaven would then be "at hand."
Jesus does not say it "will *someday be at hand if you're good!*"

How have we missed this for so long?
This kingdom is given to us "without cost" – meaning it's a *free gift from God!*
Each of us is called to use our gifts and talents to make the *here and now* a more *loving, merciful, forgiving and compassionate* place.
When we love God and our neighbor as ourselves with all our hearts the kingdom of heaven *is at hand!*

How are *you* being called to use *your* gifts and talents so that God's kingdom *can truly come?*

Listen to the song of the day "Mercy Reigns" on the *Mercy Reigns* album.

HARMONIZING WITH GOD

JULY

6

Psalm 33:2-3

Give thanks to the Lord on the harp; on the ten-stringed lyre offer praise. Sing to God a new song; skillfully play with joyful chant.

St. Ignatius said he and all people were made to *praise, reverence and serve God.*

What if we all used our talents to praise, reverence and serve God?

How are you doing this in your life?

How is God calling you to use your gifts and talents?

If you were to "give thanks" to God in the way that you use your gifts and talents, how would you do it?

As a singer/songwriter, I love to open myself to Divine Inspiration and create songs about the unconditional love of God and then share them.

What song does God want to co-create with *you?*

Whatever talents God has given you, you have also been given free will to do with them as you please.

What if you used them to show others the unconditional love of God?

Talk about a beautiful 'harmony'!

What better way could you possibly say "thank you" to the One who created you?

Listen to the song of the day "Sing a New Song" on the *Live to Love* album.

JULY

7 GRACE

Hosea 2:16

So, I will allure her, I will lead her into the desert and speak to her heart.

Sometimes we have to be in a desolate place where we have no control before we are open to hearing God's voice, before we can feel God's presence. **It's so uncomfortable to our egos to not be in control that we will seldom willingly go to such a place.**

It's as if God *lovingly lures* us to the desert for our own good. **It's not that our Creator wants us to suffer, but wants us *to be free of all the stuff that held us in bondage.*** When we are finally free of all those attachments, God can finally *commune* with us.

Did you ever feel like everything is falling apart, like all the things you were so sure about are crumbling? Welcome to the desert! **There will come times in all our spiritual journeys when we must move out of our comfort zones so that we can grow.**

As Jesus said, "No one pours new wine into old wineskins. Otherwise, the wine will burst the skins and both the wine and the skins are ruined. Rather, new wine is poured into fresh wineskins." (Mark 2:22). **For the Spirit to act in new ways we need to be open to new ways of being.** However, most of us will not *willingly* move into the desert. **We do not want to let go of all the *familiar* ways that no longer give us life but which we do not know how to part with.**

It will feel like dying. **What if we *go with the Flow* and allow it to *allure* us?**

In the desert we will be free to hear God's gentle, kind whisper in our hearts, a whisper that will always lead us to transformation, healing, wholeness and peace.

Listen to the song of the day "Take the Road Less Traveled" on the *Live to Love* album.

THE GOOD SHEPHERD

Matthew 9:36-38

At the sight of the crowds, his heart was moved with compassion for them because they were troubled and abandoned, like sheep without a shepherd. Then he said to his disciples, "The harvest is abundant but the laborers are few; so ask the master of the harvest to send out laborers for his harvest."

We *all* experience times when we feel "troubled and abandoned."
Isn't it comforting to hear that Jesus' heart was
***"moved with compassion"* for such people?**

He didn't look down at them in disdain.
Jesus mirrors the face of a *loving* God.
This is *Good News!*

Our Creator would like to guide us with the same
care and love that a *shepherd* has for his *sheep*.
Many times we find such help from others who have responded to Love's call.

Don't hesitate to ask for help.
It gives *someone else* the opportunity to *be* Jesus to *you*.

Who are those near you who are feeling troubled and abandoned?
Perhaps it is *you* who could reach out to *them* with a
comforting word, a smile or some encouragement?

Your Inner Voice will lead you if you *listen*.

Listen to the song of the day "I Will Give You Rest" on the *Live to Love* album.

JULY

9 ENDURE

Matthew 10:21-22

Brother will hand over brother to death, and the father his child; children will rise up against parents and have them put to death. You will be hated by all because of my name, but whoever endures to the end will be saved.

Whoa, this sounds very *grim*.

In other words, following Jesus will *not* be easy!

You will be met with resistance, probably even from family members and friends.

Most of the apostles literally lost their lives for following Jesus.

The bottom line is that the struggle *is* worth it.

It's the path whereby, along with God's help, we *grow* and become *whole.*

God's desire is that we become our full and complete *unique selves*.

While there may be hardships in following Jesus, there will always be a certain peace and calm amid the storms.

We have the assurance from Jesus himself that it will all be worth it if we "endure."

This life is *not* all there is.

Life after death is eternal.

Listen to the song of the day "Make Your Way" on the *Mercy Reigns* album.

RESURRECTION IN PROGRESS

JULY

10

Matthew 10:38-39

"Whoever does not take up his cross and follow after me is not worthy of me. Whoever finds his life will lose it, and whoever loses his life for my sake will find it."

When we follow Jesus it requires doing what *he* does.

Jesus returns love and compassion when persecuted.

He showed us this when he literally picked up a cross and carried it, finally forgiving those who crucified him and saying, "Father, forgive them, they know not what they do."

Following Jesus requires letting go of self-centered desires (ego) and then carrying the burdens that come with surrendering ourselves to a Greater Power.

Jesus promised that if we did this and followed his example we would lose the lives our *egos* were demanding but find the lives *God* wanted for us.

In other words, we would discover our *true selves.*

Surrender your struggles to God, follow Jesus and find true life.

As Jesus put it, "This is the time of fulfillment.
The kingdom of God is at hand." (Mark 1:15).

Listen to the song of the day "Love Will Always Lead You Home" on the *Mercy Reigns* album.

11 SATISFACTION

Psalm 37:4

Find your delight in the LORD who
will give you your heart's desire.

How *comforting* is today's verse!
So *hopeful.*
It *resonates deep within me.*

How I *yearn* – for what?
I've yearned for *many things*, but if and when those things have manifested in my life, they've *never completely satisfied the yearning.*
Maybe *briefly*.
But the yearning then *returns.*

Take comfort in knowing that *this* yearning is *built-in-the-fabric of all that is.*
St. Paul wrote about it: "We know that all creation is groaning in labor pains even until now." (Romans 8:22).
We, and *all* creation, are "groaning in labor pains."

That captures the feeling pretty well.
God is *drawing* us – *enticing* us, if you will – to *God's self.*
It's a love story.
God is the *Lover* and *we* are the *beloved.*

When you *let go* of your ego's understanding of what will satisfy that deep yearning, you can simply *go-with-the-flow* of the Love that is calling you.

This requires a *contemplative practice*, periods of meditation or Centering Prayer.

Then – even *now* – your "heart's desire" is in the *process of being revealed.*

Listen to the song of the day "May I Be Light" on the *Listen to Your Heart* album.

BE YOU

Philippians 1:6

I am confident of this, that the one who began a good work in you will continue to complete it until the day of Christ Jesus.

St. Paul knew of the infinite worth and purpose of each person he was addressing.

He knew that each person was *loved* into existence.

Each of us is *infinitely loved* and wouldn't be alive if God didn't *will* it to be.

God wants each of us to *live* our uniqueness and become *fully* the *human person* we were created to be.

That's God's plan.

It's not a contest to prove our worthiness for heaven!

On our way to *wholeness* ("holiness") we are also called to play a unique role in building a more compassionate, loving and just world (the *kingdom of God*).

Listen to the song of the day "Glorify You with Me" on the *Give Praise and Thanks* album.

JULY

13

BE OPEN

Matthew 11:25

Jesus said in reply, "I give praise to you, Father, Lord of heaven and earth, for although you have hidden these things from the wise and the learned you have revealed them to the childlike."

How often have you been *convinced* of something only to have some sudden revelation that you were *wrong*, or at least *no longer sure*?

When you look at the world from a position that you are right, you are at a *dead end.*

We must keep a "childlike" openness to something new or we will never grow.

Just ponder for a moment the vastness of the universe and the amazing intricacy of the trillions of cells that make up one human body.

Allow this experience to humble you to be open to discovering something *new* and *awe inspiring.*

In today's scripture passage, Jesus seems to say that those whose egos are in full command, who are self-righteous, who believe themselves wise are essentially *blind.*

Those who are able to *let go* of their egos and *humbly open themselves* to *mystery* with the *awe and wonder of a child* will see *great works of God.*

Are you able to *listen* and *look* with *childlike curiosity?*

If so, get ready for a *wondrous adventure to begin!*

Listen to the song of the day "You'll Lead Me" on the *Listen to Your Heart* album.

CALLED BY GOD

Jeremiah 1:5-7

Before I formed you in the womb I knew you. Before you were born I dedicated you, a prophet to the nations I appointed you. "Ah, Lord God!" I said, "I know not how to speak; I am too young." But the Lord answered me, Say not, "I am too young." To whomever I send you, you shall go; whatever I command you, you shall speak.

What is God asking *you* to do?
Usually it has something to do with your talents, but sometimes you may not be aware of a talent that God wants to develop in you.

Is there an "inner yearning" to do something?
God is calling *you!*

Our egos will make excuses because our egos think our lives are all about *us.* Our lives are actually about *God* and God's *love story*, God's *dream* for the world.
You and I are a part of that!

Jeremiah's excuse was that he was "too young" to speak out as a prophet.
What is *your* excuse?

You are never *too young* or *too old* or *too short* or *too tall* or *too anything* for God to work with *you!*

God doesn't call the *qualified*, but qualifies the *called!*

Listen to the song of the day "Singing My Song" on the *Live to Love* album.

JULY

15 MODEL FOR TRANSFORMATION

Matthew 19:39

"Whoever finds his life will lose it, and whoever loses his life for my sake will find it."

This is an example of one of Jesus' teachings that for many people probably goes in one ear and out the other.

In reality, it is a *core* teaching.

Living the Gospel, *following* Jesus, requires *letting go* of our *egocentric desires.*

That means all the things we *think* will bring us happiness but are mostly centered in our *childhood programs for happiness*, things that are based on *security, control* and *esteem.*

These pursuits will never *truly satisfy* our cravings but will only lead us to *wanting more.*

That will lead you to a life of *endless, meaningless* pursuits.

When you *let go* of that stuff and, in a sense, *lose the life* that popular culture entices you to and instead seek to be a loving presence to life as it unfolds, you actually find your true self.

It's the life you were meant to take part in.

It's the very life of God.

Listen to the song of the day "Breathe On Me" on the *Listen to Your Heart* album.

KINGDOM OF GOD IS AT HAND

JULY

16

Luke 17:20-21

Asked by the Pharisees when the kingdom of God would come, he said in reply, "The coming of the kingdom of God cannot be observed, and no one will announce, 'Look, here it is,' or, 'There it is.' For behold, the kingdom of God is among you."

What do you think of when you hear the phrase: "The kingdom of God"?

Many jump to thoughts of *heaven and eternal life*, but this does *not* seem to be what Jesus is talking about!

He says, "The kingdom of God is *among* you."

This is also sometimes translated as "within you."

Could it be we can begin to enter the kingdom of God when we are truly *loving God* and *loving our neighbor as ourselves?*

We are meant to be a part of building the kingdom of God in the *here and now!*

This is *your* mission.

Don't miss it!

Listen to the song of the day "Shall We Sing" on the *Listen to Your Heart* album.

JULY

17

WONDERFULLY MADE

Psalm 19:2

The heavens declare the glory of God;
the sky proclaims its builder's craft.

Take a look at a beautiful blue morning sky or a clear night sky glimmering with stars.

Take a look at all the marvels of nature surrounding you.

Look beyond the skies to the vast universe.

The Great Artisan is still at work *creating.*

You and *I* are a part of God's beloved Creation.

How are we responding with our gifts and talents to work with God in creating this unfolding masterpiece?

How are we proclaiming our builder's craft?

We do it by simply *being our true selves.*

We are loved by our Creator for simply *being us.*

We *don't* have to do *anything* to *earn* God's love.

We are loved *just as we are.*

When we *live in this awareness*, that is when God's glory shines!

Listen to the song of the day "The Way You Are" on the *Mercy Reigns* album.

CYCLE OF LOVE

Luke 21:3-4

He said, "I tell you truly, this poor widow put in more than all the rest; for those others have all made offerings from their surplus wealth, but she, from her poverty, has offered her whole livelihood."

The poor widow contributed two small coins, but that was *all* she had.

The wealthier people had no doubt donated many more coins, but it was nothing they would *miss.*

How much of *ourselves* do we give to God?

Do we give of ourselves when it's *convenient?*

Do we give of ourselves only on Sunday when and if we go to a church?

Do we ever even *think* about giving of ourselves in our daily lives for God's desires and purposes?

What *are* God's purposes for *each* of us?

What is *my* unique mission?

To simply be the unique me.

In being my *true self,* I am called to use my gifts and talents *each moment* to reflect the same unconditional love that I receive from my Creator.

How am I called to serve others in a compassionate, just and loving way?

Listen to the song of the day "Make Me a Channel" on the *Listen to Your Heart* album.

JULY

19 SOUL DESIRE

Luke 18:41-43

Jesus asked him, "What do you want me to do for you?" He replied, "Lord, please let me see." Jesus told him, "Have sight; your faith has saved you." He immediately received his sight and followed him, giving glory to God.

Interesting question from Jesus to a blind man, isn't it?
"What do you want me to do for you?"

The blind man had been calling out to Jesus to "have pity on me." Jesus showed great humility and respect in not taking for granted that he *already knew* what the man wanted.

So, what do you want Jesus to do for *you?*
Is what you want something you really *need* for your *wholeness* and *goodness?*

Contemplate that question in the silence of your heart.

The blind man had *faith* that Jesus would provide him what he needed.
He also had the *courage* to *step out of his comfort zone* and ask Jesus for help.
Then in *response* to receiving his sight, he *followed* Jesus "giving glory to God."

Do we have the courage to *step out of our comfort zones,*
call out to Jesus* and *boldly ask him to help us?
We can either accept the *status quo* in our lives and *remain stuck* in our spiritual growth, or we can *follow Jesus* on the path to our *true selves* and *enlightenment.*

That path *won't be easy,* but will lead you to *peace and freedom.*

Listen to the song of the day "Heal Me" on the *Live to Love* album.

TOP PRIORITY

JULY 20

Matthew 4:21-22

Jesus walked along from there and saw two other brothers, James, the son of Zebedee, and his brother John. They were in a boat, with their father Zebedee, mending their nets. He called them, and immediately they left their boat and their father and followed him.

How amazing it is that two brothers would *drop* their *way of life*, say *goodbye* to their father and *immediately follow* Jesus.

They left *their* plans *behind.*

The *same choice* confronts us today.

Do we follow our *egos' plans* to build *our own* kingdoms, or do we 'die to ourselves' and *follow* Christ in building God's kingdom here on earth?

When we decide to *follow* Jesus we embark on a great adventure in which God gives us our heart's desire and we discover our *true selves.*

Listen to the song of the day "I Want to Follow You" on the *Listen to Your Heart* album.

JULY

21 TRUE LIFE

Luke 1:38

"May it be done to me according to your word."

Letting go of our ego's *self-centered* desires is the key to allowing our *true selves* to *come forth.*

To make this happen, you almost have to have some *contemplative practice*, some *method* of literally *letting go of the ego's constant attempts to remain in control.*

Some form of meditation is one way to *practice being present,* allowing your non-stop thoughts to slow to a trickle and then stop.

However, most of us are *addicted* to our thoughts and *constant commentaries.*

Those are all distractions from living in the present.

It is only from the "now" where you can open your heart for a Divine message.

It is only then that you can get an *inkling* of your *true self* and begin *living your purpose.*

It is only then that you can echo Mary's words above:
"May it be done to me according to your word."

Listen to the song of the day "Let It Be Done to Me" on the *Mercy Reigns* album.

MARY MAGDALENE

JULY
22

John 20:18

Mary of Magdala went and announced
to the disciples, "I have seen the Lord,"
and what he told her.

Mary Magdalene is *finally* getting the recognition *due* her.
Pope Francis upgraded the July 22 "memorial" in her honor
to an official "feast" on the Church's liturgical calendar.
A decree formalizing the decision was titled "Apostle of the Apostles."

Her recognition is *long* overdue. (For years, Mary was falsely remembered
as a prostitute based on no evidence to support such a claim.)
**The canonical gospels say that Mary Magdalene was present at the crucifixion,
present when Jesus' body was taken from the cross and
present when he was put in the tomb.**

What strength and courage!
How *eventful* and *noteworthy* that Jesus selected her to be the *first* witness to his
astounding resurrection and to be the *first* person instructed by Jesus *himself* to
announce the *most amazing* news that *had* ever – or *would* ever – happen!

**In a world dominated by men, where women were servants and
had no rights, it was Mary of Magdala who was selected to
inform the other disciples of the Good News!**
I wonder how well that went over with the other disciples?
In St. Luke's account, the disciples did not believe.

**It may be uncomfortable for each of us at times to be messengers of the Good
News that *God's love is unconditional and triumphs over death.***

On such occasions, *take courage*, and think of Mary of Magdala.

Listen to the song of the day "Salvation" on the *Live to Love* album.

JULY

23 BE STILL

Matthew 12:38

Then some of the scribes and Pharisees said to him, "Teacher, we wish to see a sign from you."

How often do we do the *same* thing – ask God for a *sign?*

While the scribes and Pharisees were asking to *test* Jesus,
what if we in good faith ask for a Divine *sign?*

There is nothing wrong with this as I think there is a
Loving Goodness at work Who delights in giving us signs.

Did you ever wonder how many signs we might be *missing* simply because we are too *busy* and *distracted* by the "noise" we are constantly immersed in and *are immersing ourselves in?*

Do you ever experience *silence?*

How often is your *own mind* the *source of noise*
with its endless *critiquing, judging* and *commentary?*
Stop and *observe your rambling thoughts.*
***Who* is the *one observing* those thoughts?**
You, the *real you.*
Allow your *true self* to *emerge.*

Set aside 10 to 20 minutes today to simply *sit in silence* and *let go* of your thoughts.
Then make it a practice to really *be present* to your life.

Observe your surroundings without *judgement* or *critique.*

You just may find that Divine messages *abound.*

Listen to the song of the day "Turn Off the Noise" on the *Listen to Your Heart* album.

JULY

24

DYING AND RISING

2 Corinthians 4:11

For we who live are constantly being given up to death for the sake of Jesus, so that the life of Jesus may be manifested in our mortal flesh.

St. Paul understood what Jesus meant when he said, "Unless a grain of wheat falls to the ground and dies, it remains just a grain of wheat; but if it dies, it produces much fruit." (John 12:24).

If we *let go* of our *ego's* desires, *die* to *self-centeredness, new life* will *rise* in us.

This is the emerging of the *true self.*

As we follow the example of Jesus, *letting go* of *attachments* to things that *won't last,* we'll discover the joy of *giving* ourselves for a *Greater Good.*

We'll be taking part in a *creative process* with *eternal designs.*

Then the life of Jesus will start being "manifested in our mortal flesh."

We will become *more* and *more* the *unique* person we were *meant* to be.

So what feels like "dying" will actually lead to the *fullest life* you could *ever* imagine.

It's never too late or too early to start your unique journey in Christ.

How about *now*?

Listen to the song of the day "Pour Me Out" on the *Give Praise and Thanks* album.

JULY

25

STAND IN THE LIGHT

Matthew 13:22-23

"The seed down among thorns is the one who hears the word, but then worldly anxiety and the lure of riches choke the word and it bears no fruit. But the seed sown on rich soil is the one who hears the word and understands it, who indeed bears fruit and yields a hundred or sixty or thirtyfold."

Jesus tells us that we are like *seeds* scattered on the ground.
God's *word* is our *nourishment.*
It is a fertilizer that gives life through *unconditional love* and *forgiveness.*
It is like the sun – always shining down upon us.
We experience such growth and blossoming if we
allow this fertilizing Love to *saturate* us.
Sometimes we get *overwhelmed* with the thorns of *anxieties* and *troubles.*
We also get *lured* by the thorns of *material goods* and *wealth.*
God's Presence and nourishment is meant to give us abundant
life and the fruit of coming to know our *true selves.*
Then we can become the fruit of God's love to others.
God's nourishment is constantly being offered to us through each of our senses,
but at the same time our senses are being bombarded with all kinds of other poisons.
We have to strengthen ourselves with contemplative prayer or meditation,
spiritual reading, or doses of *communing* with God in nature.
We have to allow the water of God's love to spur our
growth through *reflection* and *discernment.*
Otherwise we wither.

If we stay *present* to God's loving *Presence* we will grow *even amidst the thorns,*
blossoming fruit that we could never have imagined.
One wonderful way of *cultivating* the soil of our life situation
is by following the examples set by Jesus.

Listen to the song of the day "I Stand in the Light" on the *Mercy Reigns* album.

LOVE CONQUERS HATE

JULY

26

Psalm 69:8-10

For your sake I bear insult, shame covers my face. I have become an outcast to my kin, a stranger to my mother's children. Because zeal for your house consumes me, I am scorned by those who scorn you.

Have you ever been ridiculed for doing the *compassionate* thing?
When you follow the model Jesus gave us for living our lives, *reaching out* to the *excluded* and the *poor*, working for *justice* while showing *compassion* and *mercy* – you *will* face insults. You *will* be scorned.

Sometimes when you follow God's call to *love all people* you are met with derision and rejection from those who define themselves by *whom* they are *against.*
Sometimes the worst assault may come from those *closest* to you who feel uncomfortable about how *you've* changed when *they* haven't.

Jesus felt the *same scorn* when he returned to Nazareth. He said, "A prophet is not without honor except in his native place and in his own house." (Matthew 13:58). So if you've ever felt this way, *you* are in *good company.*

Your persecutors are actually your *greatest teachers.*
They are the *hardest* to love and yet that is *exactly what you are called to do!*
Don't lose heart!

Follow Jesus and speak the words he inspires, even though it may lead you down a road less traveled.

Live from the *reality of oneness* that is *hidden* by the *delusion of separateness.*
Lives will be changed for the *better*, including *yours.*

Listen to the song of the day "Take the Road Less Traveled" on the *Live to Love* album.

JULY

27

GOD'S PLAN FOR YOU

Luke 10:40-42

Martha, burdened with much serving, came to him and said, "Lord, do you not care that my sister has left me by myself to do the serving? Tell her to help me." The Lord said to her in reply, "Martha, Martha, you are anxious and worried about many things. There is need of only one thing. Mary has chosen the better part and it will not be taken from her."

What is your motivation?
If it is to *serve*, then serve joyfully.
If it is to *listen and learn*, then listen and learn joyfully.
While Martha was running around trying to make sure everyone was fed,
her sister Mary was calmly sitting by Jesus listening to him.
Martha is also "anxious and worried about many things."
***That's* her problem**.
If she simply was serving as a response to her *inner calling*,
she would not be *judging* Mary.
Mary was following her heart, and also breaking all the rules.
**Sitting at the teacher's feet for instruction would
have been reserved for only the men at that time.**
Jesus endorses her "rule breaking."
She was included in the group of men that he was instructing.
Serving others like Martha was doing is definitely what we are *all* called to do, but without listening to the Lord for direction we will be lost as to our *true purpose.*

Are you taking time each day to sit at the Lord's feet and *listen* to him?
**Why not reflect on scripture, perhaps this reading,
and then sit in silence and just *listen.***

**Listen to the song of the day "Listen to Your Heart" on
the *Listen to Your Heart* album.**

THE ONE THING

JULY
28

Psalm 81:10

There must be no foreign god among you; you must not worship an alien god.

What *is the* foreign god *among us?*

What idol has *displaced* our Creator from first priority in our lives?

Could it be a material possession, or maybe power, control or prestige?

Could it be vanity?

Could it be the need to be right?

What is the *one thing* in your life that you
could not let go of* if God *asked you for it?

What is blocking God from *giving you* what will truly bring you peace?

Do not allow it to have top priority.

Stop *clinging* to it so your hands can be *opened* to what God wants to give you.

Listen to the song of the day "God Is the Goal" on the *Live to Love* album.

JULY

29 GROWING COMPASSION

Matthew 13:31

Jesus proposed another parable to them. "The kingdom of heaven is like a mustard seed that a person took and sowed in a field."

The kingdom of heaven is evolving in the *here and now.*

Just like a tiny mustard seed under the dirt, it is growing.

It is usually not seen because it is hidden from plain view.

Nonetheless, it's sprouting.

***Each* of us is expected to be a *sower* of this seed.**

Jesus clearly expected us to *take action* as God's instruments in bringing about the *kingdom of heaven* in the here and now.

How are we being called to sow the seed of God's kingdom so that it grows in this time and place?

To know, we must be awake and alert to the *Divine Presence*, which means we must be focused on the *present moment.*

That is where our Loving Creator dwells, always *loving us* and *wanting to commune* with us.

Now is the time and place where we can channel Love and Light as *only each of us uniquely can* by planting seeds of God's kingdom, or we could call it, God's *peaceable community.*

Listen to the song of the day "May I Be Light" on the *Listen to Your Heart* album.

DIVINE GUIDE

Psalm 25:4

Make known to me your ways, Lord;
teach me your paths.

We always seem like we are on the *fast-track* to *somewhere*, but *where?*

Are we pursuing possessions, prestige, position –
or perhaps we are on a treadmill to *nowhere?*

We each have to ask ourselves: Am I pursuing *my* plan, *someone else's* plan for me, or am I open to *God's* plan for me?

God has a plan to bring you peace and contentment.

It comes when we allow God to live *through* us.

The Word became flesh in Jesus.

How does the Word want to become flesh in *you?*

Listen in your heart for the Spirit's gentle voice and
awaken to the Presence of God in each moment.

Enter into the *co-creative dance* with your Creator.

Then, you will always be on the *right* path, even in times of struggle.

Listen to the song of the day "Shall We Sing" on the *Listen to Your Heart* album.

JULY

31 GLORY

Psalm 71:16

I will speak of the mighty works of the Lord.

I highly recommend keeping a journal to write about what is going on in your life.

When I look back over each day's happenings, usually I can find one or two things that seem to be *outpourings* of God's grace, sometimes many more.

There are incidents that have been life-giving or eye-opening.

Sometimes I can see a *subtle thread of grace* running through what appeared to be meaningless events.

When you start noticing the "mighty works of the Lord" in your midst, *it will change you.*

Then you will want to tell others about it.

You will understand that you are *part* of something *magnificent, wondrous and glorious.*

There is a Love embracing and supporting *all* of creation.

You and I are a part of this *unfolding* masterpiece.

That is reason to *smile* and *rejoice.*

Listen to the song of the day "How Magnificent, Wondrous and Glorious" on the *Mercy Reigns* album.

PRICELESS

Matthew 13:45-46

Again, the kingdom of heaven is like
a merchant searching for fine pearls.
When he finds a pearl of great price,
he goes and sells all that he has and buys it.

Jesus interchangeably talks about the kingdom of "heaven" and the kingdom of "God." He also talks about that kingdom being "among" you or "within" you. (Luke 17:21).

It's the peaceable kingdom of *love, mercy, forgiveness* and *compassion*, a *state-of-being* when you *know* that *you are accepted by God.*
It's being in a state of *communion* with your loving Source.
This state-of-being is *always available*, like a "fine pearl" right under our noses.
It's there for the taking on *one condition*: We must be *present* to the *Divine Presence*.

This takes *letting go* of all the other distractions and attractions – *not renouncing* them – but simply *not being attached* to any of them.

Of course, our egos are attached to *many* things, so this is not an easy process.

You can practice this "letting go" through *Centering Prayer* and other forms of *meditation.*

The pay-off is *inner peace* and finding your *true self*, the person you are meant to be in service of God's kingdom.

As Jesus put it, "Whoever loses his life for my sake will find it." (Matthew 10:39).

What else could be more important than finding your *real life?*

Listen to the song of the day "I Will Give You Rest" on the *Live to Love* album.

AUGUST

2 BE YOU

Matthew 13:54-57

He came to his native place and taught the people in their synagogue. They were astonished and said, "Where did this man get such wisdom and mighty deeds? Is he not the carpenter's son? Is not his mother named Mary and his brothers James, Joseph, Simon, and Judas? Are not his sisters all with us? Where did this man get all this?" And they took offense at him.

Some people seem to think that *not changing* is a medal of honor.
They *praise* people for *holding tight to a position* and
they *ridicule* people who *change a position.*
But listening to new information, weighing it, and then changing your view is many times the mark of a *wise* person.
Life can change a person as well.
It's supposed to.
It *ought* to broaden your viewpoint.
That's because there are many, many other viewpoints different than just your own.
When you follow the *self-emptying path* of Jesus your life is *meant to change.*
We are meant to "die" to our own *self-centered* desires so that our *true self* can *rise.*
On a trip to Jerusalem at age twelve, Jesus was said to have "astounded" the teachers in the temple with his understanding. And then the scripture says, "Jesus advanced [in] wisdom and age and favor before God and man." (Luke 2:52).
He *grew.* He *changed.*
After his *transformational experience* in the desert following his baptism by John the Baptist, Jesus returned to the town he grew up in. He was a man with a *mission.*
The people there "took offense at him."
To be your *true self,* you must be willing to follow your calling.
This *will lead you to change.*
This will *challenge others to change as well.* Then, you can count on others to "take offense."
If and when this happens, it's helpful to find a community to support you.
Know this: The living Christ will *never abandon you.*
Have faith in this, and *live.*

Listen to the song of the day "Changed" on the *Give Praise and Thanks* album.

SOUL LONGING

Psalm 84:3

My heart and flesh cry out for the living God.

Is there a *yearning* inside of you?
Is there an *inner emptiness?*
What is your heart and flesh *crying out to have?*

What will satisfy this longing?
If you relate to having this inner yearning, you are not alone. St. Paul said this: "We know that all creation is groaning in labor pains even until now." (Romans 8:22).
That's right, *all of creation.*
It seems God has installed this longing in everything.

Many mistakenly believe that they can satisfy the yearning with something *material* or *physical.* This is what your *ego* will tell you.
As St. Augustine expressed to God, "Our heart is restless until it rests in you."

The *longing* is a *spiritual* one.
It's on the *soul* level.
Only the Unconditional Lover that created you can *satisfy* it.

When you *let go* of all the things that *don't* matter, and *let go* of your fixation to *control* everything, you will fall into the arms of your loving Creator.
At the *same time*, you will discover your *true self.*

As Thomas Merton wrote in *New Seeds of Contemplation*, "Therefore there is only one problem on which all my existence, my peace and my happiness depend: to discover myself in discovering God. If I find Him, I will find myself, and if I find my true self I will find Him."

What are the things *you* need to let go of to truly *live?*

Listen to the song of the day "Breathe On Me" on the *Listen to Your Heart* album.

AUGUST

4

LISTEN

Mark 9:7

Then a cloud came, casting a shadow over them; then from the cloud came a voice, "This is my beloved Son. Listen to him."

This is one of those major moments in the life of Jesus known as "The Transfiguration" when Peter, James and John heard God's voice giving them a powerful message: Jesus is the *beloved Son of God* and they should *listen* to him.

As *followers* of Jesus, *we also are called to listen to him.*

How do we do this?

Try spending some time in solitude reading Jesus' words in the Gospels and then sit in silence and allow those words to speak to you in the *depths of your heart.*

"Listen to him."

These are God's words to *each* of us.

Are we taking time to listen?

St. John of the Cross said, "God's first language is silence."

That's why some form of *contemplative prayer* is also important, a time of *silent listening* to allow your *incessant thoughts to cease.*

If you make this a practice, I promise that your life will change for the better.

Trust and you will be led to *new life, inner peace* and your *true self.*

Listen to the song of the day "Slow Me Down" on the *Mercy Reigns* album.

EVERYONE HAS A CALLING

AUGUST

5

Matthew 17:3-5

And behold, Moses and Elijah appeared to them, conversing with him. Then Peter said to Jesus in reply, "Lord, it is good that we are here. If you wish, I will make three tents here, one for you, one for Moses, and one for Elijah." While he was still speaking, behold, a bright cloud cast a shadow over them, then from the cloud came a voice that said, "This is my beloved Son, with whom I am well pleased; listen to him."

As we continue with the transfiguration of Jesus today, we see
two other leaders from salvation history appear with him.
From this vision we can look at that history and see that while God's people
repeatedly wandered off course, God *never* abandoned them.
God had always sent *another* messenger to guide them.

God will surely see through to completion the great work of creation.
Jesus, the very incarnation of God, shows us the path to life and wholeness.
The path is one of love for *God, self* and *others.*
This path is *not* an easy one.
It is a way of life that will be met with persecution.
We *will* falter.
Fear not!

Jesus showed us that *love* ultimately *wins.*
Death does *not* have the final say!
So *listen* to the words of Jesus and then act on what your heart is telling you.
You are also meant to be God's messenger of hope!

Listen to the song of the day "I Want to Follow You" on the *Listen to Your Heart* album.

AUGUST

6 THE WAY OF LOVE

Matthew 16:23

"You are thinking not as God does,
but as human beings do."

We tend to base so much of our lives on our own ability to *reason* and yet Jesus was quite clear in his response to Peter that *our* thinking can be *far* from God's.
Who would *not* have sided with Peter when he rejected Jesus' prediction that he would suffer greatly at the hands of the religious leaders and be killed?
Peter based his response on the faulty premise that Jesus was to be their new king who would lead them out of bondage and into power.
That was not the mission of Jesus.

Jesus wanted to show that God was *intimately with all people and all creation.*
He wanted to show that God's love was not just for some but everyone, *especially the poor and disenfranchised.*
Love was the purpose of everything.
This is what got him killed.
How else could God show us what true *unconditional* love is?
How else but to be *hated, persecuted,* and *crucified* so he could then respond to the most *heinous injustice* with *loving forgiveness!*

This was *not* a *payment* to God or a *punishment* he suffered in place of us.
God can forgive without limits. Jesus told *us* to forgive an *infinite* number of times, *so why wouldn't God do the same?*
What Jesus gave us was a model to follow, a *model of living* that will lead us to *transformation* and *new life.*
This is the way in which the kingdom of God truly comes!
Jesus is inviting us into a *life-changing, life-transforming* journey of *letting go* of the ego-generated *false self* so the *true self* can emerge and God's love can be manifested in *this* time and place.

As St. Paul says, "Be renewed in the spirit of your minds, and put on the new self, created in God's way in righteousness and holiness of truth." (Ephesians 4:23-24).

Listen to the song of the day "Salvation" on the *Live to Love* album.

SWEET SURRENDER

AUGUST

7

John 12:24-26

"Amen, amen, I say to you, unless a grain of wheat falls to the ground and dies, it remains just a grain of wheat; but if it dies, it produces much fruit. Whoever loves his life loses it, and whoever hates his life in this world will preserve it for eternal life. Whoever serves me must follow me, and where I am, there also will my servant be."

This is a *key teaching* of Jesus to help you discover *who you are.*
In order to discover our *true selves,* we have to *let go* of our *false selves.*
The *false self* is the person our *ego* creates, which is usually based on what our culture tells us is the definition of *success.*
It is usually about *power, prestige* and *possessions.*
All these things will *not last,* nor will the *false self.*
The worst case scenario is that they all disintegrate when we die. How awful it would be to see it all slipping away on our death beds and to realize *we were never our true selves!*
Jesus said the false self must *fall to the ground and die.*
If we *love the life this world wants for us* we will *lose the life we were meant to live.*
But if we *hate the life that this world tells us to live,* we will *find the life meant for us.*
This requires us to *change.* Most of us *don't like change.*
To be a Christian we *must* change. It requires *letting go of our egos' desires,* letting them *die,* so that God's desires can grow in us.
Jesus shows us the way.
That's why being a *fan* of Jesus is practically *meaningless.*
We must actually *follow* him!
This will take you on the path of *dying,* then *rising.*
It will require making changes in how you live your life, how you treat people and the environment. It will require some painful yet exciting and growth-filled transitions.
The payoff will be *inner-peace, being a positive influence in the world, experiencing a taste of the kingdom of God* and *discovering your true self.*

Listen to the song of the day "You'll Lead Me" on the *Listen to Your Heart* album.

AUGUST

8 DIE TO LIVE

Matthew 16:24-26

Then Jesus said to his disciples, "Whoever wishes to come after me must deny himself, take up his cross, and follow me. For whoever wishes to save his life will lose it, but whoever loses his life for my sake will find it. What profit would there be for one to gain the whole world and forfeit his life?

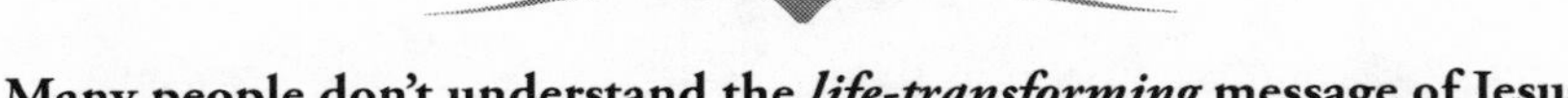

Many people don't understand the *life-transforming* message of Jesus.

Unless you "deny yourself" – meaning *let go of the false self that your ego has constructed* – and "take up your cross" – meaning *accept the hardships and struggles that come with following* – you will not find the life that was *meant* for you.

You must shed the *masks* of your *false self* so that your *true self* can be unveiled.
That *true self* is *not* something you *achieve* or *accomplish.*
It's your *soul-self,* your *spiritual essence* that was *loved-into-existence* by a Love that is *unconditional* and *eternal.*
You could actually gain much power, prestige and many possessions in following your ego's desires and *never know your true self.*

How *sad* that would be!
The more you uncover your true self, the more you are living in the flow of God's Presence.

This requires a regular practice of *being present* and *listening.*

It won't be easy picking up your cross and following your heart, but *paradoxically* you will find inner *satisfaction, peace* and *freedom.*

Listen to the song of the day "Make Your Way" on the *Mercy Reigns* album.

FULLNESS OF LIFE

Matthew 18:3-4

"Amen, I say to you, unless you turn and become like children, you will not enter the kingdom of heaven. Whoever humbles himself like a child is the greatest in the kingdom of heaven."

In our culture, the *greatest* is the person who stands with
arms raised in triumph after winning a title.
Not so in the kingdom of heaven.

Jesus turns our culture *inside out.*
He said that the *greatest* in the kingdom of heaven is *not* the gold medal winner,
the one who wins the trophy, the champion, or the brash celebrity.
The greatest in God's kingdom is someone who
humbles **himself or herself** ***like a child.***

This is not something you can *fake.* It has to be genuine.
A child tends to live *very keenly in the present moment.*
A child is ***open*** **to the** ***awe and wonder of the moment*** **in the** ***simplest*** **of things.**
A child is playfully present.
Being ***totally enthralled*** **in the** ***present moment*** **is the**
entrance way **into the** ***kingdom of heaven.***
It's the place where you are *detached* from all *ego enticements of power, prestige and possessions* so that the *Divine Presence* might be *fully experienced.*

The paradox is when you are ***humbly present,*** **you actually** ***discover your true self.***

It's *never too late* to enter God's kingdom.
All it takes is ***letting go.***
You can start *right now.*

Listen to the song of the day "Shall We Sing" on the ***Listen to Your Heart*** **album.**

AUGUST

10 POUR ME OUT

Matthew 17:22-23

As they were gathering in Galilee, Jesus said to them, "The Son of Man is to be handed over to men, and they will kill him, and he will be raised on the third day." And they were overwhelmed with grief.

When you stand up for *Love* in the face of *hate* sometimes you pay a *heavy price.* Witness what happened to the peaceful civil rights protesters in the 1960's or more recently in Charlottesville, Virginia in 2017.

All *non-violent* protesters of hateful extremists are examples of Jesus. He, too, stood up to injustice with non-violence and it led to his crucifixion.

Back in Jesus' time, his followers believed he would be the long-awaited *military* Messiah that would lead them to freedom. How devastated they must have been to hear him say that he would be killed!

God's ways are not *our* ways.

Jesus would instead be the *suffering servant* Messiah to demonstrate that while the path of Love leads to persecution it *also* leads to *waves of good works.*

It *ushers in the kingdom of God.*

Jesus showed us that the way to God's kingdom, to *true life*, is through dying to our own desires, our ego's cravings, *emptying ourselves* so that *God's desires* could *rise* in us.

In letting go of your *ego-created false self* you find your *true self.*

This is the same way that God's kingdom can *break into the present.* It led Jesus to call on those who held the power and wealth to care for those on the margins, the sick and poor. He called for the end of divisions.

Jesus knew, of course, that this would *not* be accepted by those who held the power and wealth in government and religion. They *wanted divisions.*

He knew that eventually this path would lead him to the cross.

Every step of the way, Jesus showed us that it is only through *self-emptying* love, *dying to our ego*, that we experience *new life* whether in our *daily struggles* or at the *end of our earthly lives.*

When we surrender ourselves to God's purposes amazing things happen.

Love *triumphs* over hate and new life *overwhelms* death *every time.*

Listen to the song of the day "Pour Me Out" on the *Give Praise and Thanks* album.

BE FREE

Matthew 19:23

Then Jesus said to his disciples, "Amen, I say to you, it will be hard for one who is rich to enter the kingdom of heaven."

What does it mean to "enter the kingdom of heaven"?

Certainly we all hope to enter upon death but Jesus seemed to be focused on the *now* and *not* some *future* "reward."

When a scribe agreed with Jesus that the two greatest commandments were *to love God with all your heart, soul, mind and strength* and *to love your neighbor as yourself,* Jesus told him, "You are not far from the kingdom of God." (Mark 12:34).

Jesus was clearly talking about experiencing the kingdom of God in the *present.*

A rich person has an abundance of power, prestige and possessions. It's easy to get caught up in *defending* and *protecting* all of that to the point that there is no time for God or anyone else.

It's not the power, prestige and possessions *in themselves* that are bad, it's the *attachment to them.*

To *be present* to the Divine Presence is *to be free of clinging to anything.*

It's to be free to live in a *loving relationship* with *all that is.*

Then, you will be experiencing the *kingdom of God* or the *reign of God* right *now.*

What is blocking me from being truly present to God's love in this moment?

Listen to the song of the day "How Wonderful to Me" on the *Live to Love* album.

AUGUST

12 DIVINE PRESENCE

Matthew 19:16-17

"Teacher, what good must I do to gain eternal life?" Jesus answered him, "Why do you ask me about the good? There is only One who is good. If you wish to enter into life, keep the commandments."

Eternal life is a *gift*, it's not something we *merit*.
So the man's question to Jesus is *nonsensical*.
You can't "score points" to be rewarded with heaven one day.
This is what has *so many* Christians *confused*.
The man asking Jesus how to "gain" eternal life was also attached to many possessions and viewed eternal life as a commodity to gain through his own works.
If you had to *earn* heaven, you'd be on a *never-ending-treadmill* of trying to do good deeds that would *never-be-good-enough*.
This would make for a very *frustrating* and *guilt-laden* life!
Jesus makes the issue very *present*. He tells the man that if he wishes to "enter into life," he should keep the commandments.
In other words, as St. Catherine of Siena reportedly said, "It's heaven all the way to heaven."
***Now* is what matters. It's how you are *present* to *others* and *all of creation*.**
We each receive an outpouring of love from the "only One who is good" (*God who is love* (1 John 4:8)). So we are meant to *receive* that Love and *share* that Love.
That's why Jesus said that the greatest commandments were *to love God, and to love your neighbor as yourself*.
While we know that certain acts are good and others are bad, labeling anything as either "good" or "bad" is generally *not* a good idea.
God can use all that happens for good. As St. Paul said, "We know that all things work for good for those who love God." (Romans 8:28).
In my life there have been many times when something happened that *appeared* to be *bad* at the time but in the long run turned out to be very *good*.
My whole experience of having a ruptured appendix appeared to be the *worst* thing that ever happened to me at the time, but in retrospect I now view the experience as one of the most *deeply spiritually transforming* ones of my life.
So it was actually *very good!*
Jesus goes on to advise this man to sell his possessions, give to the poor, and then to "come, follow me." (Matthew 19:21). Jesus knows that the man is *attached* to his many possessions which are what is keeping him from engaging in *life*.
The question for each of us is, "What attachments do *I* need to *let go* of in order to follow the path of love *right now?*

Listen to the song of the day "Glorify You with Me" on the *Give Praise and Thanks* album.

ALL ARE ONE

Matthew 19:29-30

"And everyone who has given up houses or brothers or sisters or father or mother or children or lands for the sake of my name will receive a hundred times more, and will inherit eternal life. But many who are first will be last, and the last will be first."

The kingdom of God throws this world's values *upside down.*
Those who are *first* by our *culture's* standards, meaning those who *win* and reap huge *monetary rewards*, will be *last* by *God's* standards.
God does not measure success in power, prestige and possessions, but in *love.*

When we reach the end of our days on earth, God will not ask us how much money we made, but how much we *loved.*
Jesus said the greatest commandments were to love God with your whole heart, soul and mind and then to love your neighbor as yourself. (Matthew 22:37-39).
Jesus pretty much laid out what God holds as important when he said, 'For I was hungry and you gave me food, I was thirsty and you gave me drink, a stranger and you welcomed me, naked and you clothed me, ill and you cared for me, in prison and you visited me.' (Matthew 25:35-36).
The key is *relinquishing all self-centered attachments,* which is the *path of Jesus.* This transfers our attention from our ego's desires to the needs of *others* and *all of creation.*
Then we truly enter into the *present moment* and *God's Presence.* In that awareness, nothing is interfering with our openness to God.
This *eternal now* is where the *kingdom of God* is *manifested.*
It's where *God's dream* for us can be known.
Here, there is no such thing as being *first* or being *last.*
All are *equal* and *one.*
This is what *God* wants. Do *we?*

Listen to the song of the day "All Are One" on the *Mercy Reigns* album.

AUGUST

14 EXPRESS YOURSELF

Psalm 96:1

Sing to the Lord a new song;
sing to the Lord, all you lands.

All of creation metaphorically *sings a song in its very being.*

Every living thing, through its very nature, pours out all that it is without any *indecision* or *hesitancy* – except us *human beings!*

We have freedom of choice.

Many times, we *compare* ourselves to others and determine that we are not *good enough*. We *envy* others or wish we could be *different* or try to *out-do* others.

This is because our egos are in charge.

Your ego must *diminish* so your true self can *emerge!*

What if we simply were ourselves to the fullest extent with no filters?
What if we simply kept *in tune* with the song in our hearts and followed Jesus while pursuing our deepest passions?

What unique song is God trying to sing through *you?*

Each person has a song to share that is different than any other person's song and each is *beautiful.*

Sing *your* song.

Be *you* in *each moment.*

The Master Composer is *yearning* to make *your* song a part of the *on-going symphony of love.*

Listen to the song of the day "Sing a New Song" on the *Live to Love* album.

GRATITUDE

Luke 1:46-47

"And Mary said: "My soul proclaims the greatness of the Lord; my spirit rejoices in God my savior."

Mary is perhaps our *best example* of someone putting aside *her* desires and saying "yes" to *God's* desires *for* her.

When asked if she would be the mother of the Son of God, you can imagine how *radically* that *pulled the rug out* from under the plans Mary had for her life!

By saying "yes" Mary's life became an amazing adventure beyond any description.

God has plans for *each* of our lives.

Those plans might not be as *grandiose*, but they are plans that are *uniquely ours.*

No one else can live out the love of our Creator like *you* can.

How does God want to be *made flesh* in *you?*

How does God want to be *birthed* through *your* life?

"Tune in" to the voice of Love in your heart. Set aside time for silent prayer, meditation, scripture reading and experiencing the awe and wonder of nature.

Then listen to your *inner voice.*

What are you *drawn* to in the name of *goodness* and *compassion?*

Start moving in that direction and you will find yourself saying: "My soul proclaims the greatness of the Lord; my spirit rejoices in God my savior."

Listen to the song of the day "Lift Up Our Voices" on the *Give Praise and Thanks* album.

AUGUST

16 LIVING PRAISE

Psalm 145:10

All your works give you thanks,
O Lord, and your faithful bless you.

A flower doesn't look around and say to itself, "I'd really rather be a tree."
Nor does a dog wake up in the morning and grumble, "I wish I was a horse instead."
All living things, flowers, plants, trees, and creatures of all kinds, are just busy *being themselves* each moment of every day.

They do it quite naturally and without reservation.
Do *we?*

Humans seem to be the only beings who sometimes wish we were someone else.

Each of us is perfectly made in our uniqueness.

Spend some time doing the things you love doing – whether it's reading, writing, drawing, painting, singing, playing a musical instrument, making crafts, running, working out, acting, etc.

Enjoy your "*you-ness.*"

Be *you* with *enthusiasm.*

Think about how we have been given life, love, grace, mercy, forgiveness and eternal life, all with no strings attached.

Not only that, we've also been surrounded by the beauty of creation.

It's all gift.
Stop for a moment and take it all in.
Then *breathe deeply* and *give thanks.*

Listen to the song of the day "Give Praise and Thanks" on the *Give Praise and Thanks* album.

1 Corinthians 1:9

God is faithful, and by him you were called to fellowship with his Son, Jesus Christ our Lord.

God will *never let us go*, despite all the times *we* have *turned away* and despite all the times in the future when *we will slip and fall.*

Remember that God *is* love.

Also remember: "Love is patient, love is kind. It is not jealous, [love] is not pompous, it is not inflated, it is not rude, it does not seek its own interests, it is not quick-tempered, it does not brood over injury, it does not rejoice over wrongdoing but rejoices with the truth. It bears all things, believes all things, hopes all things, endures all things. Love never fails." (1 Corinthians 13:4-8).

Love was *made flesh* and took human form in Jesus.

Love became *human.*

Jesus said that he is "the way and the truth and the life." (John 14:6).

If we follow him, trust him, become friends with him, he will show us who we are.

There are so many influences and voices trying to tell each of us what we should do, think and act in order to be *someone.*

If you want to know why you are here, if you want to know the *real* you, your *true self* – get to know Jesus.

Listen to the song of the day "Come to Jesus" on the *Live to Love* album.

AUGUST

18 DEATH LEADS TO LIFE

1 Corinthians 1:17-18

For Christ did not send me to baptize but to preach the gospel, and not with the wisdom of human eloquence, so that the cross of Christ might not be emptied of its meaning. The message of the cross is foolishness to those who are perishing, but to us who are being saved it is the power of God.

Paul was speaking to members of the early Church about
the difficult message of Jesus' death on the cross.
While our egos seek personal gratification and are fed by worldly messages to "grab" all the pleasures we can, the *cross* has an *opposite* message.

Jesus *emptied* himself, giving *everything* he had – his very *life* –
to show us the way of God.
When we *empty* ourselves of our *egos'* desires to be satisfied, we open ourselves to *God's* desires to lead us to what we truly *need* and who we truly *are.*
This is being *saved!*

Jesus' way clashes with the world's way.
To love *unconditionally* is to give yourself for another's benefit and to respond to persecution with love *all the way to the end.*

For popular culture the message of the cross is *death.*
To *Christians*, the message of the cross is that death is *not* the end, but the pathway to resurrection and *new life.*

Giving leads to great joy.
Jesus showed us the way.

Each of us has the *choice* of whether to follow.

Listen to the song of the day "Love Will Always Lead You Home" on the *Mercy Reigns* album.

CYCLE OF LIFE

1 Thessalonians 4:14

For if we believe that Jesus died and rose, so too will God, through Jesus, bring with him those who have fallen asleep.

St. Paul's message is truly Good News!

Our salvation is not about *our* goodness or achievement, but *God's*.

Jesus said we must *die to ourselves* for that is when we fall into God's loving hands.

Following Jesus is not about learning an *evacuation plan* to heaven but learning the *process of letting go – dying to self.*

It's about being transformed in the *process.*

This is the only way to *become* our true selves.

What if we all became fully the unique people God made us to be and used our gifts and talents to *serve* others?

God's dream for the world would come to be *now.*

God's kingdom would come "*on earth* as it is in heaven."

This is God's goal.
So have no fear!
Listen to your heart.
Cooperate with God's desires for you.
The time is *now!*

Listen to the song of the day "Listen to Your Heart" on the *Listen to Your Heart* album.

AUGUST

20 LIFE CHANGING

1 John 4:9

In this way the love of God was revealed to us:
God sent his only Son into the world
so that we might have life through him.

I followed many pursuits that I thought would bring me happiness.

I was listening to my *ego* which wanted the rewards
the world said would make me happy and fulfilled.

The world's rewards are centered on power, prestige and possessions.

All those pursuits are *dead ends*.

They only led me to wanting *more* and *more*,
building a "false self" that left me in misery.

It wasn't until I was thoroughly miserable that I was able to hear a soft, loving voice in my heart telling me that I was loved for no other reason than the fact that I was a *beloved child of God*.

It seems that many times it takes becoming miserable before we can actually experience what Unconditional Love is!

Jesus showed us this Love in the way he lived his life.

Following his example is one path to discovering your *true self*
and a life abundant in love, peace and joy.

Listen to the song of the day "God Is" on the *Give Praise and Thanks* album.

"SILENCE IS GOD'S FIRST LANGUAGE."
– ST. JOHN OF THE CROSS

Mark 1:35-38

Rising very early before dawn, he left and went off to a deserted place, where he prayed. Simon and those who were with him pursued him and on finding him said, "Everyone is looking for you." He told them, "Let us go on to the nearby villages that I may preach there also. For this purpose have I come."

Notice how Jesus goes off to "a deserted place" and prays.
He gets away from any distractions to commune with God in *solitude.*
There he can *immerse* himself in the *silent Presence* of God.

Notice how Simon and the others find Jesus and try to get him to return to the people who have already experienced the power of his preaching and healing.
Does Jesus simply *go along* with what *others* want him to do? *No!*

Jesus knows his *mission* is to *move on* to *preach* and *heal elsewhere.*
How does he know?
Apparently through his *heart-to-heart* time in *silent prayer* with God.

How often do *we* do this?

Do we follow the *quiet voice* in our *hearts* or do we blindly follow the *loud voices* of *pop culture* and what others want us to do?

For us to know our *calling* and *mission*, we must take time for silence to open up a *heart-to-heart communication* with our Loving Creator.

Listen to the song of the day "Turn Off the Noise" on the *Listen to Your Heart* album.

AUGUST

22 WORTH THE STRUGGLE

2 Timothy 1:8

So do not be ashamed of your testimony to our Lord, nor of me, a prisoner for his sake; but bear your share of hardship for the gospel with the strength that comes from God.

Being a Christian is *not* easy.

Jesus *promised* that his followers would be persecuted.

Once you *know* Jesus, once you know that following him leads you to your true self, to find purpose and inner contentment, the choice is *clear.*

It resulted in St. Paul being imprisoned and finally executed.

He followed *willingly* and with courage as he relied completely on the strength given to him by God.

What else could he do?

He had found his true life in following Jesus!

He had found his *calling.*

Who are *today's* prophets and apostles?

Could it be you?

Follow Jesus, and he'll take you on the road to freedom!

Listen to the song of the day "Take the Road Less Traveled" on the *Live to Love* album.

SHINE THE LIGHT

AUGUST
23

1 John 3:2

Beloved, we are God's children now; what we shall be has not yet been revealed. We do know that when it is revealed we shall be like him, for we shall see him as he is.

The bible says we are made in God's image.
That image, as Trinity, is in perpetual, loving relationship.
Each of us is a tiny, unique reflection of the Divine Image.

However, that reflection is dimmed in us by all the superficial and unimportant ways that we express ourselves based on worldly illusions that will not last.

Jesus teaches us to *let go* of those illusions, to "die" to our *egocentric* desires so that the Divine Image can shine through.

We are meant to take part in the *Trinitarian-Relational-Flow-of-Love.*

It is the path to becoming our *true selves.*

Each moment provides us a choice of whether to let go of our ego's insatiable desires to create a *false self* or to use our gifts and talents for God's desires.

That requires *letting go* and being present to *God, everyone* and *everything else.*

Each of us has no idea what our true self will be since it is not of *our* making.

We can be sure that when we are fully present to the Divine Presence our true selves will shine brightly.

Listen to the song of the day "May I Be Light" on the *Listen to Your Heart* album.

AUGUST

24 YOUR TRUTH

John 1:38

Jesus turned and saw them following him
and said to them, "What are you looking for?"

Interesting question, isn't it?
So, *what* are *you* looking for?

Are you looking for the things that connote success in this world,
things like power, prestige and possessions?
**Those things aren't bad, in and of themselves, as long as you
don't get *attached* to any of them.**
That is the *catch*.

You can find a certain amount of pleasure from those things and
need a certain amount of those things to get by in this world.

None **of those things will ever be enough to satisfy
the *deep yearning inside your soul.***

Jesus said that you couldn't serve both *money* and *God*.

**It's really a question of whether you are looking to
build *your own* kingdom or *God's* kingdom.**

Which is your *main* motivation?

When you look to build *God's* kingdom you are using your gifts and talents to serve others in making the world a more loving, forgiving, compassionate and just place.

Jesus is a great model to follow.

**Listen to the song of the day "I Want to Follow You" on
the *Listen to Your Heart* album.**

BE AWAKE

AUGUST

25

Mark 4:18-19

"Those (seeds) sown among thorns are another sort. They are the people who hear the word, but worldly anxiety, the lure of riches, and the craving for other things intrude and choke the word, and it bears no fruit."

God's word comes to us in scripture, in rituals, in silent prayer, through music, through other people, through art, through animals, and through nature and all of creation.

There are many "seeds" being sown, but what is the condition of our "soil"?

Are we cultivating our soil?

What other words, music, TV shows, or friends might be poisoning our soil and "choking" God's seeds?

How are you cooperating in becoming the person God intended you to become?

We all need to cultivate our inner soil so that we are receptive to the spiritual nourishment God wants to give us.

Set aside 20 to 30 minutes of time for quiet reflection or meditation.

Your life will bear much fruit if you do.

Listen to the song of the day "Breathe on Me" on the *Listen to Your Heart* album.

AUGUST

26 PRAISE BE

Psalm 98:1

Sing a new song to the Lord,
who has done marvelous deeds.

The next time that you are tempted to complain,
look at the *many blessings all around you.*
What about each precious *breath* you take?

This life in *human form* has an expiration date.
We have no idea when the time will be up.
I remember vividly a brush with tragedy several years ago.
I suddenly lost control of my car on ice, narrowly missed a head-on collision,
spun around, slid off the road and overturned. It all happened
in just a few seconds, but it seemed like an *eternity.*
Somehow, I did not sustain as much as a scratch or a bruise.

It seems it takes such encounters with *mortality* to *wake up*
to how *awesome* – and yet *fragile* – life is!
Each *moment* is a *gift.*

How often am I spending those moments *lamenting the past* or *fretting over the future?*

Wake up!
Engage* with the *now*, the *only time* to engage with the *Divine Presence.
This *Holy Mystery* wants to *shower* you with Love.

You* are part of this *magnificent unfolding creation.

You have been given *life* with the promise of *eternal life*.

How *great* is the God of *all!*

Listen to the song of the day "I Stand in the Light" on the *Mercy Reigns* album.

UNCONDITIONAL LOVE AND ACCEPTANCE

Mark 1:15

"This is the time of fulfillment. The kingdom of God is at hand. Repent, and believe in the gospel."

Jesus' words tell us that the kingdom of God begins *now.*

It's *here*, not just sometime in the distant future.

Now, *this moment*, is the only time that's real.

The past is finished, the future is a mystery.

"Repent, "which means to *change your direction.*

Don't waste any time beating yourself up over
past failures or fretting over future concerns.

The gospel or *Good News* is that God loves you unconditionally *now.*

God wants to be with you now, so that you can become an expression
of love, mercy, grace, forgiveness and compassion to the world.

That is your purpose.

It will lead you to becoming your *true self.*

The process will give you enjoyment and fulfillment.

This is the moment.

Don't miss it!

Listen to the song of the day "Slow Me Down" on the *Mercy Reigns* album.

AUGUST

28 SOUL SATISFACTION

Luke 9:24-25

For whoever wishes to save his life will lose it,
but whoever loses his life for my sake will save it.
What profit is there for one to gain the
whole world yet lose or forfeit himself?

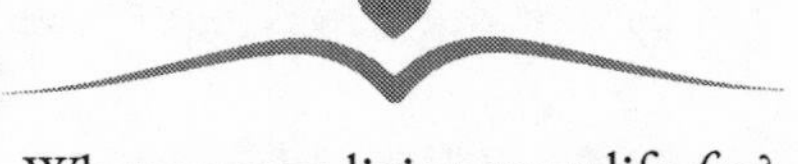

What are you living your life *for?*

What is the *purpose?*

If it is to satisfy your ego, it is to satisfy your *false self.*

As I have said in the past, "ego" stands for: "*E*dge *G*od *O*ut."

The false self will *never* be satisfied.

It relies on a *program for happiness* set up in childhood in which every whim and self-centered desire needed to be satisfied.

A great spiritual goal is to let that system for happiness *dry up.*

It is a *false* system leading *nowhere.*

Live to *love* and live to *serve.*

Follow in the ways of Jesus and you will find *soul satisfaction* and your *true self.*

Listen to the song of the day "God Is the Goal" on the *Live to Love* album.

HIGHER PURPOSE

Mark 7:8-9

"You disregard God's commandment but cling to human tradition." He went on to say, "How well you have set aside the commandment of God in order to uphold your tradition!"

Jesus made it clear that *love* is the *most important thing*, when he was asked to specify the *greatest commandment.*

This is what he said: "You shall love the Lord your God with all your heart, with all your soul, with all your mind, and with all your strength.' The second is this: 'You shall love your neighbor as yourself.' There is no other commandment greater than these." (Mark 12:30-31).

If you look at the various Christian denominations today, there are *mountains* of *rules, doctrines, dogmas, rituals and beliefs.*

How *strange,* when Jesus did *not* emphasize *rules.*
As a matter of fact, he made a practice of *breaking* them when *love demanded it.*

***Love* and *healing* seemed to be his main concerns.**

Rules and doctrines do have their place in giving us structure and a framework for discussion.
They have unfortunately been used too often as instruments to *punish, ostracize* and *inflict pain.*

Sometimes it seems we have lost the most important, foundational teaching: *to love.*

Since God *is* love (1 John 4:8), *each of us* is called to *channel* that love.

Listen to the song of the day "God's Love Is All You Need" on the *Listen to Your Heart* album.

AUGUST

30 GO FORTH

Mark 6:4

Jesus said to them, "A prophet is not without honor except in his native place and among his own kin and in his own house."

When Jesus returned to his hometown of Nazareth,
he astounded the people with his teaching.
At first they were impressed.

Then they asked, "Is he not the carpenter, the son of Mary?"
In other words, *"We remember who you were, so who do you think you are now?"*
Then, the scripture says, "They took offense at him."

Following your heart, giving your all to being the person you were meant to be (your *true self*) will mean *growth* and *change.*
Some people will not be comfortable with that.
As a matter of fact, sometimes your *closest friends* and *family* can be
the *very ones* who will give you the *hardest time.*
If they see *you* change, then *they* have to *change* in the *way they see you.*
The fact is, many people *do not like change!*

When you follow the dream God has given you and begin to *live* it, you will be *growing* and *moving out of your comfort zone.*

This will challenge others around you to do the same and they might not like it.

Your duty is *not* to please *them* but to please your *true self.*
When you do that, you are pleasing *God.*

So sing *your* song.
It's a sure path to finding your *true self* and *inner peace.*

Listen to the song of the day "Singing My Song" on the *Live to Love* album.

LET GO AND LIVE

Mark 6:8

Jesus instructed them to take nothing for the journey but a walking stick – no food, no sack, no money in their belts.

Just how *obsessed* are you with your *possessions?*

This "stuff" that *won't last* becomes such a focus of our attention.

We sometimes call certain things our "prized-possessions."

Those same "prizes" will one-day be *junk.*

How much precious time do we waste on
keeping, securing and multiplying our possessions?

It's not the stuff that is inherently bad, it's our *attachment* to it.

Jesus sent his apostles out with *nothing* so that nothing would distract
them from devoting themselves to imparting the
love, mercy, grace, forgiveness and compassion of God to *all.*

They were about the business of *building the kingdom of God.*

**"Letting-go" is not about *losing* anything of *worth*
but about *gaining more* of what *truly is.***

Start *now,* so that when it comes time for your *final* letting-go,
you will be *well-versed* in *dying and rising* to *new life.*

Listen to the song of the day "Mercy Reigns" on the *Mercy Reigns* album.

SEPTEMBER

I WHOLENESS

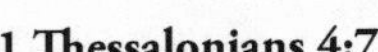

1 Thessalonians 4:7

For God did not call us to impurity but to holiness.

If whatever we are *doing* or *thinking* is not *life-giving* or *loving* either to *ourselves* or to *others*, then it is not leading us to *wholeness* (or *holiness*).

God is always calling us to become *whole*, to live *authentically as ourselves.*

When we are, we are bringing to life the *full, complete,* and *unique* expression of God's love to the world that *only each of us can.*

No one can be *you* like *you* can!

We are incapable of being whole apart from a *conscious connection* with God the Source of Life and Love.

How do we do this?

By *being present* to the *Divine Presence.*

By being *lovingly attentive* to life as it *unfolds.*

Allow the *Great Compassion* in Whom "we live and move and have our being" (Acts 17:28) to lead you.

Listen to the song of the day "Make Me a Channel" on the *Listen to Your Heart* album.

TAKE COURAGE

Luke 4:24

"Amen, I say to you, no prophet is accepted in his own native place."

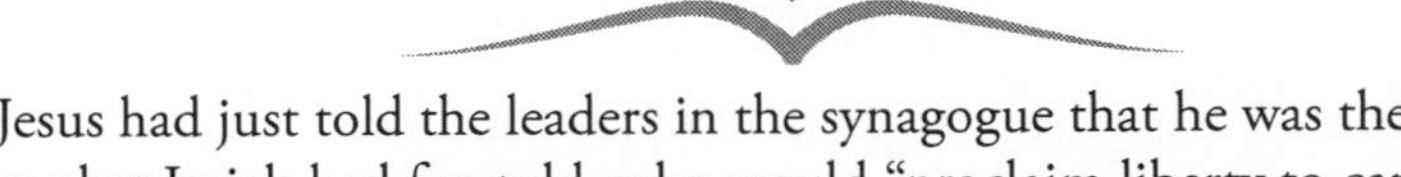

Jesus had just told the leaders in the synagogue that he was the one the prophet Isaiah had foretold, who would "proclaim liberty to captives and recovery of sight to the blind," and "let the oppressed go free."

But the leaders said, "Who does he think he is?"

They all saw him grow up as just a carpenter's son.

Have you ever been prompted somewhere deep inside to speak up for someone who was unjustly treated or to tell someone in need about the love of God?

If you followed through, did you find that those *closest* to you *looked down* on you with contempt?

Did you find that those *closest* to you now *distanced* themselves from you?

Following God's calling and being a disciple of the light is sometimes the most difficult when you're with the people who *know you best!*

Jesus felt this judgment as well, but took action *anyway*.

Turn to him for help and follow your heart.

You'll be led on the path to *freedom, wholeness* and your *true self.*

Listen to the song of the day "You'll Lead Me" on the *Listen to Your Heart* album.

SEPTEMBER

3

PERSEVERE

1 Corinthians 4:5

Therefore do not make any judgment before the appointed time, until the Lord comes, for he will bring to light what is hidden in darkness and will manifest the motives of our hearts, and then everyone will receive praise from God.

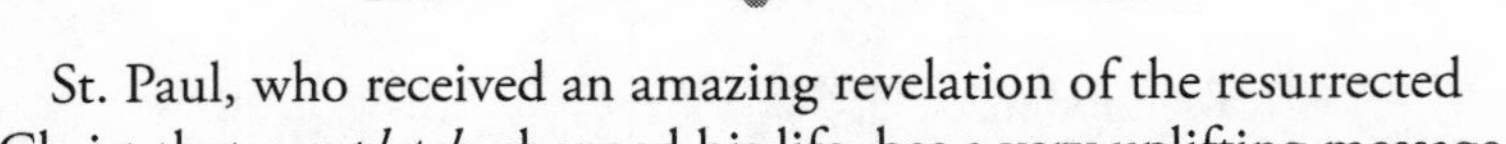

St. Paul, who received an amazing revelation of the resurrected Christ that *completely* changed his life, has a very uplifting message.

He tells us *not to judge others or ourselves,* but to *only rely on God's judgment.*

We're not here to *please others*, but to *please God.*

"Take delight in the Lord, and he will grant you your heart's requests." (Psalm 37:4).

What *yearning* has God placed *in your heart?*

Follow it!

God wants to do new and wondrous things with you!

Many are too distracted by other influences.

When we put all our hopes in God, God will lead us to the true motives of our hearts and there will *not be condemnation.*

St. Paul says, "*everyone will receive praise from God.*"

This is Good News!

Listen to the song of the day "Listen to Your Heart" on the *Listen to Your Heart* album.

GO WITH THE FLOW

Luke 5:11

When they brought their boats to the shore, they left everything and followed him.

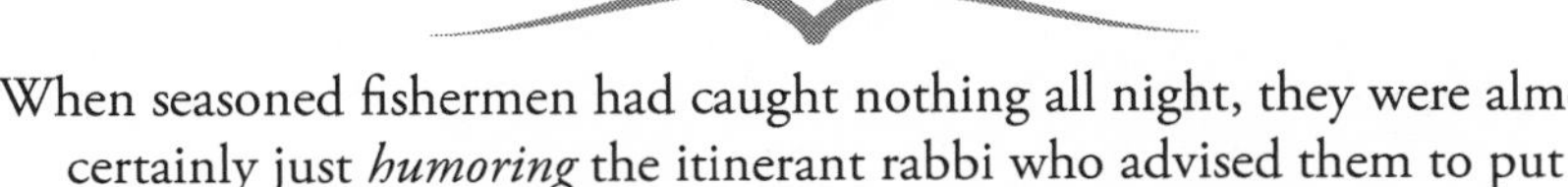

When seasoned fishermen had caught nothing all night, they were almost certainly just *humoring* the itinerant rabbi who advised them to put out into deep water and lower their nets one more time.
When this resulted in their nets being so full of fish that they nearly broke, these fishermen were shaken.
They were *so amazed*, not only by *this* feat, but by the inspiring way Jesus had been preaching about God that they "left everything and followed him."

There comes a time in life when we are given the opportunity to *wake up*.
We come to a *crossroads.*
We realize that there is a *greater purpose in life.*
The *earlier* this happens the *better!*

Your career, your house, your car, your money, your beliefs, all will *fade to oblivion.*
What are you *living* for?
Why did God *love-you-into-existence?*
Why are you here?

As scripture tells us, "God is love." (1 John 4:8). You and I are meant to *experience Love* and to *share* that Love with others.

To do so, your ego needs to *relinquish control* and *release all the attachments* that will *never* provide *lasting peace.*

We are being invited to immerse ourselves in God's *eternal out-pouring of love* in an *on-going, unfolding act of creation.*

What are *you* willing to *leave* to do so?

Listen to the song of the day "Make Your Way" on the *Mercy Reigns* album.

SEPTEMBER

5

PURPOSE IN LIFE

Luke 4:42-43

At daybreak, Jesus left and went to a deserted place. The crowds went looking for him, and when they came to him, they tried to prevent him from leaving them. But he said to them, "To the other towns also I must proclaim the good news of the kingdom of God, because for this purpose I have been sent."

Even Jesus needed to withdraw to "a deserted place" so he could better "hear" God speak in the silence of his heart.

It is from this practice of *contemplative listening* that Jesus understood his *purpose:* to "proclaim the good news of the kingdom of God."

The "good news" is that "the kingdom of God is at hand." (Mark 1:15 and Matthew 3:2) In other words, *right here, right now.*

God's Love and Presence is available to *everyone* in the *present moment* and it's entirely *free.*

You are totally accepted *as is.*

Jesus also understood that his purpose was not to bask in the accolades of his adoring fans, but to move out of his comfort zone and tell others the "good news" as well.

If you are a follower of Jesus, then it is *your* job, too.

How are *you* being called to be a messenger of the *good news* of God's *unconditional love* for *all?*

Listen to the song of the day "I Want to Follow You" on the *Listen to Your Heart* album.

KEY TO HAPPINESS

SEPTEMBER

6

Luke 6:20

And raising his eyes toward his disciples Jesus said:
"Blessed are you who are poor,
for the kingdom of God is yours."

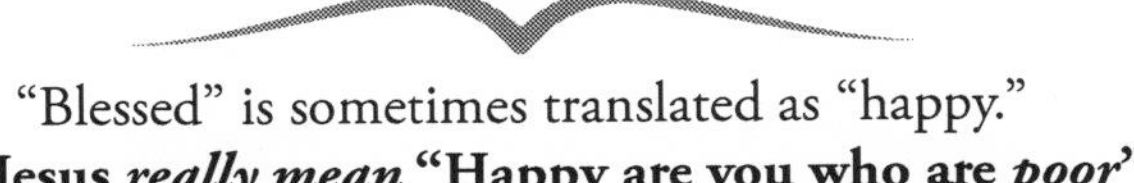

"Blessed" is sometimes translated as "happy."
Can Jesus *really mean* "Happy are you who are *poor*"?
Are we not happier when we have *wealth* and all the *stuff* that goes with it?
Well, for a *time* we are.

Think about the last time you really wanted some material thing and then got it. Did the happiness you felt *last*, or did it *fade* until you started craving *something else* to satisfy your yearning?

The deep, inner yearning we all feel is actually a *spiritual* craving, not physical. It's the groaning of our souls, our *true selves*, for *wholeness* and *oneness* with God. Our Creator wants to satisfy our inner yearning by leading us to become our true selves. **For this to happen, we must first stop seeking *fulfillment* from things that *don't last*, like *power*, *prestige* and *possessions.***

Those things all have their place in this world, but the *attachment* to them is what we must avoid.

When we *let go* of attachments and, in a sense, *become "poor"* we are then open to what God wants to give us.

When we are *present*, open to *each moment*, *letting go* of the distractions, we are indeed *poor* in *possessions* but *rich* in the *Grace of God.*

Listen to the song of the day "Singing My Song" on the *Live to Love* album.

SEPTEMBER

7

BE ENCOURAGED

Deuteronomy 31:8

"It is the LORD who goes before you; he will be with you and will never fail you or forsake you. So do not fear or be dismayed."

Do not fear **is probably the most repeated sentiment in the bible.**

Jesus also counseled against worry and fear: "Peace I leave with you; my peace I give to you. Not as the world gives do I give it to you. Do not let your hearts be troubled or afraid." (John 14:27).

Scripture also tells us that God *is* love. (1 John 4:8).

Later in that same passage, "There is no fear in love, but perfect love drives out fear because fear has to do with punishment, and so one who fears is not yet perfect in love." (1 John 4:18).

One of my main callings in life is to communicate to all who will listen that *God loves you.*

I experienced this realization in a life-changing way back in 1998 and have since experienced it *many more* times.

Turn *away* from any harbingers of fear and turn *toward* God who is *Love* itself.

You came from Love.

Love will *never fail you.* (1 Corinthians 13:8).

So go *be* the Love that you *are!*

Listen to the song of the day "The Way You Are" on the *Mercy Reigns* album.

LET GO OF EGO

SEPTEMBER

8

Luke 6:42

"How can you say to your brother, 'Brother, let me remove that splinter in your eye,' when you do not even notice the wooden beam in your own eye? You hypocrite! Remove the wooden beam from your eye first; then you will see clearly to remove the splinter in your brother's eye."

Jesus tells us not to judge others, but that doesn't mean we have to *turn our brains off.* We do have to *judge* what is in our best interest. We also can't help but to *judge* as in *determine in our own minds* whether we think what someone else is doing is a *good idea or not.*

What Jesus instructs us *against* is making any judgments about another person's *salvation* or *innate goodness.*
After all, we don't know all the reasons why people do what they are doing or what experiences might have influenced their actions.
A "wooden beam" in my eye might be obstructing a clear view of that other person and I might be *completely clueless* about that "beam" that is clouding my understanding.
Just how many beams and specks are obstructing my view of which I am completely unaware?

Perhaps if I reached out and formed a *relationship* with someone that I *disagreed with*, each of us might be changed for the better.

Loving God, help me to focus on *my* faults and not the faults of others.
Help me to see the inner beauty of all people, *especially* those who anger me.
Help me to be able to *both* disagree with someone *and* still be in relationship with them.

Listen to the song of the day "All Are Welcome" on the *Give Praise and Thanks* album.

SEPTEMBER

9 BE THE TRUE YOU

Colossians 3:3-4

For you have died, and your life is hidden with Christ in God. When Christ your life appears, then you too will appear with him in glory.

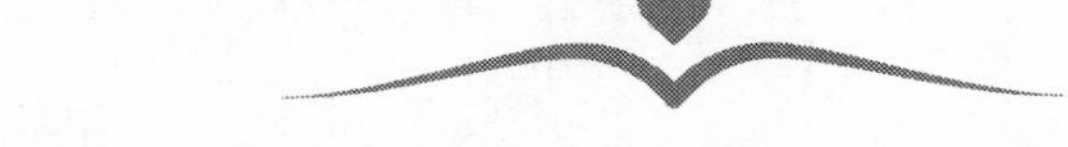

Whatever most people think is their identity, it usually *isn't.*
Your *true identity* does not come from your status, job, prestige or possessions.
It doesn't come from what others say about you.
All those things will pass away, quite *literally* when we *die.*

That will end up being quite a painful experience, unless we practice *dying to ourselves* every day, as in dying to our *false selves.* Your false self is the product of your ego and the various masks it puts on in order to fit in or to feel worthy or superior.
This is *not* who you *really are.*

Your *true self* is grounded in the love of God.
***You* are God's beloved!**

One path to living this truth is by following Jesus and his example of being present to the needs of others and not becoming *attached* to anything that is fleeting. Jesus also took time for silent prayer to be open to what God was saying in his heart.
By doing this he was able to respond to life by doing what was just and compassionate at all times, giving himself freely to others out of love, even unto death.

As St. Paul said in today's scripture, when your false self diminishes or dies, Christ grows in you and your true self emerges.

Christ, God's life, your Loving Source, wants to live in you *now.*

Open yourself to this truth and the result will be glorious.

Listen to the song of the day "Changed" on the *Give Praise and Thanks* album.

LOVE IS YOUR CALLING

SEPTEMBER

10

Romans 8:28

We know that all things work for good for those who love God, who are called according to his purpose.

Life is a long road.
As you know, there will be twists, turns and potholes in that road.

God has a plan in Creation to fulfill a purpose.
What *is* the purpose?

It's way beyond my capacity to grasp.

But, I have faith in one thing: God's plan is a great one,
better than anything I could come up with.

I'm convinced God wants each of us to know Love and be transformed by Love into a unique *reflection* of Godself.

There is *nothing* I can do to *earn* God's love.

It is always *freely given.*

We are invited to join God in a creative dance.

The choice is ours.

The process will lead us to discover our *true selves.*

As long as I stay focused on loving God and loving my neighbor (*all* people), getting back up when I fall, and with each step simply focusing on doing the next loving thing, I know *all shall be well.*

Listen to the song of the day "Shall We Sing" on the *Listen to Your Heart* album.

SEPTEMBER

11

WAKE-UP CALL

Luke 6:24-25

"But woe to you who are rich, for you have received your consolation. But woe to you who are filled now, for you will be hungry."

This is *not* a dress rehearsal.
This is your life.
Each moment is the *real deal.*
The big question is: *Why are we here?*
We must ask ourselves this question.

Pretend it is sometime in the future and you are on your death bed. Are you able to look back at your life and be at peace with how you spent it?
Jesus told us that the two most important commandments were *to love God and our neighbor as ourselves.* (Matthew 22:36-39).

***Love* is what matters.**
In today's scripture verses, Jesus *isn't* saying that being rich is bad but he *is* saying that being rich *isn't what life is about.*
That's why he said "woe to you who are rich," because if that's your *only aim in life*, you will already have received your consolation.
This is not a threat of punishment.
Jesus is telling us that it *will be distressing* for anyone who stands in the light of God's eternal Love and reviews whether they did the *one thing* that they were made for: *Did they channel Love with their life.*
Did they share their resources in the service of others or did they horde their wealth?

Jesus told us how to love: Did we feed the hungry, clothe the naked, care for the sick and visit the imprisoned (Matthew 25)?

We *come* from Love and will one day *return* to Love.
In the meantime, the only thing that truly matters, is how we *love.*

Listen to the song of the day "Make Me a Channel" on the *Listen to Your Heart* album.

AMAZING GRACE

Psalm 40:9-10

"To do your will is my delight; my God, your law is in my heart!" I announced your deed to a great assembly; I did not restrain my lips.

When we start following God's *gentle nudges* in our hearts, we *will* be led into *delight.*

Simply adhering to *laws* and *rules* will *not* lead *anyone* into delight.
Love will.
Love *changes hearts.*

Is our motivation ***love*** or ***laws?***

It usually takes some form of suffering before our egos will be forced to *let go* of *control* and our *self-centered desires* so that we can fall into the loving arms of God.

For me, it was only after I truly experienced Unconditional Love when I *least deserved it*, when I was completely without any ability to *earn* it, that I was *transformed.*
My heart melted.

It was only then that I was able to allow this love to freely *bubble-up* from deep inside of me so that *in my imperfection* I could share it.

It is my *delight* to do so.

This is what God wants for *you.*

Open your heart and receive your Creator's love *just as you are!*

Then share it freely!

Listen to the song of the day "Singing My Song" on the *Live to Love* album.

SEPTEMBER

13 NOW IS THE TIME

Psalm 84:6

Happy are those who find refuge in you,
whose hearts are set on pilgrim roads.

The more I let go of my selfish desires (the yearnings of my ego), the more I "die to myself," the more I then experience the bubbling up of God's yearnings in my heart.

It's time to turn off the noise that surrounds us and tries to lure us with false promises of happiness that will *not* last.

Let us turn to God by being *present* to the *inner silence* in our hearts.

What path is God calling *you* to take?

The way might not be clear, but God will lead you as you start following the promptings of your heart.

Wholeness and deep gladness are yours with *each* step.

Set your heart to *your* unique journey.

The time to do so is *now.*

Inner peace and joy await you.

Listen to the song of the day "Turn Off the Noise" on the *Listen to Your Heart* album.

TRUE SELF

SEPTEMBER

14

Colossians 3:9-10

Stop lying to one another, since you have taken off the old self with its practices and have put on the new self, which is being renewed, for knowledge, in the image of its creator.

It seems we all form what Thomas Merton called a "false self"
before our soul's misery will finally force us to see the *delusion.*
Most of us spend our early years *conforming* to what
our culture and/or parents want us to be.
We try to be "successful" based on the criteria of *power, prestige* and *possessions.*

There is *never enough* to satisfy our egos' need for *more.*
Usually it takes having the rug pulled out from under us, some type of *fall* or *suffering* before we *wake up* and ask: "What is my life really about?"

Your "*true self*" can only *rise* when your *false self diminishes.*
One sure way to discover your *true self* is to *follow Jesus.*
He will lead you to *cast off* your "old self with its practices" so that a *new* self, the one made "in the image of its creator" can *emerge.*

However, *the ego will not willingly give in after years of being in charge.*
The "*me*-centered" old self will demand attention.

As a Christ-consciousness begins to grow in you,
you will suddenly be able to *observe* what's happening.

It'll be an *awakening.*
Then, without judgment, you'll *allow* the old self to be *dismantled.*

What is *your* unique image of God to the world?

Listen to the song of the day "Changed" on the *Give Praise and Thanks* album.

SEPTEMBER

15 HOW TO BE YOU

Philippians 2:5-8

Have among yourselves the same attitude that is also yours in Christ Jesus, Who, though he was in the form of God, did not regard equality with God something to be grasped. Rather, he emptied himself, taking the form of a slave, coming in human likeness; and found human in appearance, he humbled himself, becoming obedient to death, even death on a cross.

I think St. Paul demonstrates in today's scripture verses that he understood Jesus famous saying, "Unless a grain of wheat falls to the ground and dies, it remains just a grain of wheat; but if it dies, it produces much fruit." (John 12:24).

Our path to being our *true self* comes through *self-emptying.*
Our way to *wholeness* (salvation) is through *letting go.*
My ego must, in a sense, *die*. It needs to take a back seat.

Jesus *saves* us by *showing us this path.*
He saves me *every day* by delivering me from the *delusional* path of materialism, *consumerism* and any other "*ism*" that separates me from the oneness of God's Love.
He gives us the "blueprint" to follow so that each of us can be the unique child of God that God intended.
When we empty ourselves of selfish desires and truly humble ourselves, we are then free of the attachments that kept us unconscious of our true divine nature.
Letting go* then becomes a *way of life*, allowing us to experience God's Presence in *each moment.

We are free to engage others from a place of love and compassion.
Then, when our physical life comes to an end one day, the transition to eternal life will be seamless, smooth, and joyful, because *dying* has always been so very *well-practiced.*

Listen to the song of the day "Love Will Always Lead You Home" on the *Mercy Reigns* album.

CHOOSE LOVE

1 Timothy 1:13

I was once a blasphemer and a persecutor and an arrogant man, but I have been mercifully treated because I acted out of ignorance in my unbelief.

Before his conversion, St. Paul (known as "Saul" at the time) was basically a *terrorist.*

He thought wiping out the new followers of Jesus was his *calling.*

He thought God *liked* what he was doing.

Paul looked on approvingly at the stoning of the first Christian martyr.

He led the persecution of Christians.

What was God's *response* to Saul? *Mercy* and *forgiveness.*
What?!

Well, *how else would Love respond?*

Because of this response, Paul was *transformed.*

He became perhaps the greatest Christian evangelist and missionary ever.

How many more potential "St. Pauls" are living today?

Who* will be the one who risks responding to hate with *love?

On the cross Jesus forgave the most *unjust* act *ever* thereby *transforming* it into the most *loving* act in *history.*

May each of us be inspired to become ambassadors of *mercy*, not *revenge.*

Listen to the song of the day "Mercy Reigns" on the *Mercy Reigns* album.

SEPTEMBER

17 PATH TO PEACE

Psalm 40:17

But may all who seek you rejoice and be glad in you.
May those who long for your help always say,
"The LORD be glorified."

What are you seeking?
There is a *deep yearning* in each of us.

The advertising industry has reaped great profits by telling us we can satisfy this yearning through gaining material things. But this will never work!
Our yearning is actually on the *spiritual* level.
It's a desire to be who we were meant to be.

St. Paul puts it this way: "We know that all creation is groaning in labor pains even until now" (Romans 8:22). *Groaning in labor pains.*
We all are in *labor pains* to give birth our *true selves.*
Your soul is trying to emerge from beneath the layers of masks and pretenses your ego has invented.
Many people fall into various addictions as they try to satisfy their soul cravings with material or physical things.

What you need is a *spiritual* solution.
It can only come from your Source.
Are you seeking the One who created you with all your heart?
When you *let go* of your *attachments* and *empty* yourself, you are *free to receive what God wants to give you.*

It happens *now,* in *this* moment.
Your yearning is actually your Divine nature groaning to *express* itself.
When you are free to *creatively express your uniqueness*, you will truly be *glad.*
In your very *beingness* God will be *glorified.*

Listen to the song of the day "Glorify You with Me" on the *Give Praise and Thanks* album.

LOVE IS THE WAY

1 Corinthians 13:1-3

If I speak in human and angelic tongues but do not have love, I am a resounding gong or a clashing cymbal. And if I have the gift of prophecy and comprehend all mysteries and all knowledge; if I have all faith so as to move mountains but do not have love, I am nothing. If I give away everything I own, and if I hand my body over so that I may boast but do not have love, I gain nothing.

St. Paul's words are profound.
Love* is the *bottom line.
It's what life is all about.
Nothing else is more important.
How *difficult* it is!
As St. Paul goes on to say: "Love is patient, love is kind. It is not jealous, love is not pompous, it is not inflated, it is not rude, it does not seek its own interests, it is not quick-tempered, it does not brood over injury, it does not rejoice over wrongdoing but rejoices with the truth."
You can carry out all kinds of good works and follow the very *letter* of the law, but if you do not do so *with love*, it is *meaningless*.
And if in carrying out the law you are not doing the loving thing, it is *meaningless*.
Jesus said the two greatest commandments are to *love God with all your heart, soul and strength and to love your neighbor as yourself.*
Love *God, everyone* and *yourself*.
God already loves *you* with *no strings attached.*
You don't have to *earn it.*
Dear God, help me to love in the same way.

Listen to the song of the day "Love God" on the *Live to Love* album.

SEPTEMBER

19 CALLING

1 Corinthians 12:27-28

Now you are Christ's body, and individually parts of it. Some people God has designated in the church to be, first, apostles; second, prophets; third, teachers; then, mighty deeds; then, gifts of healing, assistance, administration, and varieties of tongues.

What is your *purpose in life?*

St. Paul said each of us has a part to play in God's unfolding creation.

We are all here to channel God's love to the world.

Each of us does that in a unique way that only we can do because there is only one of each of us.

We are *instruments* of God's love by sharing our unique talents and gifts.

Our lives are part of a *bigger picture*: our Creator's *masterpiece in progress.*

Do what you love and you will love what you are doing.

If you are unsure of what it is you would love to do, simply open yourself to God's unconditional love and pass it along to others.

God will lead you to finding your place in the body of Christ.

This is life's great adventure!

How are you being called to bring the kingdom of God alive in *this* place and time?

Listen to the song of the day "You'll Lead Me" on the *Listen to Your Heart* album.

COUNTER CULTURE

1 Timothy 6:7, 9, 11

For we brought nothing into the world, just as we shall not be able to take anything out of it. Those who want to be rich are falling into temptation and into a trap and into many foolish and harmful desires, which plunge them into ruin and destruction. Instead, pursue righteousness, devotion, faith, love, patience, and gentleness.

In this passage St. Paul is preaching an *entirely different philosophy of living* than the *world* preaches.

The point is this: *What is your main motivation in life?*

Are you pursuing *wealth* or are you pursuing *God's desires for you?*

Wealth in itself is *not* evil, only when it becomes an *attachment.*

It is *so* easy for the pursuit of wealth to become the *main objective.*

What about simply *being present* to God and *how God sees you?*

Listen to God's voice in the *silence* of your heart.

Hear that *you* are *the beloved.*

How might you then respond by sharing your gifts and talents to channel God's love and compassion to the world?

This* is the path to *inner peace, wholeness* and your *true self.

Listen to the song of the day "God's Love Is All You Need" on the *Listen to Your Heart* album.

SEPTEMBER

21 LIFE SONG

Psalm 101:1

I sing of love and justice; to you, Lord, I sing praise.

Jesus taught that the greatest commandments were to *love God* and to *love your neighbor as yourself.* (Matthew 22:37-39).

He also taught the "golden rule:" *"Do to others whatever you would have them do to you."* (Matthew 7:12).

Each of us must ask ourselves these questions:

Do I *bring people together*, or do I *divide them?*

Do I *build up* or do I *tear down?*

Am I a *channel of God's love to the world?*

Do I *stand with the rejected and the outcast?*

What is the song that you are singing with *your* life?

When your life is a song of *love* and *justice*, then it is a *song of praise* to God.

Listen to the song of the day "My Lord and My God" on the *Live to Love* album.

CONTEMPLATION AND ACTION

SEPTEMBER

22

Luke 8:21

He said to them in reply, "My mother and my brothers are those who hear the word of God and act on it."

Jesus was good at using *exaggeration* to make a *point.*

When told that his mother and brothers were outside waiting to see him, Jesus made the above statement. He *wasn't* suggesting that his followers *shun* their families, because honoring your parents is a Commandment and Jesus was a Jewish man of integrity. **Jesus was emphasizing that a person's *top* priority, *over family*, is to *follow God's will.***

How do we do that?
By *listening to the silent voice* of God and then *acting.*
Lectio Divina* – reading scripture with the *ear* of *your heart,* is one way to *listen.
What word or phrase is *moving you, grabbing your attention?*
Allow it to *ruminate* in your heart in silence.

Another way to listen is *contemplative prayer*, simply sitting in *silence* and allowing your chattering mind to *be still.*
Since God *is* love (1 John 4:8), whatever divine message you hear will be spoken *in love.*
Notice Jesus does not stop with instructing his followers to simply listen.

He said you *must act.*
If your idea of being a Christian is only assenting to a set of beliefs but you are not acting in the cause of *unconditional love* and *justice* for *all* people, you are only a *fan* of Jesus.
He wanted *followers.*

Listen to the song of the day "I Want to Follow You" on the *Listen to Your Heart* album.

SEPTEMBER

23 LIVING YOUR LIFE

Luke 8:1-3

Afterward Jesus journeyed from one town and village to another, preaching and proclaiming the good news of the kingdom of God. Accompanying him were the Twelve and some women who had been cured of evil spirits and infirmities, Mary, called Magdalene, from whom seven demons had gone out, Joanna, the wife of Herod's steward Chuza, Susanna, and many others who provided for them out of their resources.

Are you looking for some real *purpose* in your life – something to get fired-up about and make you feel *alive?*
What was it that inspired the group following Jesus in today's scripture to make such a drastic change in their lives?

These followers were quite the mixture of people.
Besides the assorted men including fishermen and a tax collector, there was also quite the assortment of women.
Some of these women must have been wealthy because they "provided for them out of their resources."
All these people left their previous lives to follow Jesus.

He gave them a *soul purpose.*
Perhaps the more we get to know Jesus through reading about him and allowing him to speak to us in the silence of prayer, we might be equally inspired to find the *true purpose* of our lives.

It'll mean some difficult changes, as well as deep inner *joy.*

Listen to the song of the day "Let It Be Done to Me" on the *Mercy Reigns* album.

VOCATION

SEPTEMBER 24

Ephesians 4:1-3

I, then, a prisoner for the Lord, urge you to live in a manner worthy of the call you have received, with all humility and gentleness, with patience, bearing with one another through love, striving to preserve the unity of the body and one Spirit…

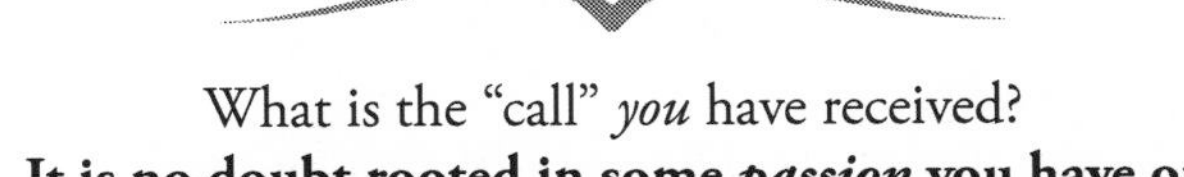

What is the "call" *you* have received?
It is no doubt rooted in some *passion* you have or *deep interest* as well as a *talent* you were blessed with.
It is never too *early* or too *late* to start *responding to that call.*

The call will lead you to *help* or to *serve* others.

This is what it's like to be a *follower* of Jesus, not simply a *believer.*

It's *not easy.* St. Paul ended up in prison and eventually put to death.
Jesus promised that his followers would be *persecuted.*

Despite the hardships, Paul urged us to treat others with *humility, gentleness,* and *patience.*

Do we *bear with one another to preserve the unity of the body of Christ*, or are we quick to *cast out* or *rejec*t those who differ with us?

We are *all* called to *work for unity.*

Jesus ate with the tax collectors and the sinners.

Do *we?*

Listen to the song of the day "All Are One" on the *Mercy Reigns* album.

SEPTEMBER

25 THE GREAT COMPASSION

Luke 9:2

He sent them to proclaim the kingdom of God and to heal [the sick].

Jesus sent his followers to proclaim the "kingdom of God."
What does *that* mean?

We know that Jesus stated his mission when he read from the prophet Isaiah in the synagogue: "He has anointed me to bring glad tidings to the poor. He has sent me to proclaim liberty to captives and recovery of sight to the blind, to let the oppressed go free." (Luke 4:18).

When those things occur, you have *peace, freedom, compassion, healing* and *justice.*
That's the "kingdom of God."

***That's* what his followers were called to proclaim.**
So are *we.*

The *kingdom of God* is a *state of being* where *compassion* reigns, not *power.*
It's when *everything* and *everyone belongs.*

We *proclaim* it whenever we *channel God's love to others* to bring them *healing* and *wholeness.*
For that to happen, we need to *let go* of our *attachments* to all the stuff we *falsely believed* would bring us happiness.

All you *really need* is God's *unconditional Love* and it's *already inside you* ready to be *tapped.*
You won't need to bring anything else on your journey.

Listen to the song of the day "Make Me a Channel" on the *Listen to Your Heart* album.

LIFE CHANGING QUESTION

Luke 9:18-20

Once when Jesus was praying in solitude, and the disciples were with him, he asked them, "Who do the crowds say that I am?" They said in reply, "John the Baptist; others, Elijah; still others, 'One of the ancient prophets has arisen.'" Then he said to them, "But who do you say that I am?"

For me, that was a *life-changing* question.
When I finally took it to heart and delved deeply into the Gospels and spent my own time "praying in solitude," I was hooked.
I couldn't get enough of who Jesus was – and *is.*

There was *no one* like him.
He became a *friend*, an *inspiration*, and my life started to *change.*
There was a sense of *excitement* and *inner peace*,
as well as *unrest* because *change* is *not* easy.
But it's *necessary* to *grow.*

Nothing would *ever* be the same.
First came a call to pick up my guitar which I hadn't touched it in ten years. Then, out of nowhere (*now–here*) came song-writing, then a return to school, then recording an album of original music about my spiritual journey titled, *Listen to Your Heart.*
Then came a change of careers, from radio news to ministry. First youth ministry and social justice ministry, then jail ministry and chaplaincy.
I now have four albums of original, inspirational music.
My life has been *utterly changed for the better*, totally by the grace of God.
How *amazing* that the more I discover about ***Jesus***,
the more I discover about my ***true self.***
So, who do ***you*** say Jesus is?

Listen to the song of the day "Pour Me Out" on the *Give Praise and Thanks* album.

SEPTEMBER

27 SHINE YOUR LIGHT

Luke 8:16

"No one who lights a lamp conceals it with a vessel or sets it under a bed; rather, he places it on a lampstand so that those who enter may see the light."

There is a Light inside each of us.
It was installed by our Creator who is Light: "God is light, and in him there is no darkness at all." (1 John 1:5).

Jesus was the embodiment of this Light bringing life to the world.
He allowed this Light to shine fully and completely through him. "The light shines in the darkness, and the darkness has not overcome it." (John 1:5).

The Light of Christ brought healing, forgiveness, mercy, comfort and compassion to the world. The Light also dispelled the darkness of oppression and hatred.

As followers of this Light, *we, too,* are meant to be *beacons* in the world.
We are called to shine the Light of Christ.
We can't do this by our own strength, but only by turning over our self-centered control to a *Higher Power.*
The holders of worldly power will not react well to this Light.
They tried to extinguish it by crucifying Jesus.

You will also experience persecution.
As Jesus said, "If they persecuted me, they will also persecute you." (John 15:20).
The Light of Love cannot be defeated!

The resurrection continues through all those who continue to shine the Light.
Allow the Light to shine through *you.*

Listen to the song of the day "May I Be Light" on the *Listen to Your Heart* album.

LET LOVE LEAD YOU

Luke 9:9

"Who then is this about whom I hear such things? And he kept trying to see him."

Herod was a ruthless ruler who had John the Baptist put to death.

When Herod heard of the miraculous things Jesus was doing, he had to find him.

Herod was jealous.

He wanted to protect his power and status and was threatened by the attention Jesus was drawing.

Jesus attracted crowds of followers despite the fact that he *never wanted fame* or ever tried to draw attention to *himself.*

Now – two-thousand years later – there is *no name* in *history* that is *more* well-known than *Jesus.*

When you *live out your calling*, let your ego *diminish* and follow the path where God leads you – amazing things *will* happen.

You will be living as your *true self.*

What else could be *more* meaningful and fulfilling?

Listen to the song of the day "I Stand in the Light" on the *Mercy Reigns* album.

SEPTEMBER

29 LET GO

Luke 9:3

Jesus said to them, "Take nothing for the journey, neither walking stick, nor sack, nor food, nor money, and let no one take a second tunic."

These instructions from Jesus to his followers are rather extreme.
His point was that there should be no distractions to the mission at hand.
There should be no *attachments* to get in the way of spreading the gospel message.
That was their *top priority.*

***We* are meant to take up that mission, as well.**
While we aren't all expected to travel as lightly as the apostles, we are expected to be *mindful* of the *attachments* that *distract* us from being bearers of the Good News.
What is the *Good News?*
That *God loves all people unconditionally.*

Each of us needs to ask ourselves:
What is blocking me from being a channel of God's love?
The more material possessions I have, the harder it is to *not* be attached to them.
There is nothing innately bad about the things in and of themselves, it's my *attachment* to *them* that separates me from my mission.

Is there anything you would not let go of, if God asked you to?
You can only find wholeness and contentment in the Unconditional Love of God.
When you are *present* to this Love, *nothing is lacking.*

"The Lord is my shepherd; nothing shall I want." (Psalm 23).
So may you be *open* to *receiving* this Love which is *always offered.*
You only have to *accept* it.
It's also the only way to experience being your *true self* and *giving glory to God* at the *same time.*

Listen to the song of the day "Glorify You with Me" on the *Give Praise and Thanks* album.

BIG PICTURE

SEPTEMBER

30

Haggai 1:6

You have eaten, but have not been satisfied; You have drunk, but have not been exhilarated; have clothed yourselves, but not been warmed; And he who earned wages earned them for a bag with holes in it.

These are the words spoken by the prophet Haggai over 2500 years ago.

Isn't it amazing that they are still true?

Do we not still try to satisfy a *spiritual* yearning with food, drink, fashion and material stuff that will *wear out* and *disintegrate?*

How will we find satisfaction for this spiritual yearning?

By loving God and our neighbor as ourselves.

Love is all you *need.*

In John 6:68 the apostle Peter said to Jesus, "You have the words of eternal life."

Read the words of Jesus and follow his ways.

Then, in the midst of struggles, your life will be filled with love, joy, peace, patience, kindness and goodness, both *now* and *forever.*

Listen to the song of the day "God Is the Goal" on the *Live to Love* album.

1 Happily Empty

Job 1:21

Job said, "Naked I came forth from my mother's womb, and naked shall I go back there. The LORD gave and the LORD has taken away; blessed be the name of the LORD!"

We *come into this world* with *no possessions* and we'll *leave it* with *no possessions.*
We come in with no prestige and whatever we have will stay here when we leave.
We enter this life with no power and whatever
power we attain here, stays here when we exit.
Yet many people spend their lives as though *possessions,*
prestige* and *power* are *all that matters.
What a *delusion!*

Sometimes it takes a *traumatic loss*, a *major suffering*,
to *wake us up* from that delusion.
For me, it was a *growing discontent* with my radio news
profession and a *traumatic ruptured appendix* episode.
Our egos must be forced to *let go of control*, so that our *true selves* can begin
to *emerge*, so that we can start *going-with-the-flow* of God's will.

What is *God's will?*
It's the path of *love* and *goodness.*
It's *channeling* that Love and Goodness *through each of us.*

As Jesus said when asked to specify what the most important commandment was: "You shall love the Lord, your God, with all your heart, with all your soul, and with all your mind. This is the greatest and the first commandment. The second is like it: You shall love your neighbor as yourself." (Matthew 22:37-39).
To love is all that matters.

Listen to the song of the day "Slow Me Down" on the *Mercy Reigns* album.

LOVE IS THE WAY

OCTOBER

2

Psalm 27:8

"Come," says my heart, "seek God's face";
your face, Lord, do I seek!

What are you *seeking?*

Your heart is *yearning* for *something.*

There is always a desire to fill the void, to satisfy what is not being satisfied by anything we've tried before.

Could it be that *God* is the only One who can satisfy that yearning in your heart?

Are you seeking God or are you seeking to satisfy this desire for fulfillment through *things of this world?*

Maybe if we searched for God's face in *all* people, in *all* creatures and in *all* creation – including *ourselves* – we just might find the *fulfillment* we are looking for.

How differently we would treat all things!

The kingdom of God would truly *be at hand!*

Listen to the song of the day "I Surrender" on the *Live to Love* album.

OCTOBER

3 BE PRESENT

Luke 9:61-62

Another said, "I will follow you, Lord, but first let me say farewell to my family at home." [To him] Jesus said, "No one who sets a hand to the plow and looks to what was left behind is fit for the kingdom of God."

Jesus is again making it clear that the only way to the kingdom of God is the *now.*
When you are *living in the present moment* the *reign of God is experienced.*

God is *always present*, it is *we* who often *are not.*
Our minds are *mulling over the past* or *fretting about the future* while the only time that is *real* – right *now* – is *missed!*
Jesus used the metaphor of someone who is plowing the land but is looking behind to see what has already happened. Jesus says to do the proper job, you must be focused on what is happening *now.*
The kingdom of God is really *an experience.*

It is available *now* – *inside* you and *around* you.
"Asked by the Pharisees when the kingdom of God would come, Jesus said in reply, "The coming of the kingdom of God cannot be observed, and no one will announce, 'Look, here it is,' or, 'There it is.' For behold, the kingdom of God is among you." (Luke 17:20-21)."
"Among you" is sometimes translated as "within you."

So allow Jesus to lead you to the abundant life of the kingdom of God.
Follow his example of how to live.
The time to follow him is *this moment*, and *this moment*, and *this moment*, etc.
Breathe.
When you are *present* the *love of God will live in you* and *lead your actions.*

Listen to the song of the day "Breathe On Me" on the *Listen to Your Heart* album.

RESTORATION – NOT REVENGE

Luke 9:52-55

Jesus sent messengers ahead of him. On the way they entered a Samaritan village to prepare for his reception there, but they would not welcome him because the destination of his journey was Jerusalem. When the disciples James and John saw this they asked, "Lord, do you want us to call down fire from heaven to consume them?" Jesus turned and rebuked them.

Years of differences between the Jews and Samaritans resulted in the Samaritans shunning Jesus. Two of Jesus' disciples asked him if they could call on God to *destroy* the Samaritans in *retaliation.*

Isn't this the *usual* human reaction – to *attack* those who have wrongly treated us?
Tit for tat.
It's been going on for years, and *years*, and *years*.
Violence* perpetuates *violence.
Jesus' answer to his disciples' question was a stern *"no."*

It takes a "non-dual" mind, a consciousness that is able to hold all things without separating and dividing, to be able to respond in a *new, nonviolent* way.
It is from this mind that Jesus said, "Love your enemies." (Matthew 5:44).
Instead of seeking *revenge,* what if we all asked for the grace to respond to those who wrong us with *both* compassion *and* a conviction for justice?
Perhaps then the world would change *one person at a time.*

***Be* the *change* that you want to see in the world!**

Listen to the song of the day "Salvation" on the *Live to Love* album.

OCTOBER

5 BE THE GOSPEL

Luke 10:1-2

After this the Lord appointed seventy[-two] others whom he sent ahead of him in pairs to every town and place he intended to visit. He said to them, "The harvest is abundant but the laborers are few; so ask the master of the harvest to send out laborers for his harvest."

Jesus wanted his followers to *spread the Good News of God's unconditional love* for *all* people.
So he sent them forth, but *not* alone.
He sent them in *pairs*.
Of course, at the time it was likely much safer to travel with a companion.
I also think this speaks of the need to *not* be a *lone ranger.*

We *all* need support!
As followers of Jesus today, we are all called to share the Good News with others and to find support in others who also want to share that mission.
You and I are being sent as *missionaries of God's love.*
In this regard, *actions* speak much louder than *words.*

Look to the example of St. Francis of Assisi.
Legend has it that he told one of his friars, "Preach the gospel always and when necessary use words."
Whether he said it or not, it fits how Francis lived his life.

The question for each of us to answer is: *Would others know who Jesus is by witnessing our words and actions?*

Listen to the song of the day "Make Me a Channel" on the *Listen to Your Heart* album.

OCTOBER

6

SILENT PRESENCE

Luke 10:41-42

The Lord said to her in reply, "Martha, Martha, you are anxious and worried about many things. There is need of only one thing. Mary has chosen the better part and it will not be taken from her."

Martha was upset that she was waiting on all the guests while her
sister Mary was sitting beside Jesus listening to his teachings.
Why was she not helping?
Doing the work to make sure the guests are taken care of is a *good* thing but what Jesus was getting at was Martha's *motivation.*

Why was she "anxious and worried about many things"?
What was Martha's *motivation* for her serving?
Was she serving from her sense of being an *instrument of God's love – or* serving her ego's need for *recognition?*
Was she carrying out the *call in her heart* with *joy*
or was she *judging others with a critical eye?*
Jesus seems to recognize that *Mary* was carrying out the call in her heart, which was to *listen* to him.

There is a time for *action* but there is also a time for *listening*, especially when the speaker is *Jesus.*
At that time, women would not have been welcome to sit at the feet of a teacher like Jesus. That place would have been reserved for *men* only. But Mary followed the calling in her heart and Jesus was quite comfortable with it.

Serving is commendable and necessary, but it is critical that we spend time listening to the Inner Voice for direction so we know *how* to *serve.*
What is God saying in *your* heart?

Listen to the song of the day "Listen to Your Heart" on the *Listen to Your Heart* album.

OCTOBER

7 DEEP GRATITUDE

Psalm 139:1-2, 7, 13-14

O LORD, you have probed me, you know me: you know when I sit and stand; you understand my thoughts from afar. Where can I hide from your spirit? From your presence, where can I flee? You formed my inmost being; you knit me in my mother's womb. I praise you, so wonderfully you made me; wonderful are your works!
My very self you knew.

King David is said to have written this Psalm in praise of God around 3000 years ago.

The same God who brought the universe into being, who wills everything to be or it would simply disintegrate, also willed you and me into being.

Scripture tells us that we are made in God's image and that our Loving Creator looks on all of creation as "good."

You and I are children of this wonderful God!

How can we celebrate this and honor God with our lives?

Bring your searching heart to the God who knows you *through* and *through.*

Listen to the song of the day "How Wonderful to Me" on the *Live to Love* album.

AWAKEN

Luke 11:13

"If you then, who are wicked, know how to give good gifts to your children, how much more will the Father in heaven give the holy Spirit to those who ask him?"

Who is the most *loving* person you know?

Well then, wouldn't God have to be that loving, and *infinitely more?*

Jesus' message to his followers was that God would never give us something that would harm us, no more than a loving parent would.

However, while like a loving father or mother to us, God is *not* like *Santa Claus.*

Just because we ask for something that we *believe would make us happy,* does *not* mean that what we ask for *would in fact do so.*

God wants us to *experience* Love, *know* Love and *be* Love.

When we are *both* receiving God's love *and* giving it away, we are fully *present* to the moment.

This "free-flow" of *giving-and-receiving* love is basically the personification of the Holy Spirit.

When we ask for more of *that,* get ready for *life to the full.*

We would then become the fully unique gift to the world that we were intended to be, right *now*, in *this moment.*

What could be a better gift than *that?*

Listen to the song of the day "The Spirit's Alive" on the *Give Praise and Thanks* album.

OCTOBER

9

BLESSINGS ABOUND

Psalm 111:2-3

Great are the works of the Lord, to be treasured for all their delights. Majestic and glorious is your work, your wise design endures forever.

Look around you at the glory of God's creation.

Whether it be the beauty of the changing colors of the leaves on the trees; or the blue sky; or the brilliance of the sunrise or sunset; or the intricate design of a tiny flower; or the song of a bird – God's glory is on display *everywhere.*

All of creation is giving God glory *in its very being.*

God's glory is also in full display in ***you***, *just as you are.*

You give your Creator glory by just being *yourself.*

So *awaken* to God's glory all around you, be *present* to it all, and *give thanks!*

May your life be a response in gratitude to God!

Listen to the song of the day "Give Praise and Thanks" on the *Give Praise and Thanks* album.

TOP PRIORITY

OCTOBER 10

Galatians 1:10

Am I now currying favor with human beings or God? Or am I seeking to please people?

Many times we get lost in a world that tells us we must conform to its ways to be somebody.
Our culture dictates certain criteria that defines "success" in its eyes, usually involving power, prestige and possessions. While those things bring "success" in the world, they have nothing to do with success in the eyes of God.

Love **is God's measuring stick.**
When we love, we are discovering our *true selves.*
Many times we can get side-tracked from being our *true selves* by seeking to please our parents, our friends or our culture.
When you are disconnected from your true self, you are also disconnected from your Source.
In the Gospel of John, Jesus likens God to the "vine grower" and himself as the vine: "I am the vine, you are the branches. Whoever remains in me and I in him will bear much fruit, because without me you can do nothing." (John 15:5).

In reality, we can never truly be disconnected from God, but *consciously* we can be.
When that happens, you will never bear the "fruit" that you were meant to bear.
We must be able to be silent enough to hear the gentle whisper of God in our hearts.
That whisper is also from our true selves yearning to emerge.

Listen for the Voice that tenderly tells you that you are loved fully and completely *as is.*
Rest in this knowledge.
Experience it.
Let it warm your heart.
How do you wish to respond?

Listen to the song of the day "The Way You Are" on the *Mercy Reigns* album.

OCTOBER

11

LET IT BE DONE TO ME

Luke 11:10

"For everyone who asks, receives; and the one who seeks, finds; and to the one who knocks, the door will be opened."

Jesus assured us that God *answer*s our prayers.

In other words, *God wants the best for you.*

Do you *believe* that?
It's true.

Jesus instructed us to pray to God, "Your kingdom come, your will be done, on earth as in heaven." (Matthew 6:10).

So instead of asking God for things that you want, why not ask God to give you the *guidance* ("holy Spirit") to ask for what is *best* for you so that God's kingdom would be more evident *here and now?*

Why not ask that *God's* will and desires for you become *your* will and desires.

God's desires will always lead you to *fulfillment*, *peace* and *joy* because you will experience all of that in the very *process* of following the Holy Spirit's guidance.
It's *in* that process that you experience your *wholeness* and *true self.*

When you ask for God's will and truly open yourself to receiving it, you *are* receiving it.

When you truly *seek* it, you *are finding* it.

Trust the *process.*

Listen to the song of the day "Let It Be Done to Me" on the *Mercy Reigns* album.

GIVE ALL

Galatians 1:22-24

And I was unknown personally to the churches of Judea that are in Christ; they only kept hearing that "the one who once was persecuting us is now preaching the faith he once tried to destroy." So they glorified God because of me.

With these words, St. Paul was giving witness to his amazing transformation.
He had gone from being a brutal *persecutor* of Christians to being a passionate *preacher* of the *way of Christ* to all people.
Paul's turnaround began with a mystical experience of the risen Christ while on the road to Damascus (Acts 9).
His transformation didn't happen all at once, but over the next few years as he spent time with the apostles.

We are all *works in progress.*
Everyone is on a unique *spiritual journey.*
God will use all our experiences for our good.
A perfect model to follow on your spiritual journey is Jesus.
Following him will lead you to *life to the full*, but it will *not* be easy.
When you try to love all people and stand up for those who are oppressed and left out, many times *you* end up being persecuted yourself (as was Paul).
***Love wins*, if not in this life, certainly in the eternal realm.**
Jesus showed us that death leads to *resurrection.*
This is true not only in death but *all through life* in the many *"dyings"* and *"risings"* that we experience in the light of Love.
Letting go of the *false selves* our egos have created and then allowing Love to *transform* us will lead us to our *true selves.*

What a perfect way to give glory to God!

Listen to the song of the day "Glorify You with Me" on the *Give Praise and Thanks* album.

OCTOBER

13 GLORY BE

Ephesians 1:11-12

In him we were also chosen, destined in accord with the purpose of the One who accomplishes all things according to the intention of his will, so that we might exist for the praise of his glory.

St. Paul's words are those of a *transformed man.*
He was changed from a man "breathing murderous threats" (Acts 9:1) to a man preaching the gospel.

His change came by way of *Grace.*
When Paul *least deserved it,* he had a *mystical experience* of God's *unconditional love.*

He knew that this Love was *freely given* and that it was *freely given* to *all* people.

Each one of us is God's beloved daughter or son.

Each of us is *chosen.*

How are *you* meant to exist for the *praise of God's glory?*

By simply ***being you.***

Accept that you are loved *just as you are.*
Then live your life from that place of belovedness.
Be* that Love to *all people* and *every living thing.

Be a *channel* of God's *love and peace.*

What could be more *glorious* than *that?*

Listen to the song of the day "Changed" on the *Give Praise and Thanks* album.

LACKING NOTHING

OCTOBER 14

Psalm 62:2

My soul rests in God alone,
from whom comes my salvation.

This sounds trite, but is *profound.*
It's the key to life to the full.
Only *God* will bring you to *completion* and *fullness* (salvation) and it can happen *now.*
Do not read this verse through the lens of "reward and punishment."
Read it through the lens of "unconditional love."

God is *not out to get you,* but to *love you!*
God wants you to awaken into the fullness of the unique expression of God-self.
Other than God, nothing – *absolutely nothing* – can lead you to the fulfillment of your purpose.

How can you "rest in God"?
Practice *contemplative prayer*, spending time in silence, allowing all distractions and thoughts to drift away so that your soul will experience truly resting in the Divine Presence.
The more you do this, the more that Silent Presence will manifest itself amidst the struggles and busy-ness of your day.

"Be still and know that I am God." (Psalm 46:11).

Be still and know that I am.

Be still and know.

Be still.

Be.

Listen to the song of the day "I Will Give You Rest" on the *Live to Love* album.

OCTOBER

15 GLORY EVERYWHERE

Psalm 113:3

From the rising of the sun to its setting let the name of the LORD be praised.

What if we started each day in gratitude to God?

With the opening of our eyes after a night of sleep, what if we said, "**Thank You** for another day. What a gift!"

What if as we turned on the shower and the warm water flowed on our heads, we said, "**Thank You,** what a gift!"

With the first bite of breakfast, "**Thank You**, what a gift!"

Driving to work, "**Thank You**, what a gift!"

Doing our work, "**Thank You**, what a gift!"

Driving home, "**Thank You**, what a gift!"

First bite of dinner, "**Thank You**, what a gift!"

Watching the sunset, "**Thank You**, what a gift!"

Talking to a loved one or friend, "**Thank You**, what a gift!"

Laying our head down on the pillow at the end of the day, "**Thank You**, God, for this day, what a gift!"

Oh, and thank You for my life!

How might I give my life in praise of You?

Listen to the song of the day "Pour Me Out" on the *Give Praise and Thanks* album.

SAVED

Galatians 5:1

For freedom Christ set us free; so stand firm and do not submit again to the yoke of slavery.

The "yoke of slavery" that most of us grapple with is the attachment to *possessions, beliefs*, and *unjust systems.*

St. Paul experienced freedom in Christ.

Following the *ways of Jesus* gave him *new life.*

He realized that death would not be the end. There would be *resurrection.*

Paul saw this pattern of *dying and rising* repeated throughout life in all our struggles.

The *valley of darkness* would be followed by *glorious mountaintops.*

Paul also realized that Jesus showed him how to live his life by *giving it away,* serving others, *letting go of attachments to things that don't last.*

This also set him free *daily.*

Paul realized that Christ revealed that *there is eternal life* and that *God loved all people with an infinite love that could not be defeated.*

You did not have to earn salvation, but it was a *free gift.*

It was all *Grace!*

Paul's message to the Galatians and to *us* is to *accept* these revelations, *live them*, and *be free.*

Listen to the song of the day "I Want to Follow You" on the *Listen to Your Heart* album.

OCTOBER

17

DIVINE HARMONY

Psalm 98:1

Sing a new song to the Lord,
who has done marvelous deeds.

Every morning birds wake up and start singing as if to say, *"I am! I am! I am!"*

By their song they proclaim God's handiwork.

By their music they add beauty to our lives.

They don't dwell on past disappointments or fret over future concerns.

Take a moment to see all the wonders and blessings
poured out in abundance in your life.

Each *breath* is a *gift.*

All of nature and creation is a *gift.*

It's *all* gift.

You don't have to prove your worthiness to *receive* these gifts.

You don't have to prove your worthiness to be *accepted* into God's kingdom.

You already belong.

Be you.

Sing *your* song!

A symphonic masterpiece is in progress and *your* notes are *eternally essential.*

Listen to the song of the day "Sing a New Song" on the *Live to Love* album.

AWE AND WONDER

Psalm 19:2

The heavens declare the glory of God;
the sky proclaims its builder's craft.

A friend of mine who is quite the astronomy buff once pointed out a bright star in the sky overhead and mentioned that it is 200 *trillion* miles from Earth.

That's right: ***trillion.***

And that's one of the closer stars!

***Ponder* that for a while.**

It is truly *mind boggling.*

Yet the same awesome God who made the magnificent universe also made *you.*

You are a part of this wondrous creation.

Your very existence *declares the glory of God!*

The stars shine in praise of the Creator.

May you also shine in praise by *simply being you* in all your *beautiful uniqueness.*

Listen to the song of the day "How Magnificent, Wondrous and Glorious" on the *Mercy Reigns* album.

OCTOBER

19 DIVINE PURPOSE

Ephesians 2:10

For we are his handiwork, created in Christ Jesus for the good works that God has prepared in advance, that we should live in them.

God has uniquely crafted each of us.
We have been created by *Love itself.* ("God is love" – 1 John 4:8).

We in turn have a choice to either live in our uniqueness by using our gifts and talents for our *own* purposes (*ego*-centered), or for *God's* purposes (*Love*-centered).

We have the opportunity to be a *channel* of our Creator's unconditional love.

Jesus showed us the way: *Die* to *self-serving* desires so that *God's* desires can *rise* in us.

***Let go* of the ego's craving for power, prestige and possessions, all fixed on building a *false self,* so that our *true self* can be revealed.**

You are God's "handiwork" – God's beloved work of art – *just as you are.*

Allow that understanding to *settle in your soul.*

How will you use your gifts and talents to do good works?

Know* your *belovedness.

Feel the *peace* that it brings.

Then simply do the *next loving thing.*

Experience being in the flow of God's love right *now* and truly have life to the *full.*

Listen to the song of the day "Make Me a Channel" on the *Listen to Your Heart* album.

HIGHER CALLING

OCTOBER

20

2 Timothy 4:16-17

At my first defense no one appeared on my behalf, but everyone deserted me. May it not be held against them! But the Lord stood by me and gave me strength, so that through me the proclamation might be completed and all the Gentiles might hear it.

Just because you do the right thing *doesn't* mean you'll be rewarded by *this world.*

Many times you will be persecuted by the *powers that be.*

When you see an injustice, a Higher Power will touch your heart to do something.

How *else* can *God's will be done?*

In today's scripture, St. Paul tells us of a time when everyone deserted him.

Sometimes we have to go it *alone.*

Sometimes the road to fulfilling your destiny will be a lonely road.
It may look dark and dangerous.

When you follow your *calling* you will feel an *inner strength, comfort and peace.*

The Love that made you is leading you to fulfill a compassionate purpose greater than you could ever have devised on your own.

Listen to the song of the day "Take the Road Less Traveled" on the *Live to Love* album.

21 BE MESSENGERS OF MERCY

Luke 10:8-9

"Whatever town you enter and they welcome you, eat what is set before you, cure the sick in it and say to them, 'The kingdom of God is at hand for you.'"

Jesus sent out his messengers to tell everyone the *Good News* that would *free* them and *heal* them.

It's very simple: God's love is *unconditional.*

It does *not* have to be *earned.*

It does *not* depend on your *performance* or *achievement.*

God's love is such that it *pours itself out for the beloved, even to the point of death.*

Jesus showed us this in his path to the cross.

Pure love *heals.*

It *comforts.*

It *restores.*

Be a *channel* of this Love.

Pass along God's mercy, forgiveness and compassion to others not only through your words but through the *way you live your life.*

Whenever you do this, the *kingdom of God is at hand.*

Listen to the song of the day "Mercy Reigns" on the *Mercy Reigns* album.

BE FREE

Luke 12:15

Then he said to the crowd, "Take care to guard against all greed, for though one may be rich, one's life does not consist of possessions."

Jesus consistently said things *counter* to what our *culture* upholds as the ideal.
Our society basically tells us that *greed* is *good.*
Advertising is based on convincing us that we *need more.*
We *need* whatever item is being peddled.
Our society idolizes those who are rich and famous.

Yet, to "not covet our neighbor's goods" is one of the Ten Commandments.
Coveting is *promoted* by our capitalistic and consumerist culture.

While the possessions *in and of themselves* are not evil, they easily become *attachments*, keeping us focused on *holding on to them* while distracting us from our *calling* in life.

Jesus demonstrated how to *both* enjoy things *and* to let them go.
It was not an "either-or" scenario, but a "both-and."
You can *both* enjoy the possessions you are presented with *and* let them go, giving them freely to those in need.

This *freedom from attachments* is *key* to being able to *go with the flow of the Spirit's call in your life.*

Otherwise, you are imprisoned by your possessions, shackled from acting in love, and distracted from the Divine Presence in each moment.

Listen to the song of the day "Turn Off the Noise" on the *Listen to Your Heart* album.

OCTOBER

23 PRACTICE PRESENCE

Luke 12:37

"Blessed are those servants whom the master finds vigilant on his arrival."

Jesus says that "blessed" (or *happy*) are those who are *willing to serve* and are *living in the moment.*

This, again, is *counter-culture.*

Our society glorifies *being served*, not *serving.*

When we *let go* of our egos, realize that there is a *bigger picture*, and live for a *larger purpose than ourselves*, we are able to see the needs of others.

But only if we are *present.* (Or, as Jesus says, "vigilant.")

We must practice silencing our minds' *constant* thoughts.

When we are not *rehashing over and over* the past, or *fretting over and over* about the future, we can actually *be present* where the *Divine Presence always dwells* and is, therefore, *always arriving.*

When we are *present* we find the *Master* (God), our *true selves*, and *happiness* as well.

Listen to the song of the day "Slow Me Down" on the *Mercy Reigns* album.

UNMERITED PRESENT

Ephesians 3:7

Of this I became a minister by the gift of God's grace that was granted me in accord with the exercise of his power.

Have you ever looked back something good that happened in your life and wondered *how in the world it ever came to pass?*

If anyone had told me 20 years ago that I would one day be ministering to the sick, the imprisoned, and the poor, and would have four albums of original music along with published books of daily devotions, I would have said you were crazy.

At that time, I was quite miserable delivering bad news as a radio news anchor.
I felt like I was *acting*, like I was a *phony*.
While I was good at the job, I knew deep inside that I was
meant to do something else, but I had no idea what.

I had to run out of all of my *own* options to find relief first, before I finally *surrendered.*
That happened late in the afternoon on the first Friday of March in 1997 when I "heard" what would become life-changing words in my heart.
It was the start of a slow process that led me to ministry.
Today, I have never felt more *inner peace, contentment* and *joy.*

It has all happened by *God's grace and power.*
I am *very thankful!*

What is *your* calling?
Are you listening to God's *silent voice in your heart?*

Listen to the song of the day "Listen to Your Heart" on the *Listen to Your Heart* album.

OCTOBER

25 THE BLUEPRINT OF LOVE

Luke 13:18-19

Then he said, "What is the kingdom of God like? To what can I compare it? It is like a mustard seed that a person took and planted in the garden. When it was fully grown, it became a large bush and 'the birds of the sky dwelt in its branches.'"

There is something *beautiful* happening *unbeknownst* to
many who are lost in the *rat race* of the world.
Like a *tiny* mustard seed sprouting *unnoticed*, the
kingdom of God* is *growing in our midst.

Make no mistake, it *is* growing.
An eternal Love is the catalyst.
Some people are *tending* to this growth, *choosing* to *nourish* the seed by being *consciously present* to it. These are the people who are *loving God and their neighbor as themselves.*
These are the people *living the Beatitudes.* (Matthew 5:3-12).

In today's scripture verse above, Jesus is again making it clear that the kingdom of God begins in the *here and now*, not in some *future* heaven.
We *each* can *cultivate* the growth of God's kingdom through
acts of forgiveness, mercy and compassion *this very day.*

Receive* God's unconditional love, *allow* it to *change* you, then *pass it along.

Like the mustard seed, you must *surrender* a *static life*
in order to be *transformed* and *grow.*

Say "yes" to participating in Love's flourishing.

Listen to the song of the day "Love God" on the *Live to Love* album.

LOVE IS CALLING

Romans 8:22-23

We know that all creation is groaning in labor pains even until now; and not only that, but we ourselves, who have the first fruits of the Spirit, we also groan within ourselves as we wait for adoption, the redemption of our bodies.

All that God has created shares in our yearning for more.
St. Paul says that not only is creation "groaning in labor pains"
but that each of us also "groan within ourselves as we wait for adoption."
Our innermost being is yearning for completion and wholeness,
which I think is the true meaning of "salvation."

While our culture offers all kinds of things to satisfy this inner-groaning, like material possessions, power, prestige, celebrity, alcohol, sex, etc., the solution is spiritual.
The Rolling Stone's Mick Jagger sang, "I can't get no satisfaction."
That's because God is the only One who can satisfy
this groaning for completion and wholeness.

God is the only One who can fill the hole in your heart and tell you who you are.
God alone can satisfy your *inner groaning.*
You can find your way to God now by following Jesus who told us
that he was "the way, the truth and the life." (John 14:6).

Following Jesus will require making changes in the way we live our daily lives.
It will require following him in how we vote, treat others, how we eat,
what we buy, what we watch on social media, etc.
It will not be an easy road, but one full of life, adventure and fulfillment!

Listen to the song of the day "Breathe On Me" on the *Listen to Your Heart* album.

OCTOBER

27

LET YOUR LIGHT SHINE

Ephesians 5:8

For you were once darkness, but now you are light in the Lord. Live as children of light.

When each of us believes our *ego* is the *center of the universe* and everything revolves around "me," we are in *darkness.*

It is living a *delusion* since in reality we are all *one* with God and unified as one Body of Christ.

When we let go of this delusion and the "false me" of my ego (that little voice that keeps saying, "What's in it for *me?*") then God's light shines ever more brightly through us.

The more our egos *diminish*, the more Christ *grows* in us, the more God's Light *shines.*

Loving God, may *Your* will be done, not *mine.*

May I be a reflection of Your Light to the world.

Listen to the song of the day "May I Be Light" on the *Listen to Your Heart* album.

LOVE PREVAILS

Romans 8:38-39

For I am convinced that neither death, nor life, nor angels, nor principalities, nor present things, nor future things, nor powers, nor height, nor depth, nor any other creature will be able to separate us from the love of God in Christ Jesus our Lord.

St. Paul at one time was a persecutor of Christians and most certainly was a collaborator in causing their deaths. As he carried out his persecution, Saul (as he was known at the time) thought he was doing God's *will.*

However, he experienced a total change through the *unmerited grace* of God. Saul had a mystical encounter with the risen Christ as he traveled one day on his way to capture more Christians. (Acts 9:1-22).

After the incident, his life slowly changed and became an amazing, inspirational adventure that continues to touch millions and millions of people. St. Paul (as he became known) wrote much of the New Testament.

How do we account for such a *radical* change?
St. Paul experienced the overwhelming, *unconditional Love of God in Christ.*

What he learned was that **NOTHING** (no matter what you've done) can separate you from the love of God in Christ.

That is *Good News!*
If you want to live an amazing, inspirational *adventure:* follow Christ.

Listen to the song of the day "Pour Me Out" on the *Give Praise and Thanks* album.

OCTOBER

29 DEATH TO LIFE

Romans 8:16-17

The Spirit itself bears witness with your spirit that we are children of God, and if children, then heirs, heirs of God and joint heirs with Christ, if only we suffer with him so that we may also be glorified with him.

You and I are *children* of God and heirs of God, "joint heirs with Christ."
You *know* this is true because the *Spirit bears witness* of this to your *heart.*
That is *Good News!*

St. Paul also tells us that this is "if only we suffer with him so that we may also be glorified with him."
When the unconditional love and compassion of God became flesh in Jesus, those with the wealth and power opposed him.
They *didn't want equal love and fairness for all.*

Jesus showed us true unconditional love and compassion, even when he was rejected and executed.
He showed us that the path of unconditional love is one of self-emptying, one of "dying to self" in order that our *true selves* can *rise* and be *vessels* of Unconditional Love to the world.

We are *called* to do this as followers of Jesus.
Be assured that through the hardships and suffering you encounter you *will* be *transformed!*
You will become whole ("holy") and experience a *peace that the world cannot give.* (John 14:27).

Life is a series of trials, *little deaths* and *resurrections.*
If we follow Jesus, New Life will always result!

Listen to the song of the day "Love Will Always Lead You Home" on the *Mercy Reigns* album.

HAVE FAITH

Ephesians 6:16-17

In all circumstances, hold faith as a shield, to quench all the flaming arrows of the evil one. And take the helmet of salvation and the sword of the Spirit, which is the word of God.

St. Paul uses imagery of a warrior battling spiritual attacks against us.

Notice he does *not* suggest doing any *violence.*

Your shield is your complete *trust* in God's *unfailing love.*

The only weapon Paul suggests using is the "sword of the Spirit, which is the word of God."

God's "word" will *always* be one of *unconditional love* for all.

It will always defuse negative attacks and lead you to the *fullness* of *who you are* – your *true self.*

If we immerse ourselves in the words of the prophets and of Jesus himself and then *live* those words, we will be able to deal with any adversity that comes our way and our lives will be *transformed.*

Then we will *become* the *transformation* that will help transform this world into the *Kingdom of God.*

This is our *mission.*

Listen to the song of the day "You'll Lead Me" on the *Listen to Your Heart* album.

OCTOBER

31 UNCONDITIONALLY LOVED

Philippians 1:6

I am confident of this, that the one who began a good work in you will continue to complete it until the day of Christ Jesus.

St. Paul speaks to us from experience.

He had been changed from a man who persecuted others in the name of religion to a man who would die to spread the news that God is an *unconditional* lover.

An encounter with the unconditional love of the risen Christ is what changed him.

He had done *nothing* to *merit* such an encounter!

God has more than enough time to work with you and wants nothing more than for you to know that you are *whole* and *complete* as you *are.*

You* are God's *beloved.

Do not compare yourself to *anyone.*
You already *are* and have *always been* a masterpiece of God.

There is *nothing* you have to *do* to be *more* wonderful or worthy.

You were *born* wonderful and worthy!

Open yourself to Christ and allow him to lead you.

Focus your attention on each moment as the process unfolds.

Then the kingdom of God will truly be *at hand!*

Listen to the song of the day "Changed" on the *Give Praise and Thanks* album.

THE CALL TO SERVE

NOVEMBER

I

Romans 6:8

"If, then, we have died with Christ,
we believe that we shall also live with him."

Everything gives itself over in death so that there might be new life for another.

You see it in nature.
Animals give themselves over as food for others.
Leaves wither and fall from trees, dying to nurture the ground below.

Jesus spoke of this when he said, "Unless a grain of wheat falls to the ground and dies, it remains just a grain of wheat; but if it dies, it produces much fruit" (John 12:24).

As humans, we have a *choice* whether to willingly enter this dynamic, life-giving cycle *each* day.

Or we can choose to spend our time seeking to gain power, prestige and possessions.

That path leads to a *dead end.*

Jesus modeled the *self-emptying path* that leads to *abundant life*, a path that exemplified, "Not my will but God's be done" (Mark 14:36; Luke 22:42).

For when we *die* with Christ, letting go of our egos' desires in deference to serving another, we *rise* with Christ.

When we do this, we get *life to the full* both *now* and *forever*.

Listen to the song of the day "Glorify You with Me" on the *Give Praise and Thanks* album.

NOVEMBER

2

LOVE RULES

Luke 14:5-6

Then Jesus said to them, "Who among you, if your son or ox falls into a cistern, would not immediately pull him out on the Sabbath day?" But they were unable to answer his question.

Jesus had just healed a man in front of the Pharisees (the religious leaders) on the Sabbath day.

This broke the Jewish law which banned any sort of work on the day of rest.

Jesus broke that law.

However, Jesus told them that *love* is *always* the *determining factor* when it comes to our actions.

Love wins out over the law.

The Pharisees (and many people today) are stuck in an "either-or" mind.

For them, the *law* is the *determining factor.*

Either you keep the law and are *in*, ***or*** you don't and are *out.*

Jesus is saying we need a "both-and" mind.

I can ***both*** keep the law ***and*** break it when ***Love*** **says to do so.**

Following the rules can make someone "right" but also *self-righteous* and *heartless.*

Compassion and forgiveness require an *open mind* and a *transformed heart.*

Listen to the song of the day "Mercy Reigns" on the *Mercy Reigns* album.

ETERNAL GAZE OF LOVE

Philippians 3:17

Join with others in being imitators of me, brothers and sisters, and observe those who thus conduct themselves according to the model you have in us.

It may sound arrogant of St. Paul to tell the Philippians to be more like him, but Paul is a man who was completely transformed.

He knew that he could take *no credit* for that change.

Paul had been a brutal *persecutor* of Christians but became a man totally dedicated to *following* and *serving* Christ. His transformation came about through a mysterious encounter with the risen Jesus (Acts 9).

Paul realized that it was *Grace* that saved him, nothing he *merited* or *earned.*

Then Paul *became* the one *persecuted!*

Despite the persecution, he had found a new inner peace and joy.

Paul discovered that in the *process* of *letting go* of his *ego's* desires, the life of Christ *rose* within him.

This is the *path* to a truly *abundant life* and to living as your *true self.*

If you want the same contentment and fullness of life, *imitate Christ.*

I assure you, you will be *changed* for the *better.*

Listen to the song of the day "Changed" on the *Give Praise and Thanks* album.

NOVEMBER

4

FREE TO BE

Psalm 22:31-32

And I will live for the LORD; my descendants will serve you. The generation to come will be told of the Lord, that they may proclaim to a people yet unborn the deliverance you have brought.

From generation to generation, each of us is given the responsibility and the joy to pass along the Good News.
What is this *Good News?*

You do not have to *prove* yourself to God.
You cannot *earn* or *merit* God's love.

It has already been forever given!

Jesus showed us that even *killing him* could not stop God's love!
Forgiveness was *free!*
Death does *not* win.
The resurrection shows us that God's love triumphs.

Let the experience of this Love overwhelm you!
Let it inspire you to pass it on to all people and all of creation!
Following Jesus and serving others sets us free to be our true selves.
In following Jesus we all have the way to peace, fulfillment and everlasting happiness.

That is "deliverance."
That is the way to the Kingdom of God!
That is *Good News!*

Pass it on.

Listen to the song of the day "I Want to Follow You" on the *Listen to Your Heart* album.

POUR ME OUT

Philippians 2:5-7

Have among yourselves the same attitude that is also yours in Christ Jesus, Who, though he was in the form of God, did not regard equality with God something to be grasped. Rather, he emptied himself.

St. Paul's advice is that we have the same *self-emptying* attitude of Christ.

The idea is to stop operating out of your *ego* which is always wanting to *make itself look good and special.*

That is a very *self-centered* way of living.

Instead, St. Paul advises us to *let go* of those *egocentric desires.*

Such desires are usually *"wants"* and not *"needs."*

When the ego is allowed to *fade to the background* the *true self is able to emerge.*

The paradox is that when you let go of your attachments (those things that you think you must have in order to be you), you are able to discover your *genuine self.*

Then you can live and bloom from the *self-less* place of *Love.*

As Jesus stated, "Unless a grain of wheat falls to the ground and dies, it remains just a grain of wheat; but if it dies, it produces much fruit." (John 12:24).

Listen to the song of the day "Pour Me Out" on the *Mercy Reigns* album.

6 SOURCE OF MEANING

Philippians 2:13

For God is the one who, for his good purpose, works in you both to desire and to work.

When we *yearn* to do something for the sake of doing *good*, the *Source* of that yearning inside us is *God.*

Sometimes Christians call this the movement of the Holy Spirit.

In order to allow this yearning to well-up from the Ground of Being deep in our hearts so that we act on it, we must *surrender* to it.

We must *detach* from all the *distractions* and *glittery enticements* luring us with the false promise of satisfaction.

We must *let go* of our ego-generated *false selves.*

Nothing will satisfy the deep yearning you feel but God.

Or we could say, nothing but *Love*, since God *is* Love (1 John 4:8).

When you are living from this foundation of Love, your desires and your works will bear fruit.

You will be *taking part in God's creative flow.*

You will see amazing things happen because you will be living as your *true self!*

Listen to the song of the day "Show Me…Me" on the *Listen to Your Heart* album.

CALLED TO SHARE

NOVEMBER **7**

Romans 12:6

Since we have gifts that differ according to the grace given to us, let us exercise them.

What are your talents?

Each talent is a *gift* from God.

Whatever passions you may have, they are *gifts* from God.

They were all freely given to you, *built in* at birth.

How are you developing them and cultivating them?

That is *your* responsibility.

Your talent might be singing, artistry or dancing – or such things as critical thinking, math ability, public speaking, teaching, cooking, hospitality, healing or making others laugh.
You may have a talent to make money or to make others feel welcome.

Whatever our gifts are, St. Paul in today's scripture verse is urging us to use them to make the world a more *loving, merciful, forgiving, compassionate* and *just* place.

The kingdom of God is on the verge of *breaking into the present moment* if only we cooperate.

This is also the key to finding your *true self* and the *path to true joy and freedom.*

Listen to the song of the day "Listen to Your Heart" on the *Listen to Your Heart* album.

NOVEMBER

8 TRUST

Luke 17:5-6

And the apostles said to the Lord, "Increase our faith." The Lord replied, "If you have faith the size of a mustard seed, you would say to this mulberry tree, 'Be uprooted and planted in the sea,' and it would obey you."

So many times we want answers but Jesus *seldom gives them.*

Instead, he gives parables and sayings that disrupt the *usual patterns* of our thinking.

The important thing is to *live the question* so that you can be transformed in the process.

Answers alone *bypass* the importance of the *journey* and the *discoveries* God wants to *reveal* to *each* of us.

Jesus seems to be saying to stop looking for answers and simply *believe* in God's providence.

Let go of your *need* to be *in control*, your *need* to be the center of the universe.

You just may be *surprised* at the amazing and *seemingly impossible* transformations that await you!

Listen to the song of the day "I Stand in the Light" on the *Mercy Reigns* album.

COME TOGETHER

NOVEMBER

9

1 Corinthians 3:9

For we are God's co-workers.

This life is *not* about carrying out our *ego's* desires.
It's not about our own *personal fulfillment.*
Each of us begins our lives mistakenly believing that he or she is at the *center* of the universe.

It's painful coming to the realization that we are not.
We all start out believing it is all about "me."
The sooner we realize in our hearts that it's really about *God* and what *God is doing*, the more peace and joy we will experience.

As Jesus said, "For whoever wishes to save his life will lose it, but whoever loses his life for my sake will find it." (Matthew 16:25).

The ego *must surrender* so a *bigger life* can *rise*.

We are all part of something bigger than ourselves.

There is a grand creation *in progress* and we are invited to be *co-creators.*

How else will God's kingdom come on earth as it is in heaven?

This is the purpose of our lives.

When we *go with the flow* of this *Loving Process* we become *singers of the sacred song* and *dancers in the divine dance.*

Let Love lead you *now.*

Listen to the song of the day "Shall We Sing" on the *Listen to Your Heart* album.

NOVEMBER

10 DIVINE INTIMACY

1 Corinthians 3:16

Do you not know that you are the temple of God, and that the Spirit of God dwells in you?

It seems like we spend a lot of time *looking* for God, trying to *find* God, when God is already with us!

It is true that God is in all of Creation, but God is also as close to you as your very *breath.*

The Creator of the universe is *intimately close* to you, in your inner-most-being.

Open* yourself to that *awareness.

Set aside some time for silent meditation and quiet walks.

Empty yourself of the desires to possess things and people and *allow* God to fill you *more* and *more.*

In the process, you will *experience* being the true you, the beloved daughter or son of God.

Listen to the song of the day "Breathe on Me" on the *Listen to Your Heart* album.

MAKE YOUR MUSIC

NOVEMBER

11

Psalm 98:4

Shout with joy to the Lord, all the earth;
break into song; sing praise.

All the earth (and universe) is *continuously being filled* by God's *life-giving energy.*

Grace *abounds!*

Love is perpetually being poured out.

All creation returns this love by *giving back all that it is,* by *being itself to the fullest.*

We as humans seem to be the only created creatures that have a *choice* as to how to *respond* to such Unconditional Love.

As St. Irenaeus said, "The glory of God is the human person fully alive."

How are we being "fully alive"?

When we *drop all our masks,* all the *pretenses* and *ego-created constructs.*

When we *receive* God's love and then *share it* with the world we live as our *true selves* and our lives become songs of praise.

Sing *your* song.

Listen to the song of the day "Sing a New Song" on the *Live to Love* album.

NOVEMBER

12 GOD IS PRESENT

Luke 17:20-21

Asked by the Pharisees when the kingdom of God would come, he said in reply, "The coming of the kingdom of God cannot be observed, and no one will announce, 'Look, here it is,' or, 'There it is.' For behold, the kingdom of God is among you."

I think this is an amazing teaching from Jesus since my experience tells
me that most people think that the "kingdom of God" is something
that comes when we *die* or at the *end of time.*
Don't most people think of the "kingdom of God" as heaven –
a final reward that we hopefully reach one day?
**That would make your life your own little "private salvation project"
(Thomas Merton's term) and avoid any real responsibility
to anyone else or the rest of creation.**

This teaching of Jesus is probably ignored by most people because it short-circuits the notion that God's kingdom is *distant – out there* somewhere, sometime in the future.
**It requires a whole new mindset to understand this
and it just might *transform* you.**
This is a very important teaching to sit with and to ponder.
"For behold, the kingdom of God is among you."
That means *now.*
This line is also sometimes translated, "The kingdom of God is within you."
If God *is* Love, then the Source of Love is *among* you and *within* you.
Are you aware of this?
If not – why?
Let this awareness sink into your whole being.
May others experience this kingdom through *your* presence!
When you know the kingdom of God is *here*, it *requires you to respond.*

**Listen to the song of the day "Make Me a Channel" on
the *Listen to Your Heart* album.**

LOOK AND LISTEN

Psalm 37:4

Find your delight in the LORD
who will give you your heart's desire.

What is your "heart's desire"?
I'm thinking lots of people can say what their *minds' desires* are,
but I'm not so sure about their *hearts'*.

This type of desire would seem to be one that would satisfy a person's *soul yearning.*

I think we all have a *deep yearning* for something that will
fill us and make us *whole* and *complete.*
Something is *missing.*

Most of the time, we try to satisfy these *primal pangs* with *material things.*
It works for a while, but not long.

Your *heart's desire* can only be satisfied by *God*, or the *Highest Form of Love.*
To experience this, we must first *relinquish our self-centered desires.*
In the *on-going-process* of this *letting-go*, we begin to uncover our heart's desire.

How to begin?

By *being present* to the *Divine Presence.*

Practice *letting go of everything*, and simply *be.*

Peace and contentment can be experienced right *now.*

Delight in God's Presence and see what happens.

Listen to the song of the day "I Surrender" on the *Live to Love* album.

NOVEMBER

14 BECOMING YOUR TRUE SELF

Luke 17:33

"Whoever seeks to preserve his life will lose it,
but whoever loses it will save it."

Life is a process of *letting go.*

It's just the *opposite* of what our egos and our culture tell us.

They say *grab all you can* and *stockpile* it and *define* yourself by it,
whether it is *money, material possessions, degrees or titles.*

**Jesus says that if you *cling* to these things you will never discover
your *true self*, the life that you were meant to have.**

All those things will sooner or later deteriorate and eventually disintegrate.

When you are willing to *release* those things from your grasp, enjoying
them for what they are, but not defining yourself by them,
you will actually discover your true self, the *you* that God *intended.*

**You are ultimately a *child of God* and *loved infinitely* for no other reason
than *that.***

**Listen to the song of the day "Turn Off the Noise" on
the *Listen to Your Heart* album.**

AWE AND WONDER

Psalm 150:6

Let everything that has breath
give praise to the Lord! Hallelujah!

The Love of God is what energizes *everything that is.*

God's grace is flowing *everywhere.*

God's *constant, never-changing* love is what makes all things exist.

Through *being* all things give *praise* to God.

A tree is praising God each second by whole-heartedly *being a tree.*

Stop and truly *be presen*t to God.

***Awaken* to the Divine Presence *within you* and to your oneness with all that is.**

The Maker of the universe who *willed you into existence* loves you with an *eternal* love that is *unconditional – just as you are.*

This is *salvation.*

***Accept* it.**

God *is with you.*

May your life, *this* day and *forever* more, be a resounding "Hallelujah"!

Listen to the song of the day "How Magnificent, Wondrous and Glorious" on the *Mercy Reigns* album.

NOVEMBER

16 YOUR HOLY LONGING

Luke 18:40-43

Jesus asked the blind man, "What do you want me to do for you?" He replied, "Lord, please let me see." Jesus told him, "Have sight; your faith has saved you." He immediately received his sight and followed him, giving glory to God.

Do you pursue Jesus as the blind man did? – who, even after being told to be silent, kept calling out to Jesus as he was passing by?

What do *you* want Jesus to do for *you?*

Have faith that he will provide you what you *need.*

However, what you *need* may be different than what you *want!*

Notice how Jesus was *not* concerned with any *belief system* the blind man had, only that he had *faith* that Jesus would *heal* him.

Notice also that when the man was given sight, he *followed* Jesus.

The outcome was a *changed life.*

It's not just *physical* healing that Jesus wants for us, but *inner* healing and *transformation*, so that we also *follow* him with a *transformed* way of life that leads to *wholeness* and *inner* peace.

Listen to the song of the day "You'll Lead Me" on the *Listen to Your Heart* album.

FIND YOUR LIFE

Revelation 3:17-18

For you say, 'I am rich and affluent and have no need of anything,' and yet do not realize that you are wretched, pitiable, poor, blind, and naked. I advise you to buy from me gold refined by fire so that you may be rich, and white garments to put on so that your shameful nakedness may not be exposed, and buy ointment to smear on your eyes so that you may see.

Those who are wealthy are not bad people because of their wealth.
The question is, what is their *top priority?*
Our first motivation must be to love God and love our neighbor as ourselves.
Wealth does make this challenging. It's easy for wealth to blind us to the needs of the poor and make it appear that we are doing just fine without God as well.
The book of Revelation is rich in symbolism. The writer says we all need God's grace and spiritual healing, so that we can see as God sees.
God scolds us to change our ways as a parent whose motive is love.
God wants to *save* us, not *punish* us.
God wants us to experience the wholeness of living as our true selves.
In the Gospel of Luke, Jesus says: "For the Son of Man has come to seek and to save what was lost."
Jesus showed us how to *die to ourselves*, to let go of our ego's desires.
He showed us that such *dying* always leads to new life.
How am I lost?
What "affluence" is blinding me to those in need of my compassion?
How is this blocking me from living as my *true self?*
Like gold from a refiner's fire, it sometimes takes an experience of suffering before we are able to drop our attachments to things that don't matter so that we can attend to the things that do.

Listen to the song of the day "The Way You Are" on the *Mercy Reigns* album.

NOVEMBER

18 ALIVE

Psalm 96:11-12

Let the heavens be glad and the earth rejoice; let the sea and what fills it resound; let the plains be joyful and all that is in them.

All things give glory to God in their *being-ness.*

All that has form is simply being itself to the full and thereby praising God's *wondrous creativity.*

We humans seem to be the only living creatures that have a *choice* as to *how* we will be *ourselves.*

We have a conscious choice in *how* we will live in the form we've been given.

God loves *everything* and *everybody.*

In your *belovedness*, how do you *respond?*

How do you *express* God's love for you to the world?

What do you enjoy doing with your creative talents?

Joyfully *live these questions* and you will discover your *true self!*

Listen to the song of the day "Listen to Your Heart" on the *Listen to Your Heart* album.

FOLLOWING JESUS

NOVEMBER

19

Luke 19:41-42

As he drew near, he saw the city and wept over it, saying, "If this day you only knew what makes for peace–but now it is hidden from your eyes."

Jesus wept as he looked over Jerusalem.

He probably knew that his earthly journey might end there.

The people did not *get* it.

They didn't understand that the kingdom of God was *not* about power, might and prestige but about *mercy, forgiveness, compassion, humility and oneness.*

Jesus would confront the domination systems of religion and government with truth, but in a *non-violent* way.

He would willingly give the ultimate example of God's *unconditional* love, forgiveness and solidarity, allowing himself to be crucified so that he could look upon all of his persecutors and say, "Father, forgive them, they know not what they do." (Luke 23:34).

Now we are called to follow his example of *self-emptying* love, compassion and oneness with *all.*

As Jesus looks over the world today, is he weeping?

How am I working for peace, compassion and solidarity in a non-violent way?

How am I using my gifts and talents in following Jesus?

Listen to the song of the day "Salvation" on the *Live to Love* album.

NOVEMBER

20 OMEGA POINT

Luke 21:6

"All that you see here–the days will come when there will not be left a stone upon another stone that will not be thrown down."

Jesus' words predicting the destruction of the temple are just as true about *any material thing we have or will ever have.*

That beautiful, shiny sports car will one day be a rusted piece of *junk*; that beautiful multi-million-dollar mansion will be in *ruins*; that high-fashion, designer clothing will be in *tatters*.

Our *power, prestige* and *possessions* will all *disappear*, either slowly over time or quite suddenly when our earthly lives end.

Our* kingdoms will *disintegrate* but *God's* kingdom will *never end.

It starts *now* for those who are willing to experience it!

Jesus said when you love God and your neighbor as yourself you are not far from God's kingdom. (Mark 12:34).

When we *accept* God's Love and *share* it we are part of an *Everlasting Flow* of on-going creation moving toward a magnificent climax.

Are you living for something that is destined to *disintegrate*, or are you living for something that's *Dynamic* and *Eternal?*

Listen to the song of the day "God Is the Goal" on the *Live to Love* album.

THE TRUE YOU

Luke 21:17-19

"You will be hated by all because of my name, but not a hair on your head will be destroyed. By your perseverance you will secure your lives."

Jesus promised his followers that they would be persecuted.
When you preach love and equality for *all*, you can expect to be targeted by those who disagree with you, especially those in power.

Jesus also promised that if we *persevere in following him* our lives will be *saved.*
My advice is to please stop thinking of being "saved" as avoidance of hell.

God has no plans to punish anyone, only to *love all.*
That's what Love does!
"Whoever is without love does not know God, for God is love." (1 John 4:8).

Following Jesus puts you on the path to *wholeness.*
This path allows your *true self* to emerge from the chaos ("salvation").
Jesus will lead you *through struggles to new life.* He gave us the ultimate example in his death and resurrection.
Any struggle can lead to a deeper and fuller spiritual awareness and experience of God's love if we *let go of our ego's desires* and *go with the flow of Goodness.*

Death and defeat do *not* have the *final say!*
God's desire is that *each* of us has *life to the full.* (John 10:10).
It is then that we will have inner peace and joy even amidst the trials.

We will become more fully alive as Christ lives more fully in us.
What could be more important than to discover the true you as a beloved child of God?
That's who you are, right *now*, and *that* is something to be truly *thankful* for!

Listen to the song of the day "Lift Up Our Voices" on the *Give Praise and Thanks* album.

NOVEMBER

22 GIVE GENEROUSLY

Luke 21:1-3

When Jesus looked up he saw some wealthy people putting their offerings into the treasury and he noticed a poor widow putting in two small coins. He said, "I tell you truly, this poor widow put in more than all the rest."

How *attached* are we to our *stuff?*
How *preoccupied* are we with our *money?*

The "poor widow" was apparently able to *let go* of the *little* she had for the better of others.

She was willing to make a true sacrifice for the sake of *mercy.*

In God's economy, the more you *give,* the more you *receive.*

When you pour love into the world, it creates *ripples of goodness* that will return to you in *waves.*

Do you yearn to give of yourself to something bigger than yourself – to use your life to make a difference?

What* do you need to *let go* so your *true self* is free to *take flight?

If you give a *little* to God, you will get back a *little.*
If you give *all* that you are, you will get back *more than words can describe.*

Are you ready to start?
No better time than *now!*

Listen to the song of the day "Glorify You with Me" on the *Give Praise and Thanks* album.

EXPRESS YOURSELF

Revelation 4:11

"Worthy are you, Lord our God,
to receive glory and honor and power,
for you created all things;
because of your will they came
to be and were created."

Everything that *is* — is being animated by a *Creative Force.*

God is in the *being-ness* of *everything.*

When Moses asked for God's name, God is quoted as stating, "I AM" (Exodus 3:14).

God's very nature is *Existence* itself.

Science tells us that around 13.8 billion years ago, there was a big bang.
From one *small point* there was an explosion
from which the entire material world began.

The universe continues to expand today as God's creativity goes *on and on.*

Each of us is a part of this *creative-masterpiece-in-progress.*

Since God *is love* (1 John 4:8), the creative spark igniting it all is *Love* itself.

**We are invited to take part in this *on-going-creative-flow* of love.
That is our mission now and forever.**

Listen to the song of the day "How Wonderful to Me" on the *Live to Love* album.

NOVEMBER

24 VOCATION

Matthew 4:21-22

Jesus walked along from there and saw two other brothers, James, the son of Zebedee, and his brother John. They were in a boat, with their father Zebedee, mending their nets. He called them, and immediately they left their boat and their father and followed him.

The gospels were not written like news accounts are written by reporters today.
The writers of the gospels wanted to impart a *deeper* truth.

I'm thinking it's unlikely that James and his brother John simply *dropped everything* and walked away from their father and their livelihood when Jesus yelled out to them.
The deeper truth is they did eventually make a *radical choice* of following Jesus as their top priority.

It is a *life* choice.
It's *not* just a decision to *go to a particular church* or *agree to certain beliefs.*

To be a *Christian* is to *follow Jesus.*
That means *doing what he did.*

That means ser*ving the poor and troubled, all those on the margins.*
It means *feeding the hungry, welcoming the stranger, clothing the naked, caring for the sick, visiting the imprisoned.* (Matthew 25).

This is your *calling* as a human being: *Love one another.*

As Jesus said, "As I have loved you, so you also should love one another." (John 13:34).

Listen to the song of the day "I Want to Follow You" on the *Listen to Your Heart* album.

COMPASSION

John 1:47

Jesus saw Nathanael coming toward him and said of him, "Here is a true Israelite. There is no duplicity in him."

Jesus could read people very well.

Since he was fully committed to *emptying* himself in the *loving service of God*, he had the ability to see inside the hearts of others and to sense their motivations.

Jesus sensed that Nathanael had pure motivations and was not "two-faced."

How often do we really examine our *own motivations* as to *why* we do the things we do?

Here's a question to ask ourselves before we speak or act:

Am I motivated by loving and serving *God* or is my motivation to satisfy my *ego* and *its desires?*

If my motive is love, I enter into the *flow* of God's *goodness* and *creativity.*

Before I can ever judge *someone else's* motivations, I certainly need to be quite clear about my *own.*

This should keep me busy for the rest of my life.

Listen to the song of the day "God Is the Goal" on the *Live to Love* album.

NOVEMBER

26 GIVING GOD PRAISE

Psalm 50:23

Those who offer praise as a sacrifice honor me.

When a tree is being a tree, it is giving praise to God.

When a dog is being a dog, it is giving praise to its Maker.

They really have *no choice* in the matter.

You and I *do* have a choice.

We can choose whether we will be the unique people God made each of us to be, or whether we will choose to be someone else and wear masks pretending to be what we aren't.

When we take off the masks and are simply our *true selves*, we are the *unique person* God made us to be.

We sacrifice all the endless yearnings of our egos to be a *false self* catering to its own whims and glory.

When each of us is simply the unique masterpiece that God made us to be, we are *praising God.*

Be *you.*

***No one else* can do it!**

Listen to the song of the day "Give Praise and Thanks" on the *Give Praise and Thanks* album.

BE STILL 27

Jeremiah 7:23

This rather is what I commanded them: Listen to my voice; then I will be your God and you shall be my people. Walk in all the ways that I command you, so that you may prosper.

God speaks in the *here* and *now.*

"This is the time of fulfillment. The kingdom of God is at hand. Repent, and believe in the gospel." (Mark 1:15).

Jesus said this so that we would know that "God's reign" (or *God's dream for you*) is possible in *this very moment,* not just some distant time in heaven.

Our Loving Creator wants each of us to be a part of building the kingdom of God *right now*, using our gifts and talents to make a more compassionate world.

But it's not possible if we are holding on to past hurts or are constantly worrying about the future.

What are the "ways" God is asking *you* to walk in *now* so that you truly prosper, as in grow, feel vibrantly alive and become your true self?

There is no way you can know if you are not *listening* for God's *gentle, silent, inner voice.*

To do this, we must "repent" which literally means, "to turn" or to "change directions."

***Turn* to God.**

God is *always* speaking, but are we *listening?*

Listen to the song of the day "Slow Me Down" on the *Mercy Reigns* album.

NOVEMBER

28 FREE OFFER

John 5:30

"But you do not want to come to me to have life."

Jesus promises us the *abundant life*, but are we *choosing* it?

Our society claims the "abundant life" is about accumulating possessions, power and prestige.

Jesus says it's about "dying" to those desires because when you "lose your life" (let go of worldly success) in choosing to follow Christ you will paradoxically find your *real life* (true self) and inner peace. (See Matthew 16:25.)

Psalm 106:19-20 states, "At Horeb they fashioned a calf, worshiped a metal statue. They exchanged their glorious God for the image of a grass-eating bull."

Lord, what idol am I worshiping in place of You?

Am I trying to please *You*, or *others*, or my *ego?*

Listen to the song of the day "Listen to Your Heart " on the *Listen to Your Heart* album.

COUNTER CULTURE

NOVEMBER

29

Matthew 23:11-12

"The greatest among you must be your servant. Whoever exalts himself will be humbled; but whoever humbles himself will be exalted."

The way of life that Jesus espouses in the above statement is the *opposite* of what the popular culture espouses.

Instead of striving to *be served,* to *win* and *be on top*, Jesus says to strive *to serve those who are losing* and *be with them at the bottom.*

Instead of *ascending* society's ladder of success to gain power, prestige and possessions, Jesus says to *descend* that ladder and help the lowly, the poor and the outcast.

And the kicker is this: it's only through following Jesus' example of *self-emptying* for the sake of others that we paradoxically find *meaning, wholeness* and *completion.*

In other words, we find our *true selves.*

We become the unique manifestation of Love that we were intended to be.

The kingdom of God is at hand right *now*, in *this* moment, depending on which philosophy we choose.

I've tried both. One leads to a *dead end* while the other leads to *abundant life.*

***Each moment* provides us with a brand new opportunity to choose.**

Listen to the song of the day "Pour Me Out" on the *Give Praise and Thanks* album.

DIVINE COVENANT

Isaiah 42:6-7

I formed you, and set you as a covenant of the people, a light for the nations, to open the eyes of the blind, to bring out prisoners from confinement, and from the dungeon, those who live in darkness.

God spoke these words through the prophet Isaiah about the coming Messiah 700 years before Jesus was born.

Jesus would read these words and identify them with who he was and his mission.

God is very patient and creative, yearning to have us *all* take part in a wonderful love story that has been evolving for *billions* of years.

There were many characters in this story leading up to Jesus and there have been many after.

You and I are among the *current* characters in God's great, unfolding love story.

It's a unique part that only *you and I* can play.

If you are a follower of Jesus, then you are also meant to take part in his mission of *unconditional love and justice* stated above.

If you use your unique talents and passion to carry out this mission, you will reflect God's light to the world and will discover inner peace as well as your *true self.*

Listen to the song of the day "May I Be Light" on the *Listen to Your Heart* album.

WALK THE WALK

Matthew 7:24

"Everyone who listens to these words of mine and acts on them will be like a wise man who built his house on rock."

Listening to Jesus' words means more than just *hearing* them or *believing* in them.

That asks *nothing* of you.

We have to allow his words to *settle into our minds* and *hearts* so that they cause us to *change.*

His words should make a difference in our lives.

Jesus didn't just leave it at *listening to his words.*

He said we must *act* on them.

It would be helpful to make a regular practice of listening to Jesus' words in scripture.

Then after listening, we need to discern what the words are calling us to *do.*

What are his words saying to your heart?

When we do this and then take action, Jesus promises that even when the storms of life come, we will be grounded in a solid sense of *peace* and *security.*

Listen to the song of the day "You'll Lead Me" on the *Listen to Your Heart* album.

DECEMBER

2

LISTEN AND LIVE

Isaiah 48:17

Thus says the Lord, your redeemer, the Holy One of Israel: I, the Lord, your God, teach you what is for your good, and lead you on the way you should go.

As it was a *thousand years* before the Prophet Isaiah was born, as it was when Isaiah wrote this *700 years* before Jesus was born, as it is *today:*
God is our Redeemer.

God *was, is* and *will be* teaching and leading *all* people
because God is our *Loving Creator.*

Love* is what we *came from* and *where we are going.

God is leading us to the fullness of *who we are* and to the fullness of *Love.*

We have a great guide in Jesus.

He gave us the *model* for living our lives.

Numerous times he instructed those who listened to him to follow him.

We can still listen to him by reading the gospels.

We also can make time for *contemplative prayer.*

Set aside 15 to 20 minutes each day to sit in *silence*, allowing your thoughts to *drift away.*

Empty* yourself, *clear a space* for God to *fill.

Prepare to be taught what is for your *good* and to be led on the way you should go.

Listen to the song of the day "Make Your Way" on the *Mercy Reigns* album.

LIVING PRAISE

Psalm 145:10-11

All your works give you thanks, O Lord, and your faithful bless you. They speak of the glory of your reign and tell of your great works.

All living things are *themselves* with every ounce of their being.

They are *all in, as is.*

They don't wish they could be something else.

They do not look in envy on anything else, comparing or judging.

They have no schemes or ulterior motives.

They live with clear purpose.

Trees, birds, animals, insects, etc. simply are *themselves* to the fullest extent of their being.

In doing so they are in a *constant state of thanksgiving, giving glory to their Maker.*

May we be mindful of this and do the same in each moment of our lives.

Simply be *present.*

Be *yourself.*

It's the only way that God's kingdom can come and God's will can be done "on earth as it is in heaven."

Listen to the song of the day "Show Me…Me" on the *Listen to Your Heart* album.

DECEMBER

4

LIVE YOUR CALLING

Psalm 25:4

Make known to me your ways, Lord;
teach me your paths.

Isn't it true that we spend a lot of our time trying
to get *our* way and blaze *our* path in this world?

This is the agenda of our *egos.*

God's agenda for our lives will likely have *nothing* to do with our *ego's* agenda.

Which* agenda will lead to *inner peace* and *happiness?

You were made for a purpose.

Wouldn't it make sense that your Maker would know that purpose?

**How will you ever know *God's ways* and *God's paths* for
your life if you never ask your Creator to show you?**

God gives you free choice.

**Why not set aside silent time to listen to the small, gentle,
loving voice speaking inside your heart?**

**Listen to the song of the day "Listen to Your Heart" on
the *Listen to Your Heart* album.**

RADICALLY YOU

Matthew 11:18-19

For John came neither eating nor drinking, and they said, 'He is possessed by a demon.' The Son of Man came eating and drinking and they said, 'Look, he is a glutton and a drunkard, a friend of tax collectors and sinners.' But wisdom is vindicated by her works.

Appearances are *deceiving*.

John the Baptist was believed to be demented, someone mentally unbalanced.
Not so!
His consciousness was likely far advanced from others.

Jesus was not the mighty, warrior Messiah that the people expected.
He spent time with so-called sinners.
He was accused of being a glutton and a drunkard.

Who is Jesus to *you?*

It would be a good idea to re-read his words in the Gospels
and allow the words to speak to your soul.
They may call you to make some changes.

Fear not!
They are for your good.
God loves you *unconditionally!*
Open your heart to the One who wants to help you become the unique person that God intended.

Listen to the song of the day "Mercy Reigns" on the *Mercy Reigns* album.

DECEMBER

6

MERCY CHANGES EVERYTHING

Matthew 21:31

Jesus said to them, "Amen, I say to you, tax collectors and prostitutes are entering the kingdom of God before you."

The religious leaders did not take kindly to these words from Jesus. **They seemed to be the *only ones* whom Jesus criticized.** They were always focused on following the rules and *rigidly* holding people to those rules *without any measure* of *mercy.*

Instead of *unconditionally loving* their neighbors, they were *judging* them by a standard that was very "black and white." Of course, they were also *self-righteous*, pretending as though they did not have their own moral shortcomings.

On the other hand, the tax collectors and prostitutes had been breaking the rules but were trying to change their ways after encountering the unconditional love of Jesus. **It was *Mercy* that transformed their hearts, not *chastisement.***

When Love invites us to turn away from things that hurt our relationship with God and then to begin to mirror this unconditional love to the world, we begin to enter the kingdom of God *here and now.*

Instead of concerning myself over making *someone else* change, why not concern myself over how *I* can change in order to be more compassionate to others in need?

Listen to the song of the day "Radically Okay" on the *Mercy Reigns* album.

LOVE LIGHTS THE WAY

DECEMBER

7

Matthew 1:20

Behold, the angel of the Lord appeared to him in a dream and said, "Joseph, son of David, do not be afraid to take Mary your wife into your home. For it is through the holy Spirit that this child has been conceived in her."

Did you ever have something unexpected happen to you out of the blue that shook your foundation?

Sometimes we simply cannot make *sense* of it and there is *no way* around it.

These are the times that we need to rely on a *Greater Power* than our own.

Joseph, like Mary, must have been very much *attuned* to this Greater Power. Instead of clinging to a very rigid "either-or" mentality as in *either* Mary is a virgin and is not pregnant *or* she is not a virgin and she is pregnant – he opened himself to a "both-and" perspective: Mary is *both* a virgin *and* pregnant.

I think the real lesson here is: *Do we really believe that all things are possible with God* (as Jesus stated in Matthew (19:26)*?*

Joseph and Mary show us how to set aside *our* plans and be open to *God's* plans.

Are we open to the possibility that God wants to *give birth* to something *new* in our lives?

That "birthing" may involve an *unexpected change!*

Listen to the song of the day "Love Will Always Lead You Home" on the *Mercy Reigns* album.

DECEMBER

8 LET GO AND LIVE

Luke 1:38

Mary said, "Behold, I am the handmaid of the Lord. May it be done to me according to your word."

This is Mary's response to the angel's news that she would conceive by the Holy Spirit and give birth to the Son of God. Talk about a *major twist* in life plans!

Mary then gave us the *perfect example* of saying "yes" to God.

Wouldn't it be great if God would simply tell each of us what we needed to do to play a part in the unfolding kingdom of God on earth?

Perhaps God is doing *exactly that*, but *we aren't listening.*
For us to hear, we have to actually *be present.*
We have to open ourselves to the *Divine Presence.*

For that to happen, we have to *let go* of *ourselves.*

Each of us has to *die to self*, as in our "ego" self.
That is the only way our *true self* can rise.

A good practice is to set aside quiet time to *let go*, *detach* from our minds' *non-stop thoughts* and *constant chatter.*

We need to create a space to listen for God's *silent* voice.

Sit in silence for ten to twenty minutes and simply practice *letting go.*

What may sound like a *waste of time* will actually *change* your life for the *better.*

I *guarantee* it.

Listen to the song of the day "Let It Be Done to Me" on the *Mercy Reigns* album.

BE YOUR TRUE SELF

DECEMBER

9

Luke 1:45

"Blessed are you who believed that what was spoken to you by the Lord would be fulfilled."

Have you ever heard the voice of God in your heart?
Have you ever just had a thought pop into your mind *out of nowhere*,
that seemed to be an answer to a question or problem?
Did you ever get an internal *nudge* to do something for a good cause?

I've had many such promptings, but I *can't* say I have always *acted* on them.
Nor can I say that I have always believed that what I
thought I was hearing would *actually come to pass.*

Back when I was in the middle of my CPE (Clinical Pastoral Education) training, I was confused as to how my one calling to write and sing spiritual songs seemed to diverge from this new calling to *listen to* and *pray with* people who were sick.

Then one day while listening to a priest talk about a man who uplifted
a hospital patient with his guitar, I heard in my heart:
"What if I asked you to play for an audience of one?"

So, I talked to my CPE supervisor who said it would be a
great idea for me to bring my guitar to patient visits.

Today, many times I sing my songs to shut-ins and nursing home residents.

There are still times I have doubts when discerning God's messages and prompts, but I am *indeed blessed* when I look at prior promises *fulfilled.*

Listen to the song of the day "Changed" on the *Give Praise and Thanks* album.

DECEMBER

10 WONDROUS JOURNEY

Psalm 71:16-17

I will speak of the mighty works of the Lord; O GOD, I will tell of your singular justice. God, you have taught me from my youth; to this day I proclaim your wondrous deeds.

When I look back over my lifetime, I am in awe of the way God has worked.

As I've previously pointed to one of my favorite quotes by author and retreat leader Paula D'Arcy, "God comes to you disguised as your life."

It is a wondrous, amazing adventure of joys and sorrows through which we are embraced in Love.

Sometimes the aim of this Love is to *comfort us* and sometimes to *celebrate with us,* but *always* with the goal of *leading us to new life* and *wholeness.*

God – or *Love itself* – is *partnering* with *each* of us in a *grand plan of creation.*

The key is to *lean in, let go,* and *love.*

Listen to the song of the day "How Magnificent, Wondrous and Glorious" on the *Mercy Reigns* album.

RELEASE ATTACHMENTS

Luke 1:53

The hungry he has filled with good things;
the rich he has sent away empty.

Those who are hungry or *empty* will many times turn to God for help.

They are open to God's loving care because their backs are against the wall.

They have no other options.

Those who are rich or *filled* often believe they are just fine without God or are *completely unaware* of their true need of God.

Spiritually speaking, the *poor* can be *rich* while the *rich* can be *poor.*

Loving God, help me to allow You to dissolve my attachments to power, prestige or material possessions which block my relationship with You and all that You want to give me!

Listen to the song of the day "I Surrender" on the *Live to Love* album.

DECEMBER

12 LIFE GIVING WORDS

John 8:31-32

"If you remain in my word, you will truly be my disciples, and you will know the truth, and the truth will set you free."

What would you give to be *free?*

What about surrendering all the things your *ego* wants and handing them over to God?

After all, our Loving Creator is the One responsible for *everything* you have and *everything* you ever *will* have.

Instead of putting your trust in your *ego's* desires, why not put your trust in *God's* desires for you?

Jesus says to "remain in my word."

Do we do that?

Do we read his words in the gospels and spend time allowing those words to *sink in?*

He promises that if we do this he will lead us to truth and freedom.

You will be on the path of discovering your *true self.*

Listen to the song of the day "Singing My Song" on the *Live to Love* album.

YOU HAVE A PART

Jeremiah 17:5

Thus says the Lord: Cursed is the man who trusts in human beings, who seeks his strength in flesh, whose heart turns away from the Lord.

We spend so much time trying to *please other people* or fit into some *image* that *other people* or our *society* says is cool or "successful."

What does *God* say about us?

Why do we put so much credence in what others think or say and not our Creator?

There is a great quote in a documentary titled *The Human Experience* in which a rabbi says something to the effect that life is a grand musical composition and God is waiting for you to provide your note.

If you are trying to *please someone* or *even God* to somehow *justify your existence* – please stop!
You are *already enough.*
You are already *perfectly pleasing* to God, *just as you are.*

God loves you as a father or mother loves their child.

You don't have to do *anything* to *earn* that love.

The question is, how will you *be* the love that you are to the world?

Are you listening to God's tender voice in your heart, nudging you to *be* that *unique note* that only *your life can play*, or are you listening to human beings?

Love will lead you, if you allow it.

Listen to the song of the day "The Way You Are" on the *Mercy Reigns* album.

DECEMBER

14 CHILD OF GOD

Isaiah 49:1

The Lord called me from birth, from my mother's womb he gave me my name.

You are a creation of God, a beloved daughter or son.
God *loved you into existence.*

There is nothing you can do to change that unconditional love.

God wants nothing more than to love you *as you are* and *transform* you into a living channel of love.

Your Creator wants you to realize your full potential, not so much for your own personal fulfillment, but to take part in the *building of the kingdom of God* in the *here and now.*

That will require *letting go* of your *ego-centered* plans so God's plans can rise within you.

As Jesus put it: "Not my will but yours be done." (Luke 22:42).

What is God calling *you* to be?
***You, that's* what!**

To be your *true self* requires *letting go* of the *false self* your ego has worked so *hard* to construct.

Jesus showed us the way.

Resurrection is *assured.*

New life, your *true life*, is *promised.*

Listen to the song of the day "Breathe On Me" on the *Listen to Your Heart* album.

OPEN TO GRACE

DECEMBER

15

John 3:3

"Amen, amen, I say to you, no one can see the kingdom of God without being born from above."

The Pharisees were the religious leaders who had all the answers based on the *law.*
Jesus broke laws sometimes when he was healing people or when a loving response demanded it.

One Pharisee named Nicodemus came to Jesus in the secrecy of the night looking for *explanations.*
Jesus gave him something *beyond* religious *answers.*

Black and *white* theological information is a nice *foundation* to build on but information is not *transformation.*
Information cannot replace the *transformative journey* necessary to enter the kingdom of God in your midst.

For that there must be a *rebirth* from above.
We need a *new way of seeing*, a *new mind* as St. Paul would say (Romans 12:2).

When we are faced with dilemmas that black and white answers won't resolve, then we have the opportunity of *surrendering* to a Higher Power.
That's when we are open to experiencing the transforming unconditional love, mercy and forgiveness of God.

Then it's not about *our* goodness, but *God's.*

The kingdom of God is truly at hand right *here* and *now* for those who are willing to *die to themselves* so that God can *give birth* to something *new* and *lasting.*

Listen to the song of the day "God's Love Is All You Need" on the *Listen to Your Heart* album.

DECEMBER

16 ULTIMATE GIFT

John 6:27

"Do not work for food that perishes but for the food that endures for eternal life, which the Son of Man will give you."

Jesus said if you know *him*, then you know *God* (John 14:7).

He healed the sick, helped the poor and worked to free the oppressed.

Jesus *poured himself out* to *all* out of *unconditional love.*

His words and his very body in the Eucharist are meant to nourish us on our path to the fullness of life *now* and *forever.*

What *food* are *you* working for?

Our culture offers food that promises you happiness but instead creates an *insatiable appetite* for *more* and *more* that *never satisfies.*

I promise you that if you *read* and *ruminate* on Jesus' words, then *follow his ways*, you will find an *enduring peace* and *joy.*

You will begin to experience the kingdom of God right *now.*

For the kingdom of God is available *in your very midst* (Luke 17:20-21).

Listen to the song of the day "Pour Me Out" on the *Give Praise and Thanks* album.

UNIFY

John 15:5

"I am the vine, you are the branches. Whoever remains in me and I in him will bear much fruit, because without me you can do nothing."

Sometimes our egos can get carried away and believe it is all about *me*,
that the universe revolves around *me* and *my desires.*

Power, fame, and wealth can intoxicate us to the point
that we don't have a thought about God.
At some point there will be a great setback or suffering when the
delusion of power, prestige and possessions will become evident.

None* of those things *last!
When they crumble or can't bring us through a personal tragedy,
we can either fall apart or fall into the loving arms of God.
Our Loving Source will *never* abandon us.

By nurturing our connection with God
we will bear the fruit that God always intended.
Each of us will *live-out* the true manifestation of God that only each of us can be.
You will be the *unique* you, a branch unlike any other.
Then you will produce "much fruit."
It's only through our *conscious connection* to our Source
that we can truly find peace and joy.

One sure way, is to *follow Christ* who said he was the vine.
Listen to his words.

May you rest in the knowledge that *you* are one of
the many branches on the One Vine.

Listen to the song of the day "All Are One" on the *Mercy Reigns* album.

DECEMBER

18 DIVINE PARADOX

John 12:24

"Amen, amen, I say to you, unless a grain of wheat falls to the ground and dies, it remains just a grain of wheat; but if it dies, it produces much fruit."

This is one of Jesus' most *profound* statements and expresses a core teaching.

It is only through *dying* that we are *born* to *new life.*

This is true *all through* our earthly lives, not just at the *end.*

Whenever I *let go* of my *ego's* desires *God's* desires for me can come to light.

You can either live for your ego's insatiable desires and be trapped in a never-ending cycle of wanting *more and more* or you can surrender and let your ego *go.*

The *paradox* is that when you allow your ego to *die* your *true you* will start to *live.*

New life will sprout in abundance and you will be amazed at how little *you* had to do with it.

What will you do with *your* gifts and talents?

Your ego's desire will be to use them to build *its* kingdom, which will lead you to a cycle of dissatisfaction.

God's desire is that you use your gifts and talents to build *God's* kingdom, a place of love, mercy, forgiveness and compassion, leading you to deep joy and freedom.

Listen to the song of the day "Salvation" on the *Live to Love* album.

DIE TO LIVE

Psalm 16:11

You will show me the path to life, abounding joy in your presence, the delights at your right hand forever.

Are you on "the path to life?"
Are you living with *purpose* and *joy?*

It's hard to *always* be joyous, but when you are truly experiencing joy you are *totally present* to the *moment at hand.*
You are totally engrossed in what you're doing.
You are totally focused on whatever is happening.
You are totally *conscious.*

This means all the distractions must dissolve.
How often are our minds instead *lost* in the *noise* of constant *thoughts, judgments and worries?*
We are not present to the Divine Presence at all!

We all need a guide in life.
What better guide is there than Jesus?
His ministry was a model for us in how to "let go."
We are called to "die" to our ego's desires so that we can truly live.

Try sitting in silence and allow your thoughts to drift away.
Simply sit with the Source of all that *is*, and *allow* your path to life to *unfold.*

This path will no doubt lead you to make changes, to take risks, to *leave* something, someone or some way of life behind.

It will be *in* the change – *in the letting go* – that you will be transformed, and *in* that *transformation* you will experience "abounding joy!"

Listen to the song of the day "Take the Road Less Traveled" on the *Live to Love* album.

DECEMBER

20 PERSEVERE

Acts 20:24

I consider life of no importance to me, if only I may finish my course and the ministry that I received from the Lord Jesus, to bear witness to the gospel of God's grace.

I truly believe each of us needs to read St. Paul's words above as if we were saying them about *ourselves.*

What ministry did *you* receive from Jesus?

If you prefer, what ministry did you receive from *God?*

Or, how are you uniquely sharing unconditional Love in the way you are living your life?

We are *all* called to "bear witness to the gospel of God's grace."

How beautiful, to bear witness to the *good news* of the *gratuitous* and *unmerited* abundance of love that God *pours out* upon us!

Be present* to the *moment, receive* this Love and then *share* it through your *gifts, talents* and *passion.

That will require *letting go* of your egos' *insatiable desires* so that your *true self* can *emerge.*

Take a few minutes to *rest* in the Presence of Infinite Grace.

Trust the process.

Listen to the song of the day "God Is the Goal" on the *Live to Love* album.

YOU ARE INVITED

DECEMBER

21

John 15:16

"It was not you who chose me, but I who chose you and appointed you to go and bear fruit that will remain."

We all start out in life believing that we are the center of the universe and all things are here to cater to our every whim.

It's a good way to *start out.*

Babies need constant care and attention to know they are loved and accepted.

As we grow, we come to realize that we are *not* the center of the world.

That takes *"dying to yourself"* – *letting go* of egocentric desires – and coming to know that God is at the center of all that is.

It is not about *me* and *my story*, but about God and God's *story.*

Each of us has been loved into existence by God to be tiny reflections of the One who made us.

Each of us has been chosen to bear the unique fruit that only each of us can bear and then to share it with all.

Each of us is called to take part in the cosmic dance of creation.

Listen to the song of the day "Shall We Sing" on the *Listen to Your Heart* album.

22 THE WAY

Acts 5:19-20

But during the night, the angel of the Lord opened the doors of the prison, led them out, and said, "Go and take your place in the temple area, and tell the people everything about this life."

The apostles had been thrown in jail for preaching about the resurrected Christ. An angel freed them and told them to "tell people everything about this life."
This life.

The angel *didn't* say to tell people everything about a set of *beliefs, practices,* or *rules.* **Jesus showed us the way of life that would free us *now*, bring us salvation *now*, help us to live as our true selves *now*, help us to experience the kingdom of God *now.***

Jesus said, "I am the way and the truth and the life." (John 14:6).
The early Christians were first called followers of the "Way" (Acts 22:4 and 24:14).
It was a *way* of *life.*

The rules and guidelines are a great place to start and a necessary foundation, but don't get stuck there.

The question is: Are we living the *way of Jesus?*
For that to happen, the love of God, the *Way,* must *transform our hearts.*

Are we living examples of *mercy, forgiveness, compassion and equal justice for all?*
Are we loving our neighbors as well as our enemies?

Each of us is called to live the *Way.*

Be a part of the transformation!

Listen to the song of the day "I Want to Follow You" on the *Listen to Your Heart* album.

LIVE TO LOVE

John 5:44

"How can you believe, when you accept praise from one another and do not seek the praise that comes from the only God?"

In our mainstream culture, *ego* is *king.*
It's all about being *first* and *winning.*
It's also about the *praise* and *adulation* that comes with it.
When the *praise from others* is *what we want the most,*
we know our *egos* are in *charge.*
The *ego* and *its desires* can *never* be *satisfied.*

***Who* are we trying to please in the way we live our lives?**
Our *friends?* Our *parents?* Our *employer?*
Pleasing them can make you feel good, but it can lead
you *completely away* from your *purpose in life.*

Why did God make you? Why are you here?
It's certainly not to "accept praise from another."
In today's scripture verse, Jesus says the only praise that
matters is the praise that comes from your Creator.
That praise comes when you are *being you.*

For this to happen, your *self-centered ego* must *diminish* so your *true self* can *emerge.*
Then you will reflect the Love of God to *others* and *all*
creation through the use of your gifts and talents.

God's praise will then rain down upon you, and you,
in turn, will praise God by your *very being.*
Now *that's* something to *believe in!*

Listen to the song of the day "Glorify You with Me" on
the *Give Praise and Thanks* album.

DECEMBER

24 INNER VOICE

Luke 1:46-47

And Mary said: "My soul proclaims the greatness of the Lord; my spirit rejoices in God my savior."

Mary said *'yes'* to God and the *Word became flesh* in her.

How will the Word become flesh in *you* this Christmas?

When we empty ourselves of our selfish desires and *allow* God to fill us and Christ to live and grow *in us* we end up realizing *who we really are* – the beloved son or daughter of God!

We also find our calling.

Author Frederick Buechner said that you would find your vocation *"where your deep gladness and the world's deep hunger meet."* (*Wishful Thinking: A Theological ABC*)

It is in *that place* where each of us can *proclaim* the greatness of God Who saves us and completes us!

Listen to the song of the day "Listen to Your Heart" on the *Listen to Your Heart* album.

DECEMBER

INCARNATION 25

John 1:1-5, 14

In the beginning was the Word, and the Word was with God, and the Word was God. He was in the beginning with God. All things came to be through him, and without him nothing came to be. What came to be through him was life, and this life was the light of the human race; the light shines in the darkness, and the darkness has not overcome it. And the Word became flesh and made his dwelling among us, and we saw his glory, the glory as of the Father's only Son, full of grace and truth.

On this day as we celebrate the Word becoming flesh in Jesus, we continue to reflect on how the Word is becoming flesh in us.

Remembering the words of John the Baptist (John 3:30), how might each of us *decrease* so Jesus can *increase?*

May the life of Christ continue to grow in you so that you might become the unique expression of God that you were meant to be.

That's your call.
Embrace **it.**
Be **it!**

A peaceful and joyous Christmas to you!

Listen to the song of the day "God Is" on the *Give Praise and Thanks* album.

DECEMBER

26 GREAT AWAKENING

Matthew 7:14

"How narrow the gate and constricted the road that leads to life. And those who find it are few."

Freedom is wonderful, but sometimes it causes us to be shackled in the chains of *unlimited choices.*
With so many choices it can lead to *egos-gone-wild.*

If your ego is in charge, no amount of power, prestige or possessions will be enough to satisfy.

What gives you *life?*
What is it that truly gives you *inner joy, contentment* and *peace?*
What are the *many things* that you need to say *no* to so you can say *yes* to the *one thing* that will *set you free?*

We are *attached* to *many things.*
One exercise in *letting them go* is the practice of *presence.*

Simply sit in *silence.*
Let your mind be *still.*

Listen to God's silent voice in your heart, then go where it leads you.

You may not hear any words.
God's language is silence.

You'll carry it with you.
Take *one step at a time* on the narrow path to freedom.

Listen to the song of the day "Turn Off the Noise" on the *Listen to Your Heart* album.

THE FLOW OF GRACE

DECEMBER **27**

Matthew 5:3

"Blessed are the poor in spirit,
for theirs is the kingdom of heaven."

Our culture says: "Happy are you who are rich in power,
prestige and possessions for yours is the kingdom of this world."

Jesus says, "Happy are you who are *attached* to *nothing*,
for yours is the *kingdom of heaven*, right *now.*"

***Freedom and inner peace are available in each moment
for those who are open to receive it.***
God's kingdom is in our very *midst* but most *miss* it.

Some are too busy pursuing their worldly kingdoms.
It's not the power, prestige and possessions that are bad *in and of themselves.*
It's our *attachment* to them.
They are like chains.

**The *flow of God's Grace* is offered to everyone *without exception*,
but *each* of us must *choose* whether to enter that flow.**
We must first *let go* of our attachments to things that *will not last* so we
can experience the everlasting joy of riches that *will have no end.*

There is a great Love Story unfolding in time and space.

It is like a *Divine Dance* to which we are all invited.

Will *you* attend?

Listen to the song of the day "Shall We Sing" on the *Listen to Your Heart* album.

DECEMBER

28 MAJOR QUESTION

Matthew 16:15

Jesus said to them,
"But who do you say that I am?"

Excellent question!

Jesus asked his followers the question point blank.

Now, he is asking the question of *you and me.*

The existence of a historical Jesus who was followed by many Jews but was crucified by the Romans is backed up by much scholarly research.

Why was this movement *not squashed* by his gruesome execution?

What was it that made his followers come out of hiding and *boldly proclaim* that Jesus is the Savior of humankind?

They knew that their actions would likely lead them to their *own* executions, but *they did it anyway.*

Who do *you* say Jesus is and what effect does that have on *your* life and how you *live* it?

Listen to the song of the day "Come to Jesus" on the *Live to Love* album.

THE HEART OF THE MATTER

DECEMBER

29

Matthew 22:37-39

"You shall love the Lord, your God, with all your heart, with all your soul, and with all your mind. This is the greatest and the first commandment. The second is like it: You shall love your neighbor as yourself."

The Ten Commandments are a good foundation, a good set of rules to set a structure for our lives.

We all need to know *black and white* rules to get us started as children.

Jesus takes it to *another* level.

When asked what the greatest commandment is, Jesus says it's really *not* about rules, but about *love.*

The Trinity is a *constant flow* of love – giving and receiving, giving and receiving – *without* ulterior motive.

It sounds *simple*, but it's profoundly difficult: Love God *with all your* heart, soul and mind, AND love your *neighbor (everyone!) as yourself (as if they are* YOU!).

While only God can do this perfectly, you and I are called to try our best.

This is the path to *discovering* your true self.

Jesus is our finest teacher.

Listen to the song of the day "Love God" on the *Live to Love* album.

DECEMBER

30 THE WAY THE TRUTH AND THE LIFE

1 John 2:5-6

But whoever keeps Jesus' word, the love of God is truly perfected in him. This is the way we may know that we are in union with him: whoever claims to abide in him ought to live [just] as he lived.

Do you know Jesus?

One way to get to know him is to read his words in scripture and to let them soak in by silent meditation on them.

Speak to him in the silence of your heart throughout the day and allow more silent time to listen for his gentle response.

Make an effort to follow in his ways.

If you want to be open to the abundance of God's love, improve your relationship with Jesus.

That *won't* guarantee you a *trouble-free* life as Jesus promised that his followers *would* be persecuted.

When you love as Jesus loved, you love *all* people with *no* divisions.

This *guarantees* that some people will *not* like you.

But, you will have an *inner peace* amidst any storm.

Your life will be a source of *inspiration* and *transformation.*

Listen to the song of the day "Make Me a Channel" on the *Listen to Your Heart* album.

SHINE YOUR LIGHT

Matthew 5:14-15

"You are the light of the world. A city set on a mountain cannot be hidden. Nor do they light a lamp and then put it under a bushel basket; it is set on a lampstand, where it gives light to all in the house."

It doesn't matter what you've done in the past,
what your outer appearance is, or how you feel.

You have a Light inside of you that is a reflection of your Creator.

Scripture says that you are made in God's image (Genesis 1:27).

You are meant to shine God's light in your own *unique* way into the darkness of the world to bring *hope, compassion, mercy, forgiveness* and *restorative justice.*

It starts *now*, or in any *next* moment.

You don't have to have your life *all together* or pass any *worthiness* test to shine your light. It's always *there* and always *will be there.*

Your light is like none other!

Don't waste any more time with excuses.

Start your grand adventure in God's great love story.

You* are the *light of the world!

Listen to the song of the day "May I Be Light" on the *Listen to Your Heart* album.

About the Author

Bill Tonnis began his career delivering bad news on the radio, but now he delivers good news through ministry.

After obtaining a Bachelor of Science degree in Broadcast Journalism from Xavier University, Bill had a successful career as a news reporter/anchor at 700 WLW Radio for over twenty years. Emotionally drained by the job of delivering "bad news" daily, he had a life-changing epiphany in 1997 that led him to start writing spiritual songs and finding a new sense of purpose.

He completed a Master of Arts degree in Religious and Pastoral Studies at the College of Mount St. Joseph (now Mount St. Joseph University), left the radio station, and followed a new calling to be the Youth Minister at Our Lady of the Visitation Parish in Cincinnati. After five rewarding years in that role, Bill felt called to chaplaincy and completed the full training (four units of Clinical Pastoral Education) at Good Samaritan Hospital. He then began a new position at the parish as Pastoral Associate for Outreach, where he oversees social justice and service programs. Bill now provides pastoral care through words and music to shut-ins, hospitals, nursing homes, and jails.

Along with his work as a lay pastoral minister and chaplain, Bill shares his talents as a retreat leader/presenter, music minister, and a singer/songwriter with many organizations. His four original music albums entitled *Listen to Your Heart, Live to Love, Give Praise and Thanks*, and *Mercy Reigns* as well as all individual songs are available to download for purchase at various music service websites (such as Amazon Music). You can also purchase CDs of Bill's albums by contacting him at BillTonnisMusicMinistry@gmail.com.

Bill also writes a devotional blog at:
billtonnismusic.wordpress.com/todays-contemplation.

Made in the USA
Middletown, DE
05 November 2023